The DRI Report on
U.S. Manufacturing Industries

The DRI Report on U.S. Manufacturing Industries

Otto Eckstein
Chairman, Data Resources, Inc., and
Paul M. Warburg Professor of Economics at Harvard University

Christopher Caton
Vice President, Data Resources, Inc.

Roger Brinner
Group Vice President, Data Resources, Inc.

Peter Duprey
Associate Economist, Data Resources, Inc.

McGRAW-HILL BOOK COMPANY

New York   St. Louis   San Francisco   Auckland   Bogotá
Hamburg   Johannesburg   London   Madrid   Mexico
Montreal   New Delhi   Panama   Paris   São Paulo
Singapore   Sydney   Tokyo   Toronto

Library of Congress catalog card number
84-060518

Copyright © 1984 by Data Resources, Inc. All rights reserved.
Printed in the United States of America. Except as permitted
under the United States Copyright Act of 1976, no part of this publication
may be reproduced or distributed in any form or by any means,
or stored in a data base or retrieval system, without the
prior written permission of the publisher.

1234567890   DOC/DOC   8987654

ISBN 0-07-018969-2

The DRI Report on
U.S. Manufacturing Industries

TABLE OF CONTENTS

List of Tables		ix
List of Charts		xi
Chapter 1	**Introduction and Summary**	1
Chapter 2	**Dimensions of the Decline of U.S. Manufacturing**	6
	Comparison to Other Countries	10
	The Switch to Services	12
	The Role of a Worsening Business Cycle and Lower National Growth	13
	The Role of the Deteriorated International Trade Position	16
	Constant Share Analysis	18
Chapter 3	**Explanations of the Manufacturing Decline**	21
	Was Manufacturing Investment Too Low?	21
	Manufacturing Investment Abroad: The Boom in Japan	23
	Shifts Among Industries	25
	Investment by Type of Equipment	26
	Construction: Underinvestment in Factories	27
	The High Cost of Capital	28
	The Special Problem of Underdepreciation	31
	Total Taxation of Capital Income	32
	A Low Saving Rate	34
	The Effect of Stop-Go Policies: Some Econometric Results	35
	Did our Technological Efforts Slacken?	38
	The Role of Regulatory Policy	41
	Concluding Comments to Chapters 2 and 3	43
Chapter 4	**The Loss of Our Competitive Position**	44
	The Overvaluation of the Dollar	44
	United States and Foreign Trade Policies	54
	Concluding Comments to Chapters 1 to 4	57
Chapter 5	**Analysis of Individual Industries**	58
	Recent Developments in International Trade	70
	Conclusions	74
Chapter 6	**Is Manufacturing Industry Needed?**	76
	Higher Productivity Levels in Manufacturing	76
	A Higher Productivity Trend	78
	Static and Dynamic Economies-to-Scale	79
	Investment and Reinvestment Opportunities	80
	The Relation of Manufacturing Growth to General Economic Growth: Some Econometric Results	80
	Manufacturing Industry and the National Defense	83
	Manufacturing Prosperity and Regional Development	84
	An Earlier Example of Manufacturing Neglect: The United Kingdom	85

Table of Contents

Chapter 7	**Manufacturing In 1995: Some Alternative Scenarios**	87
	The Pessimistic Scenario: Economic Policy Without an Industrial Viewpoint	87
	The Optimistic Scenario: An Economic Policy With an Industrial Viewpoint	90
	The Results of the Optimistic Scenario	92
	Regional Implications of the Two Scenarios	99
	Concluding Comments	101
Chapter 8	**Conclusions**	103
Appendix:	**Detailed Industry Material**	109
	Food and Kindred Products	109
	Tobacco Manufactures	114
	Textile Mill Products	117
	Apparel	121
	Lumber and Wood Products	124
	Furniture and Fixtures	127
	Paper and Products	130
	Printing and Publishing	134
	Chemicals	137
	Petroleum Products	141
	Rubber and Plastics	145
	Leather Products	149
	Stone, Clay and Glass	152
	Primary Metals Including Steel	156
	Fabricated Metals	163
	Nonelectrical Machinery	167
	Electrical Machinery	171
	Transportation Equipment Including Automobiles	175
	Instruments	182

LIST OF TABLES

2.1	Production in U.S. Manufacturing, 1970-1972 to 1980-1982	7
2.2	Manufacturing's Share of Employment	9
2.3	Growth in Manufacturing Production, 1958-1982	10
2.4	Manufacturing During Seven Recessions	14
2.5	Potential GNP, 1948-1982	15
3.1	Manufacturing Shipments and Investment, 1958-1982	22
3.2	Shifts in Manufacturing Investment by Industry Type, 1958-1981	26
3.3	Shifts in Manufacturing Investment by Equipment Type	27
3.4	Effective Marginal Tax Rates on Capital Income	33
3.5	Savings Rates, Averages 1970 to 1980, Six Countries	35
3.6	Investment and Capital Stock of U.S. Manufacturing, Two Scenarios, 1960-1980	37
3.7	Econometric Model for Manufacturing Investment and Capital Stock	37
3.8	Expenditures on R & D, Selected Countries	40
3.9	Pollution Abatement Expenditures as a Percent of Investment in Plant and Equipment, 1973-1982	42
4.1	Unit Labor Costs, Multiples of U.S. Levels	45
4.2	U.S. International Balance of Payments, 1963-1982	49
4.3	A Decomposition of Services Exports	51
4.4	The Economic Impact of the Dollar's 1980-1982 Appreciation	53
5.1	Key Concepts—U.S. Manufacturing Industries	60
5.2	Manufacturing Production by Industry, 1960-1982	61
5.3	Constant Export and Import Share Production	62
5.4	Manufacturing Productivity by Industry, 1954-1981	63
5.5	Manufacturing Employment by Industry, 1950-1982	64
5.6	Profits as a Percent of Sales by Industry, 1960-1982	65
5.7	Real Plant & Equipment Investment by Industry, 1950-1982	66
5.8	R&D Expenditures as a Percent of Sales by Industry, 1960-1982	67
5.9	Trade Balances by Industry	68
5.10	Industry Wage Levels Relative to the Total Economy	69
5.11	A Breakdown of the U.S. Current Account Balance	70
5.12	A Geographic Breakdown of U.S. Merchandise Exports, January-June 1983	71
5.13	U.S. Merchandise Exports, 1980-1983	72
5.14	U.S. Merchandise Imports: 1980-1983	73
6.1	Cross-Sectional Analysis: Two Equations	82
6.2	Manufacturing: A Cross-Sectional Analysis, 1965-1982	83
6.3	Gross Income per Capita: Six Countries, 1965-1980	86
7.1	The Cyclically Corrected Budget, Selected Years	91
7.2	A Comparison of Two Projections, 1995	93
7.3	Production by Industry in Two Projections, 1995	95
7.4	Employment by Industry in Two Projections, 1995	96
7.5	Real Investment in Plant and Equipment by Industry, A Comparison of Two Projections, 1995	97
7.6	Manufacturing Employment, Effects by State—1995	100

LIST OF CHARTS

2.1	Real Value of Industrial Production as a Percent of GNP, 1920-1982	6
2.2	Manufacturing's Share of Employment, 1950-1982	9
2.3	Manufacturing Production, Japan, U.S., and OECD, 1965-1982	10
2.4	Manufacturing's Share of Total Employment, Four Countries	11
2.5	Manufacturing Productivity, Japan, U.S. and West Germany, 1965-1981	12
2.6	Manufacturing Production, 1950-Aug. 1983	14
2.7	Real After-Tax Manufacturing Corporate Profits, 1948-1982	16
2.8	The Import Penetration Rate in Manufactured Goods, 1965-1980	17
2.9	Manufacturing Exports as a Percent of Shipments, 1965-1980	17
2.10	Shares of Dollar Volume of World Manufacturing Exports, Japan and the U.S., 1965-1980	18
2.11	The Effect of Changing Trade Patterns on U.S. Manufacturing Output Growth: a Constant Share Analysis, 1965-1982	19
3.1	Manufacturing Investment as a Percent of Shipments, 1958-1982	22
3.2	Growth in the Real Manufacturing Capital Stock, 1950-1981	23
3.3	Real Manufacturing Investment as a Share of GNP, Japan and the U.S., 1965-1982	24
3.4	Shifts in Manufacturing Equipment Investment by Industry, 1958-1981	25
3.5	Shifts in Manufacturing Equipment Investment by Type, 1958-1982	26
3.6	Private Industrial Construction as a Percent of Total Private Nonresidential Construction, 1967-1982	28
3.7	Real Cost of Fixed Asset Services, Japan and the U.S., 1961-1980	31
3.8	Depreciation Adjustment to Corporate Profits as a Percent of Fixed Nonresidential Investment, 1946-1985	32
3.9	Capacity Utilization in Manufacturing, 1950-July 1983	36
4.1	Productivity: Six Countries Versus the U.S., 1968-1982	46
4.2	Labor Compensation: Six Countries Versus the U.S., 1968-1982	46
4.3	Unit Labor Costs: Six Countries Versus the U.S., 1968-1982	46
4.4	Trade-Weighted Exchange Rate, 1958-1983	47
4.5	United States Trade Balance, Goods, Services, and Total, 1950-1982	48
4.6	The Economy's Path With the Dollar Held Stable at Its Summer 1980 Level	52
4.7	Job Losses Caused by the Dollar's Rise: Differences Comparing History With Stable Dollar Simulation	52
4.8	The Impact of the Dollar's Appreciation on the Goods and Services Trade Balance	52
6.1	Output Per Worker Per Year in the Manufacturing and Nonmanufacturing Sectors, 1948-1982	77
6.2	Relative Wages: Manufacturing Compared to Nonmanufacturing, 1940-1982	77
6.3	GDP Per Capita Growth and Manufacturing Per Capita Growth, 1965-1982	81
6.4	GDP Per Capita Growth and Growth in Manufacturing as a Share of GDP, 1965-1982	81
7.1	Non-Oil Merchandise Trade Balance as a Percent of GNP, 1970-1995	91
7.2	Federal Deficit as a Percent of GNP, 1970-1995	91
7.3	Real Value of Manufacturing Production as a Percent of GNP, 1970-1995	94
7.4	Manufacturing Employment, 1970-1995	98
7.5	Real Manufacturing Investment as a Percent of Real GNP, 1970-1995	99

List of Charts

Appendix: Detailed Charts on Individual Industries
                Food and Kindred Products   111
                Tobacco Manufactures   115
                Textile Mill Products   118
                Apparel   122
                Lumber and Wood Products   125
                Furniture and Fixtures   128
                Paper and Products   131
                Printing and Publishing   135
                Chemicals   138
                Petroleum Products   142
                Rubber and Plastics   146
                Leather Products   150
                Stone, Clay and Glass   153
                Primary Metals Including Steel   158
                Fabricated Metals   164
                Nonelectrical Machinery   168
                Electrical Machinery   172
                Transportation Equipment Including Automobiles   177
                Instruments   183
                Miscellaneous Manufacturing   186

CHAPTER 1

INTRODUCTION AND SUMMARY

The recent recession has accelerated the relative decline of U.S. manufacturing industries and made it a generally recognized public issue. Production and employment in some industries shrank by a third from earlier levels. The resultant unemployment created profound economic problems for families and communities, and a major regional disparity in economic opportunities has developed.[1]

This decline of position of manufacturing is a major historical development for this country. Beginning with our industrial revolution shortly before the Civil War, the growth of manufacturing industry has been the principal vehicle of U.S. economic growth. The increasing productivity in goods production made possible by a capable labor force, innovative management, an exceptionally favorable supply of natural resources and rapidly advancing technology created a growth of total output such as the world had never seen. A century-long industrial development process raised U.S. living standards many fold, made U.S. gross national product nearly 40% of world output and provided the nation with the means to become the political leader and military protector of the western world, while concurrently meeting the social needs of its population.

---

[1]This study was undertaken at the request of nine companies that are and will be in the midst of these important changes. They are American Telephone & Telegraph Co., Bethlehem Steel Corp., Burlington Industries Inc., Deere & Co., E.I. du Pont de Nemours & Co., Eastman Kodak Company, Ford Motor Company, The Goodyear Tire & Rubber Co., and Texaco Inc. They asked Data Resources, Inc. (DRI) to undertake a detailed, factual study of the pattern and causes of the decline of U.S. manufacturing industries, to devise analyses that would help to explain the startling movements of the figures and to survey the available policy options. They turned to Data Resources, Inc. because of the elaborate collection of data available on the company's computers, and because of the industry expertise of its staff of macro- and micro-econometricians and its collection of macro and microeconometric models. This study would have been impossible without the cooperation of numerous economists of the company. We are especially grateful to Walter Carter, John Hammond and Ronald Whitfield. The sponsoring companies also provided industry information, and the comments of Carl E. Black, James Leonard, Edwin R. MacKethan, Kenneth Militzer, Paul Rehmet, Dennis W. Rich, and Robert A. Wendt were particularly helpful. But they have not had the opportunity to review the final draft of the report nor are they responsible for its content.

But, by the early 1980s, the signs had become unmistakable that other nations were surpassing some of our manufacturing industries and that America's traditional role in the world economy was much diminished. Japan has proved to be the principal challenger to our leadership but other nations, in Europe and Asia, are rapidly closing the gap between their economic performance and our own.

The implications of the decline in leadership of U.S. manufacturing industry are not yet fully clear or understood. Can the United States continue to play the role of guardian of the Western world, with its heavy political, economic and military burdens, with a weakening manufacturing economy? What are the social problems created by the reduction of job opportunities for blue-collar workers? Will the United States develop the kind of permanent regional disparities in economic well-being that haunt Great Britain, where the industrial heartland is trapped in depression while the service-based London area achieves prosperity? Can—or should—government policies act to reverse the decline of manufacturing industries?

Much is being written on these topics, seeking the causes of the problem and defining various policy remedies.[2] The question of "industrial policy" —government measures to aid U.S. industry in a coherent, logical and massive fashion—may become one of the principal economic issues of the 1984 Presidential election. A total nonresponse by the political process to this problem is hard to envisage. The issues must, therefore, be thought out and some degree of consensus of knowledgeable opinion developed before the country embarks on large-scale policy moves.

The present study is modest in some regards but ambitious in others. It focuses on the data and generally avoids simple explanations. Policy options are only surveyed, not recommended. Nonetheless, data never tell their own story. And, to the extent our findings differ from the earlier writings, we find a larger role for the macroeconomic conditions in which American business was operating than is usually acknowledged. We also find an earlier beginning to the process of decline, with 1949 and 1965 perhaps the pivotal dates.

This study applies conventional economic analysis and econometrics to search the data for explanations and to develop projections of the future of U.S. manufacturing under alternative policy scenarios. The individual analytical ideas are well known and long established in the mainstream of

---

[2]Ira C. Magaziner and Robert B. Reich, *Minding America's Business,* New York, Vintage Books, 1983; Robert B. Reich, *The Next American Frontier,* New York Times Books, 1983; Barry Bluestone and Bennett Harrison, *The Deindustrialization of America,* New York, Basic Books, 1982; and Lester C. Thurow, *The Zero-Sum Society,* New York, Basic Books, 1980. For a skeptical view, see Paul Krugman, "Targeted Industrial Policies: Theory and Evidence," *Conference on Industrial Change and Public Policy,* Federal Reserve Bank of Kansas City, August 1983, and Charles L. Schultze, "Industrial Policy: A Dissent," *The Brookings Review,* Fall 1983, pp. 3-12.

economic thought. The novelty of the study lies in its comprehensive view of the data, which ultimately yielded a theory of the decline of U.S. manufacturing. This theory does not rely so much on particular human failings of U.S. business, labor or political leadership, though these surely were contributing factors. The principal explanations of our industrial problem lie in objective historical economic forces that made some retardation of our manufacturing growth inevitable, and in generally ineffective policy responses to the external and internal challenges.

Highlights of the conclusions of this study include:

- U.S. manufacturing industries have suffered from national economic policies which have been insensitive to their needs. These policies include an overvaluation of the dollar in much of the postwar period, the injection of damaging credit cycles which disrupted the process of capital formation at least seven times in three decades, and a set of tax and regulatory policies which diverted the country's savings from productive industrial investment. Capital costs were high, and limited the ability to invest. National economic policy vacillated between political and financial viewpoints, between short-run stimulus and monetary restraint: industry was little heard in the highest councils of government; and her needs were ignored in the critical decisions about budget deficits, interest rates and exchange rates.

- U.S. manufacturing also was adversely affected by policies to aid the development of the economies of our free world allies and of newcomers to the industrial scene. While other nations aggressively promoted the development of their industries, the United States made no serious effort to assure that this worldwide thrust of industrial development would occur in an environment of free trade and competition. The United States government stood idly by as the newcomers took advantage of their privileges under the General Agreement on Tariffs and Trade to keep American goods out of their own countries while basing much of their development strategy on easy entry to the U.S. market. Though tariff rates declined, nontariff barriers became more widespread. Nor was serious action taken against the persistent protectionism of Japan, which has minimized manufactured good imports while seeking to take over many of the world's industrial markets. In its international trade policies, the U.S. government placed our economic interests second to political goals.

- Partly as a result of this unfavorable environment of economic and financial instability and weak trade policies reinforced by the high cost of capital, several U.S. manufacturing industries could not develop and execute competitive strategies that would have kept them in the fore-

front of technology, product design and international marketing. Discouraged by the paucity of good results from traditional lines, business leadership in some industries sought to escape the pressures from abroad by focussing on diversification and redeployment of assets. Some corporate managements turned to acquisitions at the expense of developing their own lines of business, took a damaging short-run point of view in many investment and marketing decisions, and mismanaged the relationships with their workers. These tendencies were reinforced by shortsightedness on the part of labor leaders, and by pressures from the financial community to sacrifice long-term business development for the sake of quarterly earnings and day-to-day stock price performance.
- But, as the data show all too clearly, the loss of market share by American industries to foreign competitors was so all-pervasive, affecting every industry, that much of the explanation must lie in more general phenomena than individual mistakes and systematic biases in the corporate culture. There are so few exceptions to the decline of the international positions of U.S. manufacturing industries that one must seek more general causes that act on the entire American economy.
- Without a strongly advancing manufacturing industry, the U.S. economy is hardly likely to maintain its progress in the decades ahead. A service economy lacks sufficient opportunity for technological progress and economies-to-scale to sustain the historical growth which the United States has so long achieved. To bet the future of our economic system on a service economy is a high-risk gamble that is hardly likely to prove successful.
- The steps that will promote a healthier development of U.S. manufacturing in the years ahead must include measures to improve the general economic environment and to encourage a more farsighted approach to business decision making. These steps include the following changes:
  — The cost of industrial capital should be reduced. Interest rates should be lowered through stronger budget policies. Preferential financing of nonindustrial investments should be curtailed. Easier access to long-term debt capital for long-lived investments should be sought.
  — The exchange rate of the dollar should be brought down to a level more consistent with relative cost positions. Lower interest rates made possible by a smaller budget deficit would go far to achieve this goal. Greater freedom of movement for capital to other industrial countries, particularly Japan, would also serve to reduce the value of the dollar by reducing the volume of foreign capital seeking investment outlets in the United States.

— U.S. international trade policies should aim to reverse the declining role of U.S. goods in world markets. They should be strengthened both in their formulation and in their execution. Stronger steps need to be taken to open up world markets to American goods, particularly in Japan and the newly industrialized countries. Where trade is to be governed by formal or informal agreements, the government must take greater responsibility to assure that the agreements achieve their purpose. Trade is an ineffective weapon for the federal government to use in our disputes with the Soviet Union. We should put greater emphasis on economic — as opposed to political — goals in the conduct of our foreign policy.
— Monetary and fiscal policies should be designed to achieve a more stable and sustainable pattern of economic growth, rather than the highly cyclic pattern that characterized the postwar period. Effective capital formation and a sufficiently long-range point of view in investment decisions require a greater stability of market growth than government policies have been providing.
— The United States should take strong actions to preserve its lead in the high technology industries. Public policy must promote a sufficient supply of scientific and technical manpower and an adequate support of basic research. Industries should be permitted joint research projects when world competition makes them necessary. We should insist on full reciprocity in the exchange of technical information with our trade partners.
— The numerous issues of regulatory and tax policies should be resolved with adequate weight given to their impact on industrial development.
- To assure a more successful development of U.S. manufacturing industries, an industrial viewpoint should be introduced into economic policy decisions. Monetary policy is a major determinant for the cost of industrial capital, for the development of domestic markets, and for the value of the exchange rate. Budget policy determines the tax burden of industry and affects the development of domestic markets, and numerous other policies have major impacts. Industrial development must become an explicit objective of economic policy.

CHAPTER 2

DIMENSIONS OF THE DECLINE OF U.S. MANUFACTURING

For much of the last 120 years, manufacturing led the growth of the American economy. After the completion of the railroad network and the electricity grid, much innovation and capital formation centered on the growth of a succession of manufacturing industries—steel, machinery, automobiles, appliances, chemicals, and computers, along with more modest but persistent growth in textiles, apparel, paper and food processing.

Chart 2.1 shows the relationship between the growth of manufacturing output and the growth of the gross national product as a whole. Until 1966, manufacturing industries grew substantially more than the economy as a whole.

Chart 2.1
Real Value of Industrial Production
as a Percent of GNP, 1920-1982

After 1966, this relationship changed. The margin of manufacturing growth over general growth disappears; and, with the economy as a whole entering a period of exceptional instability, much of the forward movement of manufacturing is lost. Productivity begins to slow, imports loom larger, and soon OPEC creates a setback for all industrial nations. The broad figures hide disparities among industries, of course, but the change in the relationship is so substantial that it already hints at a fundamental change in economic structure.

The composition of the manufacturing slowdown is shown in Table 2.1, which shows the growth rates and contributions to the total manufacturing production index between 1970-72 and 1980-82. These three-year intervals reduce the effects of cyclical swings—both periods include recession—allowing the secular changes to be identified. At the low end, the output of cotton fabrics and leather declined 25%, and steel fell 16%. Motor vehicles, appliances, TV and radio, and nonferrous metals barely rose. Other industries experiencing less than 10% growth over the decade were petroleum products, shipbuilding, railroad equipment and mobile homes, lumber, tires and metal cans. At the high growth end, electronic components rose 129%, plastic products rose 125%, and office equipment 87%. Communications equipment expanded 59%, chemical products 63%, and synthetic materials 77%.

Table 2.1
Production in U.S. Manufacturing,
1970-1972 to 1980-1982

	Cumulative Percent Growth 70-72 to 80-82	Value Added Weight-1967	Weighted Percent Growth 70-72 to 80-82	Contribution to Total Increase(%)
Electronic Components	128.68	1.63	2.55	8.41
Plastics Products, nec	124.60	1.11	2.36	7.78
Office, Service and Miscellaneous Equipment	87.09	2.99	3.07	10.12
Synthetic Materials	76.81	1.42	1.64	5.40
Chemical Products	63.23	4.78	3.08	10.50
Communication Equipment	58.77	2.62	1.40	4.63
Instruments	47.23	2.40	1.16	3.83
Miscellaneous Electrical Supplies	46.69	0.56	0.28	0.92
Aircraft and Parts	43.36	4.24	1.19	3.93
Basic Chemicals	40.23	2.89	1.32	4.36
High Growth Average	69.76	24.64	18.05	59.88

Table 2.1—Continued

	Cumulative Percent Growth 70-72 to 80-82	Value Added Weight-1967	Weighted Percent Growth 70-72 to 80-82	Contribution to Total Increase(%)
Industrial and Metalworking Machinery	33.72	4.51	1.21	4.00
Foods and Products	33.65	9.95	3.40	11.21
Printing and Publishing	30.88	5.65	1.62	5.57
Furniture and Fixtures	29.54	1.56	0.49	1.61
Major Electrical Equipment and Parts	28.33	1.98	0.53	1.76
Engines; Farm and Construction Equipment	28.12	2.91	0.81	2.68
Miscellaneous Manufacturing	25.79	1.72	0.47	1.53
Stone, Clay, and Glass	25.66	3.12	0.81	2.67
Paper and Products	25.25	3.65	1.01	3.32
Fabricated Metals	22.41	6.31	1.34	4.41
Medium Growth Average	29.01	41.37	11.69	38.76
Rubber Products Except Tires	17.66	0.75	0.14	0.46
Non-Cotton Textiles	17.53	2.36	0.48	1.59
Tobacco Manufactures	16.84	0.76	0.12	0.39
Apparel	12.72	3.76	0.45	1.49
Petroleum Products	9.36	2.29	0.20	0.66
Tires	7.12	0.68	0.06	0.18
Ships, RR Equip. and Mobile Homes	6.32	1.18	0.08	0.27
Metal Cans	4.72	0.43	0.02	0.07
Lumber and Wood Products	3.17	1.86	0.06	0.20
Appliances, TV and Radio	2.01	1.53	0.03	0.10
Nonferrous Metals	1.10	2.68	0.03	0.10
Motor Vehicles and Parts	1.07	5.12	0.06	0.19
Ordnance, Private and Government	−5.82	4.14	−0.19	−0.62
Steel Mill Products	−16.13	3.80	−0.57	−1.87
Iron and Steel Foundries	−22.37	0.99	−0.20	−0.66
Leather and Products	−24.61	0.98	−0.19	−0.63
Cotton Fabrics	−25.17	0.68	−0.14	−0.45
Low Growth Average	1.35	33.99	0.44	1.46
Total Manufacturing	30.32	100.00	30.32	100.00

A comparison of employment shows a grimmer picture. Because manufacturing normally enjoys a higher productivity trend than the economy as a whole, its employment levels grow more slowly. Lessened output growth and above-average productivity gains reduced the role of manufacturing jobs in the economy: manufacturing represented 34.0% of all payroll employment in the years 1948-52; but, by 1978-82, the share had dropped to 22.5% (Chart 2.2 and Table 2.2).

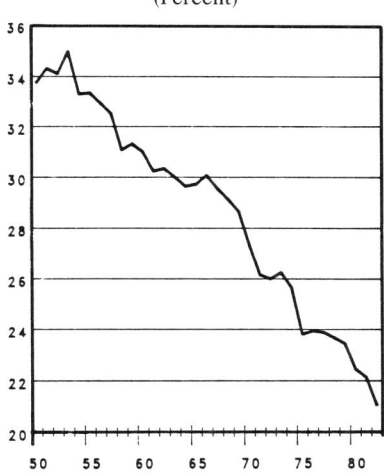

Chart 2.2
Manufacturing's Share of
Employment, 1950-1982
(Percent)

Table 2.2
Manufacturing's Share of Employment
(Millions of workers)

	1948-52	1953-57	1958-62	1963-67	1968-72	1973-77	1978-82
Total Nonfarm	46.1	51.0	53.6	61.1	70.8	78.8	89.5
Manufacturing Sector	15.7	17.0	16.5	18.2	19.4	19.4	20.2
Manufacturing Share of Total (Percent)	34.0	33.4	30.8	29.8	27.5	24.7	22.5

COMPARISON TO OTHER COUNTRIES

Manufacturing growth slowed in other countries as well. Manufacturing output of the principal industrial countries belonging to OECD rose only slightly more than in the United States (Chart 2.3 and Table 2.3). Worldwide output rose more rapidly, as newly industrialized countries such as Brazil, Hong Kong, Korea, Singapore, and Taiwan took a significant share of world markets.

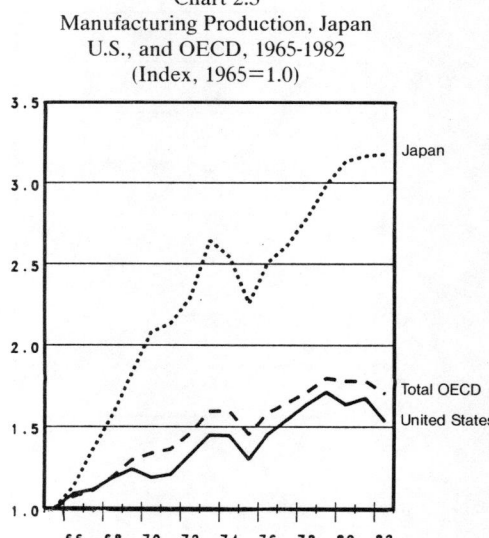

Chart 2.3
Manufacturing Production, Japan
U.S., and OECD, 1965-1982
(Index, 1965=1.0)

Table 2.3
Growth in Manufacturing Production,
1958-1982
(Percent, annual rates)

	1958-62	1963-67	1968-72	1973-77	1978-82
United States	5.8	7.2	2.8	1.6	−1.6
Japan	18.7	13.2	9.9	−0.3	3.4
Total OECD	4.8	6.4	5.1	0.8	−0.1

The international comparison of the growth of manufacturing employment shows striking results (Chart 2.4). While all industrial countries experienced declines once OPEC entered the scene in 1973, the longer-range trends show large differences. In the United States, the manufacturing share of all jobs declined by 27% between 1965 and 1982. In Germany and France, the decline was 8%. In Japan, despite a surge in productivity, manufacturing employment was as large a share of the total as in 1965.

Chart 2.4
Manufacturing's Share of
Total Employment, Four Countries
(Index, 1965=100)

The surge of manufacturing productivity in Japan was an extraordinary historical event which transformed the relationship between her economy and our own (Chart 2.5). By the end of the period, productivity of Japan's workers almost matched our own.

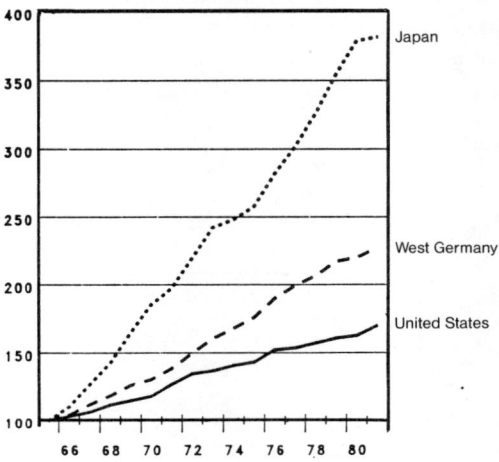

Chart 2.5
Manufacturing Productivity, Japan,
U.S. and West Germany, 1965-1981
(Index, 1965=100)

THE SWITCH TO SERVICES

Analysts of economic development have long recognized that the predominance of manufacturing growth is only a particular phase in history. Colin Clark defined three phases of development nearly 50 years ago, beginning with the "primary" agricultural stage, a "secondary" or manufacturing stage, to be succeeded by the growth of "tertiary industry", or services.[3] There are numerous reasons for the ultimate predominance of services: the pattern of consumer behavior under rising incomes emphasizes the purchase of clothing, shelter and consumer durables over a considerable range; but, at still higher levels of income, families increasingly value the use of services. These include cultural, educational and household services which are part of a leisure-oriented society: food is consumed in restaurants rather than at home; education lengthens for an increasingly complex technology and as preparation for a higher quality of life. More health services are consumed as available medical techniques become increasingly complex and costly. Public services absorb increasing shares of GNP as the society seeks to match their quality to higher levels of private consumption. The administra-

---

[3]Colin Clark, *The Conditions of Economic Progress*, 2nd ed., London, MacMillan, 1951, pp. 350-440.

tion of social services, whether of a medical, social or economic character, also requires increasing resources. Finally, industry itself makes increasing use of business services, such as legal, accounting and consulting services, as well as managerial and technical services that were previously performed by their own employees.

The trend toward services is reinforced by the changing age structure of the population. As the retired constitute a larger fraction of the population, health, household and social services become an increasing part of their consumption, whereas their needs for durable goods and even clothing are partly met by stocks of these items purchased earlier.[4]

The arrival of the "information revolution" has a somewhat more ambiguous impact on the division of activity between goods and services. In the initial stages in which the U.S. economy now finds itself, the highest growth sectors of goods output are found in the hardware for handling the information services, such as computers, word processors and the communications networks to link them. But the emphasis is shifting quickly from hardware to software, as business and consumers buy information, computer programs and communications services.

These well-recognized facts show that the above-average growth performance of manufacturing must ultimately come to an end. But the decline of manufacturing growth in recent years has been so dramatic and so sudden that its causes must be sought elsewhere.

The immediate reasons for the slowing of manufacturing growth are the increased violence of the business cycle, the economy's reduced long-term growth trend, and the decline of the American share of manufacturing activity in the world. The cycle is particularly damaging to markets and to the ability of manufacturing industries to invest. Lessened trend growth hurts the income-sensitive demand for durables. The international decline was most harmful to industries with standard technologies, large capital requirements, and high labor intensity.

THE ROLE OF A WORSENING BUSINESS CYCLE AND LOWER NATIONAL GROWTH

In part, the weakness of manufacturing growth reflected a slowing of the entire economy. National growth slowed down both because of an increasingly severe business cycle and because of a slowing in the trend of aggregate supply. There have been seven recessions since 1950, and industrial production was seriously disturbed by each one (Chart 2.6 and Table 2.4). On

[4]For an account of the impact of these changes on the society see Daniel Bell, *The Coming of Post-Industrial Society*, New York, Basic Books, 1976.

average, production declined by 11.9%, as temporarily weakened markets and inventory corrections reduced the need for factory output.

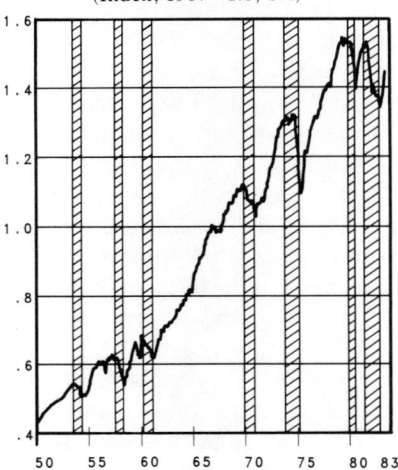

Chart 2.6
Manufacturing Production, 1950-Aug. 1983
(Index, 1967=1.0, SA)

Note: Shaded areas denote recession periods.

Table 2.4
Manufacturing During Seven Recessions

Recession Dates	Peak-to-Trough Percent Decline		
	Production	Profits	Real Investment
July 1953-May 1954	−12.1	−30.2	−13.4
August 1957-April 1958	−14.5	−34.6	−36.3
April 1960-February 1961	−9.6	−36.2	−8.9
December 1969-November 1970	−7.8	−45.4	−19.7
November 1973-March 1975	−17.3	−28.2	−15.4
January 1980-July 1980	−9.2	−33.8	−0.2
July 1981-November 1982	−12.5	−48.2	−17.4
Average	−11.9	−36.7	−15.9

The loss of sales reduced manufacturing profits, with an average profit decline of 36.7% in the seven recessions. Lower output meant that overhead costs were spread over fewer units, producing a disproportionate impact on profits. The disruption of profit growth, in turn, damaged the ability of manufacturing companies to finance investment in plant and equipment. So, after a short lag, investment also experienced substantial declines in each of the seven recessions.

Besides the recent increase in the frequency and violence of the business cycle, the long-term trend of the economy also seems to have slowed down. Potential GNP, the most commonly used measure for aggregate supply, rose by an estimated 3.5% a year until 1966 (Table 2.5). It then speeded up temporarily under the stimulus of a larger growth in the labor force, to 4.0%, even though productivity began to fade. After the 1973 jump in energy prices, the growth of potential GNP slowed down and, in the last four years, averaged 3.1%.

This slowdown in the growth of potential GNP combined with a higher average unemployment rate to produce an even more substantial reduction in the trend growth of actual output. Whereas trend growth was 3.8% until 1973, since then it has been only 2.2%, and in the most recent years lower still.

Table 2.5
Potential GNP, 1948-1982
(Annual growth rates)

	1948-66	1967-73	1974-82
Potential Output	3.5	4.0	3.1
Actual Output	4.0	3.7	2.2

Because durable goods have a higher income elasticity of demand than nondurable goods and services, their growth is curtailed more than proportionately when the economy turns down and when its trend weakens. While companies can adjust more effectively to a lower trend than they can to cyclical disturbances (responding, for example, with a lower rate of growth of capacity to preserve utilization rates and profit margins), the reduced growth of end markets holds down the opportunity for modernization and economies-to-scale, and limits the resources available for investment.

The slowing of output growth had a magnified impact on the profitability of manufacturing companies. Chart 2.7 shows the real volume of manufacturing profits after inventory and capital consumption adjustment, indicating little growth since the mid-sixties. With the capital stock continuing to expand, the rate of return on capital was falling very substantially.

The change in the mix of demands of the economy also worked against the growth of manufacturing output, but was only of small influence in the total picture. Federal purchases to strengthen our strategic military forces and to fight the Vietnam War boosted manufacturing sales in the 1960s, but faded away in the 1970s. On the other hand, the demand for capital goods actually became quite strong in the late 1970s, and military spending began to rise again.

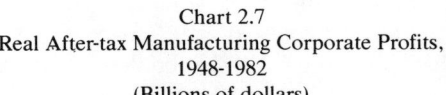

Chart 2.7
Real After-tax Manufacturing Corporate Profits,
1948-1982
(Billions of dollars)

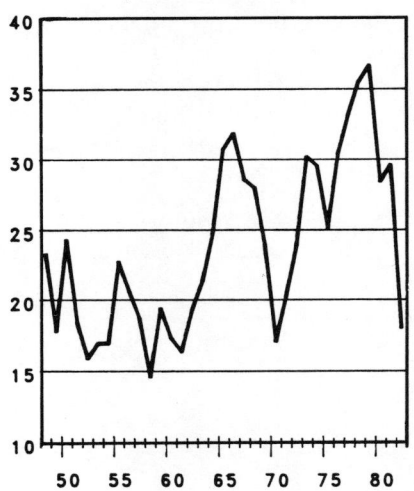

THE ROLE OF THE DETERIORATED INTERNATIONAL TRADE POSITION

The output of American factories grew less in recent years because of the rising market share of imports in U.S. markets and the diminishing U.S. market share in world markets. Chart 2.8 shows the import penetration ratio for all manufactured goods, with this ratio defined as the share of total domestic use supplied from abroad. In 1965, 4.3% of available goods were imported; by 1980 the figure had risen to 13.5%, a rise of 9.2%. It will be seen in the next chapter that virtually every industry suffered from a major worsening of import penetration.

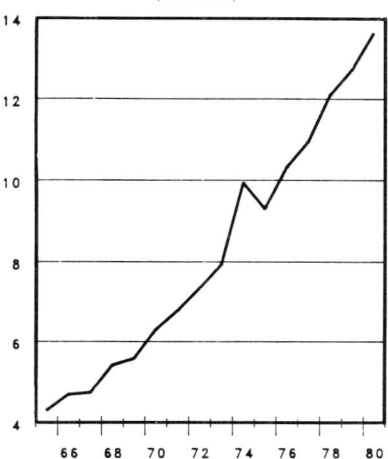

Chart 2.8
The Import Penetration Rate in
Manufactured Goods, 1965-1980
(Percent)

Exports also expanded rapidly, as world trade grew more rapidly than world output. Whereas exports represented 5.1% of U.S. shipments in 1965, they rose to 10.7% by 1980 (Chart 2.9), a rise of 5.6%.

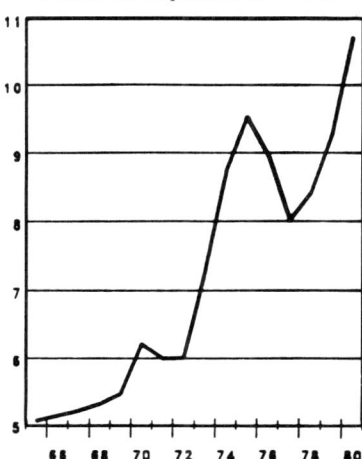

Chart 2.9
Manufacturing Exports as a
Percent of Shipments, 1965-1980

Despite a sizeable rise of exports, the U.S. share in world goods markets shows a large decline. In 1965, the U.S. share of world manufacturing exports was 22.1%. By 1980 it had dropped to 15.2%; and, as Chart 2.10 shows, the deterioration was going on steadily over most of the period. Japan's share, on the other hand, rose until 1973, and held its own even in the face of a much larger role for oil in world markets.

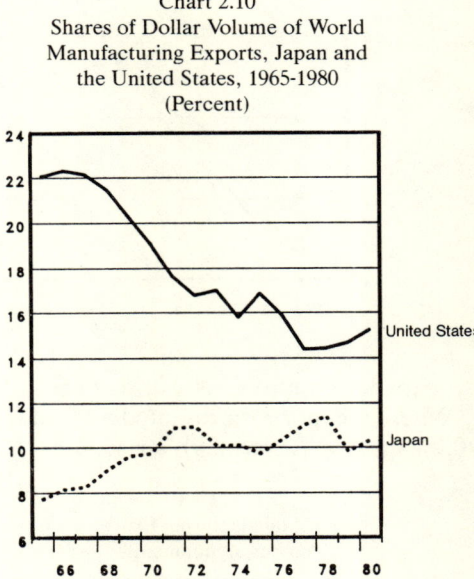

Chart 2.10
Shares of Dollar Volume of World Manufacturing Exports, Japan and the United States, 1965-1980
(Percent)

CONSTANT SHARE ANALYSIS

To estimate the impact of the changed trade position on manufacturing output, a constant share analysis has been calculated, assuming that imports provided a constant share to domestic markets and exports were a constant share of shipments, both set at their 1965 values. As Chart 2.11 shows, output would have been 4.1% greater in the years 1979-81 if the shares had held constant, and would have been 5.2% larger by 1982.[5] The trade-induced

---

[5]These results are similar, but not identical to, the conclusions reached by Robert Z. Lawrence in a series of studies prepared for The Brookings Institution. Lawrence concludes that there was no net loss, but rather a small gain, of manufacturing output due to international trade in the periods 1970-80 and 1973-80, whereas the present study finds a loss of 2.7% over the latter interval.

loss of output growth is worsening rapidly during the current recovery, with the merchandise deficit growing from $27.5 billion in 1979-81 to nearly $60 billion in 1983.

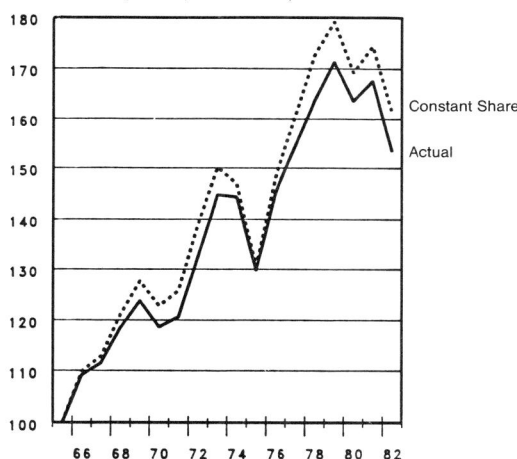

Chart 2.11
The Effect of Changing Trade Patterns on U.S. Manufacturing Output Growth: a Constant Share Analysis, 1965-1982
(Index, 1965=100)

As a result of this performance, manufacturing played a significantly more negative role in the production growth of the U.S. than in other industrial countries. Declines were universal and relatively similar after the 1973 OPEC revolution. But, while employment fell 27% in the U.S. compared to 1965, the decline in the EEC was only 7%, and in Japan it only retraced the

---

There are various methodological differences that produce this range of results. The Lawrence study uses estimates of deflated value-added originating as the basic data set for analysis, whereas the present study uses nominal values of shipments. Elaborate, but not necessarily identical, input-output analyses underlie both studies.

The years 1970-80 and 1973-80 do not show a big deterioration in our trade position for manufacturing industries because these were the years when we were beginning to pay for the high cost of oil. The dollar fell in value in the 1970s and, for a considerable interval, was quite cheap, helping our trade balance. Indeed, in the absence of the secular downtrend, our manufacturing trade balance should have become substantially more positive over this interval. The big deterioration in trade came at the end of the decade and in the early 1980s, as the dollar resumed its high value. See Robert Z. Lawrence, "Is Trade Deindustrializing America? A Medium-Term Perspective," *Brookings Economic Papers*, 1:1983, pp. 129-161, and "Changes in U.S. Industrial Structure, The Role of Global Forces, Secular Trends and Transitory Cycles," paper presented to Conference on Industrial Change and Public Policy, Federal Reserve Bank of Kansas City, August 1983.

gains scored in the late 1960s (Chart 2.4). In the United States, the cyclical swings were superimposed on an already established downtrend.

So far we have only described the basic situation. How did it happen? Before turning to industry-specific analyses, we examine broader theories that can explain this historical experience.

CHAPTER 3

EXPLANATIONS OF THE MANUFACTURING DECLINE

The list of potential explanations of the relative decline of U.S. manufacturing is very long.[6] Here the more macroeconomic factors are explored, including the following:

1) Was investment too low; and, if so, what were the reasons?
2) Was there a slackening in our effort to maintain technological advantage?
3) What was the role of such policy-related factors as the tax system, government regulation, inadequacies in the provision of skilled and technical manpower, and underinvestment in infrastructure?
4) Why did our international competitive position decline; and what were the roles of exchange rates, relative cost performance and international trade policies?

WAS MANUFACTURING INVESTMENT TOO LOW?

There was no measurable decline in the rate of manufacturing fixed investment in the United States in the last two decades. Indeed, as Chart 3.1 and Table 3.1 show, there was, if anything, an increase in the relationship between manufacturing investment and manufacturing shipments. In the period 1978-82, manufacturing invested 6.0 cents of every dollar of revenue from shipments, somewhat above the historical average.

---

[6]See the references in footnote 2 for some writings advancing various hypotheses, most of them focussed on particular aspects of corporate decisions and processes.

Chart 3.1
Manufacturing Investment as a Percent
of Shipments, 1958-1982

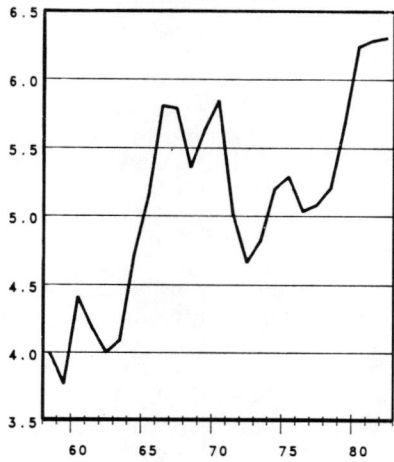

Table 3.1
Manufacturing Shipments and Investment, 1958-1982

	1958-62	1963-67	1968-72	1973-77	1978-82
Fixed Investment (Billions of Dollars)	14.9	25.4	34.9	55.8	108.1
Shipments (Billions of Dollars)	366.4	491.4	661.1	1,095.1	1,805.6
Investment as a Share of Shipments (Percent)	4.1	5.1	5.3	5.1	6.0

While more cyclical than other investment, manufacturing investment represented a roughly constant share in normal years, about 31% of the total investment.[7] Thus, one cannot argue that the relative industrial decline is directly attributable to a diminished willingness to invest.

---

[7]The petroleum industry is excluded from manufacturing in this calculation, because many of its investment and production activities are actually in mining.

Nor do the data show any slowdown in the rate of growth of the manufacturing capital stock (Chart 3.2). While unstable because of the business cycle, they show, if anything, an acceleration in its growth, averaging 2.8% in the 1950s, 3.7% in the 1960s, and 3.8% in the 1970s. Even this decade, with its recession-ridden beginning, shows a pretty considerable 6.2% rate of growth of this capital stock in its first two years.

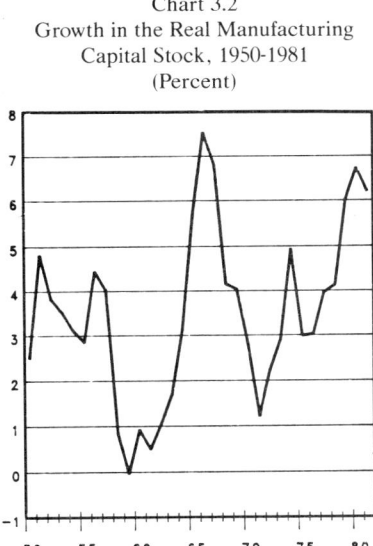

Chart 3.2
Growth in the Real Manufacturing
Capital Stock, 1950-1981
(Percent)

The shortfall in capital formation must, therefore, be found in other dimensions. At least four viewpoints can be distinguished: (1) we invested less than other industrial nations, particularly Japan; (2) the investment was concentrated in a few new industries and technologies, while the older "smokestack" industries were neglected; (3) investment was insufficient for the modernization, cost reduction and expansion of our factories and was concentrated in other forms of investment instead; and (4) a rising share of the investment had to be devoted to pollution control.

Manufacturing Investment Abroad: The Boom in Japan

Investment in U.S. manufacturing was "normal" in relation to our own previous historical experience, but it was grossly inadequate in terms of the challenges posed by other countries, particularly Japan. Chart 3.3 shows the percentage of total GNP devoted to investment in manufacturing for the United States and Japan. In the United States, the share was roughly constant when averaged over business cycles, averaging 3.9%; but Japan engaged in a massive wave of investment in her manufacturing industries in the late 1960s and the early 1970s. The share of GNP devoted to this purpose was 7% or higher from 1968 to 1974. This was an enormous amount of investment to build new factories, and gave Japan a manufacturing production establishment which, in many industries, was the most modern in the world.

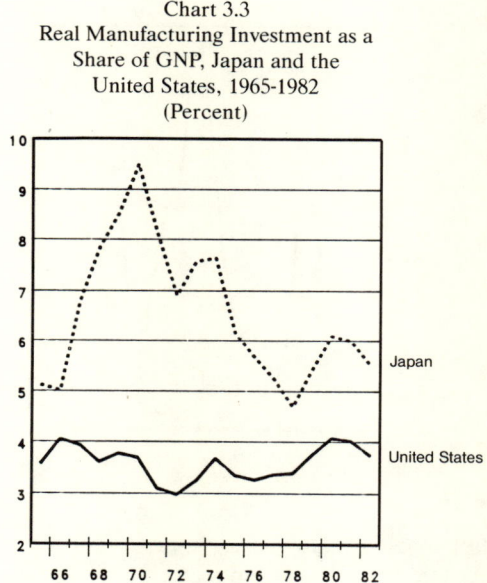

Chart 3.3
Real Manufacturing Investment as a Share of GNP, Japan and the United States, 1965-1982
(Percent)

To some extent, this extraordinary national investment in manufacturing industry was a matter of national strategy, an expression of Japan's industrial policy. These were the years when the Japanese automobile industry advanced from being a minor player in the international game to being the world leader. Her steel industry had benefited from earlier investments, but was expanded and kept up to date in technology during these years as well. The Japanese takeover of the world consumer electronics market was also a result of this extraordinary effort.

Japan's effort to become the world leader of manufacturing in the last 18 years could not have succeeded if it were only a desire of national policy. But the investments occurred in an environment which was peculiarly favorable to their success. These matters will be explored in more detail later in this chapter.[8]

Shifts Among Industries

A relatively stable rate of U.S. manufacturing investment as a whole also hides some disparities among industries. Chart 3.4 and Table 3.2 show the division of investment between the more traditional manufacturing industries and a broadly defined high-tech sector. The aggregate of investment of such industries as food, textiles and apparel, paper, petroleum refining, rubber, stone, clay and glass, primary metals, fabricated metals, and automobiles received a declining share of the total manufacturing investment dollar. On the other hand, the broadly defined high-tech sector, including chemicals, nonelectrical and electrical machinery industries and instruments received rising shares of investment.

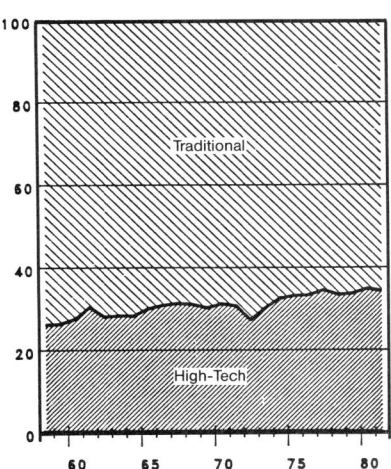

Chart 3.4
Shifts in Manufacturing Equipment
Investment by Industry, 1958-1981
(Percent of total)

[8]For an analysis of the critical role of capital formation in the differential in the growth of labor productivity, see J.R. Norsworthy and D.H. Malmquist, "Import Measurement and Productivity Growth in Japanese and U.S. Manufacturing," *American Economic Review*, December 1983, Vol. 73, No. 5, pp. 947-967. The authors conclude, " ... the remarkable record of labor productivity growth in Japan is attributed in large part to the growth of the capital stock," (p.958).

Table 3.2
Shifts in Manufacturing Investment
by Industry Type, 1958-1981
(Percent of total)

	1958-62	1963-67	1968-72	1973-77	1978-81
High-Tech Industries	27.7	29.8	30.1	32.8	34.1
Traditional Industries	72.3	70.2	69.9	67.2	65.9

Investment by Type of Equipment

The type of investment good that was actually acquired confirms the same general picture. As Chart 3.5 and Table 3.3 show, investment in the high technology types of equipment, including electronic, photographic, communication and office machinery represented an increasing share of total investment, rising from less than 30% in the years before 1972 to 45% in the last five years. The more traditional types of machinery, such as general-purpose industrial machinery, construction equipment and transportation equipment received a diminished share, with industrial machinery down from 24.1% to 16.5%.

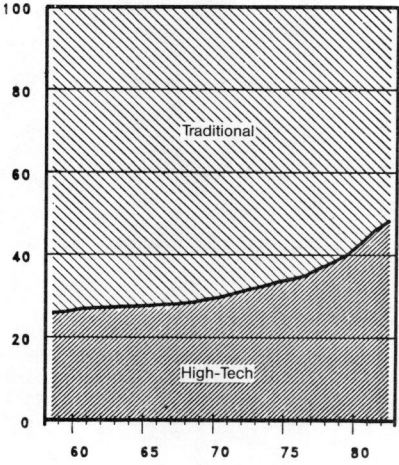

Chart 3.5
Shifts in Manufacturing Equipment
Investment by Type, 1958-1982
(Percent of total)

Table 3.3
Shifts in Manufacturing Investment
by Equipment Type
(Percent)

	1958-62	1963-67	1968-72	1973-77	1978-82
High-Tech Equipment	26.5	27.6	29.9	34.0	45.4
Office Machinery	8.4	8.7	9.2	11.2	19.2
Communications Machinery, Photo and Electronic Equipment	18.1	18.9	20.7	22.8	26.2
Traditional Equipment	73.5	72.4	70.1	66.0	54.6
Agricultural Equipment	7.2	6.9	5.6	6.0	4.1
Construction Equipment	4.7	5.1	4.6	4.5	3.3
Industrial Machinery	25.4	24.8	22.5	20.5	17.4
Transportation Equipment	25.7	26.4	27.6	26.5	22.3
Autos, Trucks, and Buses	18.6	18.7	20.0	21.0	17.2
Airplanes, Ships and Railroad Equipment	7.1	7.7	7.6	5.4	5.0
Other: Engines, Service Machinery and Household Equipment	10.5	9.1	9.8	8.6	7.5

Construction: Underinvestment in Factories

Another clue to the inadequacies of U.S. industrial investment can be found in the pattern of construction activity. Partly for reasons of the tax laws, and partly because of the relative unprofitability of manufacturing compared to the service sector, a rather small share of total construction was devoted to industrial investment in the United States. Chart 3.6 shows the relationship between industrial construction and total nonresidential construction. The industrial share declined sharply, from 31% in 1967 to 15% in 1982, as the country enjoyed a wave of construction of shopping malls, office buildings and utility capacity. Tax shelters subsidized the building of stores, apartments and warehouses; office buildings could be built with much leverage, while the financing of factories competed for scarce investment dollars in the tough capital budgeting struggles of industrial corporations.

The available data suggest that Japan pursued a very different emphasis in her construction activities. Industrial construction represented a rising share of all nonresidential construction, and absorbed more than twice the share of GNP as in the United States. Whereas U.S. plant construction was generally limited to our more successful industries and to plants of modest scale, Japan constructed large industrial plants; and, where basic capacity was needed, she did not hesitate to build it.

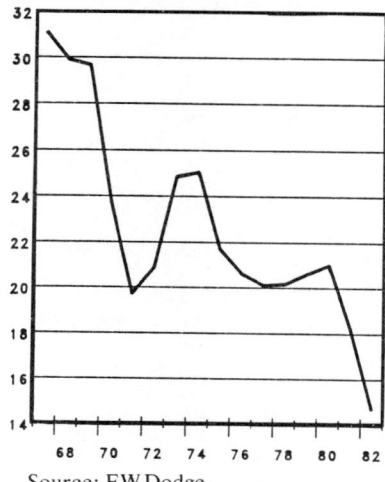

Chart 3.6
Private Industrial Construction as a Percent of
Total Private Nonresidential Construction, 1967-1982

Source: F.W.Dodge

THE HIGH COST OF CAPITAL

The causes of the inability of American manufacturing industry to respond to the challenge of Japan and other new competitors can be traced to numerous factors. But high on the list was an exceptionally high cost of capital, a cost far higher than in other sectors of the economy, and higher than in our principal foreign competitors.

A manufacturing company finances the larger part of its investment by means of internal and external equity sources. On the debt side, bank loans and commercial paper are routinely used to finance inventories and other working capital needs; and bonds can be sold in limited quantities. But access to debt is relatively limited, as the financial community insists on preservation of strong balance sheets which are largely defined in terms of relatively low debt-to-equity ratios. Thus, even though debt-equity ratios rose in recent decades, debt represented only about one-third of the balance sheet of the typical large capital-intensive manufacturing company at the end of the period.

Other sectors of the economy are able to make greater use of debt. Residential and commercial construction are largely financed by mortgages, with equity representing a relatively small percentage. The electric utility industry, which uses immense amounts of capital, shows debt representing nearly 60% of its balance sheet.

Equity capital is expensive. The return that has to be paid on it is not deductible in calculating corporate income taxes, doubling the effective cost compared to debt financing. Further, equity financing, particularly the issue of new stock, dilutes existing ownership by surrendering to the new providers of capital a share of the permanent ownership of the business. Thus, the typical cost of equity capital is more than twice as high as the cost of debt capital.

Why is manufacturing so limited in its use of debt? There are two primary reasons. First, because of the continued prevalence of the business cycle and the vulnerability of the demand for manufactured goods, earnings of manufacturers are relatively unstable. Consequently, if debt financing were the principal source of capital, many companies would be making large losses in recession times because of their leveraged balance sheets; and some of them would be forced into bankruptcy. Thus, because of the lender's risk on debt capital in an unstable economy, it is necessary to hold down the share of debt in total financing.

Second, the tax laws are less favorable to debt financing in manufacturing. Many provisions of the tax code push in that direction. Despite tax provisions that lower average effective rates, many manufacturing companies pay corporate income tax at the margin in the general range of the statutory tax rates. Financial institutions, on the other hand, are able to reduce their corporate taxes to very low figures, giving them an advantage in attracting capital. Further, tax shelters provide cheap equity capital for the financing of commercial and residential construction, and put a premium on leveraging that equity capital with the heavy use of debt to make large tax loss writeoffs possible. These differences in the cost of capital help create differences in profitability.

Utilities are also able to use more debt capital than manufacturing. Their earnings are less volatile, and their prices are set on a cost-plus basis by regulation. Because they provide services that are relatively essential in the short run, their volume is less variable over the business cycle. Prices are set by regulation, so the heightened price competition of recession has less effect. As a result, utilities are able to obtain 50% to 60% of their capital from debt sources.

The Japanese economy suffers less from these disparities. One of the elements of her strategy of industrialization has been the use of cheap debt capital to finance large-scale manufacturing investment. The close relationships between the Bank of Japan, the commercial banks and the large industrial corporations operating under the friendly eye of the government make possible a preponderant use of debt, even in manufacturing. While high historical growth may have reduced the risk of such debt financing, Japan's industries also suffer from the business cycle and from earnings swings. It is the close relationships among the public and private and financial and nonfinancial sectors which allow Japanese manufacturing to make much heavier use of debt than is done in the U.S. Indeed, in recent years, Japanese financing has moved toward the American pattern. But in the period of particularly high manufacturing investment, heavy use of debt financing was a key supporting element.

The Japanese government has understood the important role of a low cost of capital to a successful industrialization process. In the last four years, the cost of capital in the United States was boosted by a monetary policy designed to bring an end to double-digit inflation. Japan also pursued a vigorous policy of disinflation—but avoided the use of high interest rates, limiting the use of credit by more quantitative guidance, whereas the United States relied almost entirely on the price mechanism of record interest rates.

A recent study by Hatsopoulos[9] analyzes the cost of industrial capital in the United States and in Japan. The study calculates the typical composite rental price of capital, using the actual cost of debt and equity capital as the two financing sources. As Chart 3.7 summarizes, the after-tax cost of industrial capital for fixed investment in Japan was 7.8% in 1980, whereas in the United States it was 20.8%.

One of the most common observations of critics of U.S. business decisions is their myopic character. Every industry is rife with stories of decisions made on too short a focus, decisions which ultimately proved very damaging to long-range competitive positions. Japanese business, on the other hand, is credited with greater farsightedness, including willingness to build new basic capacity and create worldwide marketing and distribution systems. The typical American corporation must use high "hurdle" rates in judging investment proposals, given the high composite cost of capital that it pays. While internally generated funds may appear to be very cheap to management, they become, in effect, very expensive when their supply falls far short of the investment opportunities open to the firm. In the typical capital budgeting process, projects compete for the scarce funds; and the high hurdle rate is one mechanical rule which reflects the high opportunity costs. If the firm has to raise external capital, it faces the constraints on long-term debt financing or must pay the very high effective returns on new stock issues.

---

[9]George N. Hatsopoulos, *High Cost of Capital, Handicap of American Industry,* American Business Conference, Inc., Thermo Electron Corporation, April 26, 1983, p. 118.

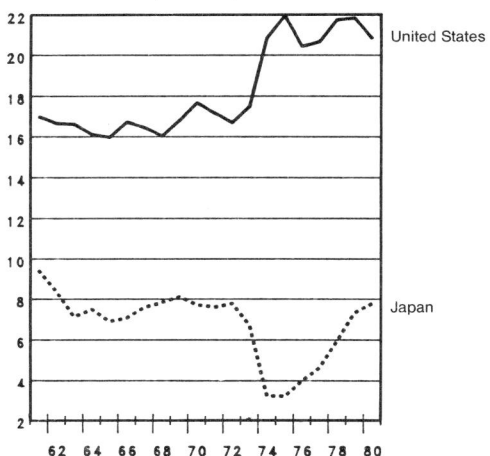

Chart 3.7
The Real Cost of Fixed Asset
Services, Japan and the
United States, 1961-1980
(Percent)

In summary, the difference in the cost of industrial capital between Japan and the United States can explain much of the difference in the levels of industrial investment. It also affects the degree of farsightedness or myopia which governs investment strategies in the two countries.

Comparisons with European countries produce intermediate results. The use of debt is greater in Germany and France than in the U.S., though not as high as in Japan. One reason for their greater willingness to use debt is the lesser role of stockholders and of stock markets. Lenders of debt, particularly banks, play a larger role than in the United States; and so there is less emphasis on steady earnings-per-share growth on common stocks.

The Special Problem of Underdepreciation

The high cost of capital in U.S. manufacturing industry is also partly attributable to the depreciation provisions of postwar tax laws. While there were liberalizations of depreciation allowances in 1954, 1962, and 1971, these changes were insufficient to keep pace with the accelerating consumption of capital and the increasing inflation. Economic lives were shortened and the depreciation paths were made more generous, but the basic principle of depreciation remained the writing down of historical cost. As inflation worsened, the gap between the funds needed to replace capital and the depreciation allowances generated by historical cost writeoffs widened. Only with the adoption of the Accelerated Cost Recovery System in the Economic Recovery Tax Act of 1981 was the average depreciation allowance raised to an economic level; but differences among industries remain great, with high-tech industries gaining little benefit.

The Bureau of Economic Analysis of the Department of Commerce publishes estimates of the under—or over—depreciation, which is, of course, on a replacement basis. Chart 3.8 shows these government estimates. It can be seen that there was underdepreciation until the reforms of 1981, except for the years following the depreciation reforms of 1962.

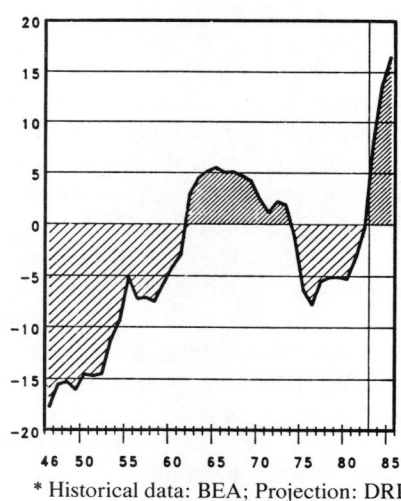

Chart 3.8
The Depreciation Adjustment to Corporate
Profits as a Percent of Fixed
Nonresidential Investment, 1946-1985*

* Historical data: BEA; Projection: DRI

Total Taxation of Capital Income

While depreciation is a particularly important aspect of the tax system, federal and state tax rates and local property taxes also affect the total burden of taxation of capital. A recent study by King and Fullerton[10] analyzes the total burden on taxation of capital income. Their study calculates marginal rates on a typical investment yielding a 10% pretax return. As Table 3.4 shows, the marginal tax rate on capital income in manufacturing is about four times as great as the marginal tax rate in nonmanufacturing industry. The commercial sector pays intermediate marginal tax rates. Their study also shows that the burden of taxation of capital rises substantially with the inflation rate, ranging from a marginal rate of 38.4% in the absence of inflation to 49.0% at 10% inflation in the case of manufacturing.

King and Fullerton also analyze the effective marginal tax rates on capital financed by different methods. These results are even more extraordinary

Table 3.4
Effective Marginal Tax Rates on Capital Income Following the
Tax Equity and Fiscal Responsibility Act of 1982 (Percents)[a]

Capital Income	Inflation Rate		
	Zero	6.77	10.00
Industry			
Manufacturing	38.4	46.4	49.0
Other industry	7.9	11.4	12.4
Commerce	29.6	30.5	30.5
Financing			
Debt	−8.9	−23.5	−29.1
New issues of stock	57.8	87.7	101.2
Retained earnings	43.9	57.3	61.7

Source: Mervyn King and Don Fullerton, eds., "The United States," *The Taxation of Income from Capital*, Discussion Paper No. 37 (Princeton University, Woodrow Wilson School of Public and International Affairs, December 1982), Figure 6.28.

a. Present value of federal income tax, state income tax, and state and local property tax paid as percentage of the return to one dollar of additional investment on the part of all owners of the specified asset. (Assumes all investments begin with a 10 percent pretax return.) For an explanation of the economic model used to generate these results, see Mervyn King and Don Fullerton, eds., "The Theoretical Framework," in *The Taxation of Income from Capital: A Comparative Study of the U.S., U.K., Sweden, and West Germany*, Discussion Paper No. 36 (Princeton University, Woodrow Wilson School of Public and International Affairs, December 1982).

[10]Mervyn King and Don Fullerton, eds., "The United States," *The Taxation of Income From Capital*, Discussion Paper No. 37 (Princeton University, Woodrow Wilson School of International and Public Affairs, December 1982).

and cast light on the disparities in the cost of capital between the United States and Japan. Debt-financed capital actually faces a negative marginal tax rate, i.e., a disguised subsidy; and, as the rate of inflation rises, this subsidy grows. This negative tax rate is produced by the reduction in the real burden of debt under inflation, a reduction which is not recognized by the tax law which allows all interest to be deductible.

On the other hand, the marginal tax rate on capital derived from new stock issues is extremely high, and at high rates of inflation exceeds 100%. A 10% return in a period of 10% inflation is actually no return at all, yet whatever nominal profit is earned is subject to taxation, making the effective tax rate over 100%. Capital obtained from retained earnings also shows a heavy tax burden, worsening with inflation; but the figures are not quite as extreme.

In summary, then, the high cost of capital was very much at the heart of the problems of U.S. manufacturing industry. Because of the inability of manufacturing to have access to large amounts of debt financing and because of the particular provisions of our tax laws, manufacturing capital is extremely expensive. Obtained at high costs, business allocates this capital as if the opportunity cost were very high. This means that less is invested and that it is invested on a relatively shortsighted basis. Japan, on the other hand, maintains a much lower cost of capital, making it possible for her industry to invest more, to undertake larger projects, and to accept longer periods of payback. These are matters which can be remedied, and some of the tax changes of 1981 have done so. But the cost of capital remains high; and, if our manufacturing industry is to stage a major revival, it will have to have access, one way or another, to cheaper capital on terms competitive with other sectors.

A Low Saving Rate

While institutional and tax factors played a critical role creating the high cost of capital for U.S. industry, the relatively low level of national saving was also of importance. The United States has operated with a substantially lower personal saving rate than the other principal industrial countries (Table 3.5). The personal saving rate has varied from 6% to 8% over the last 20 years, and became even lower in 1982-83. In Japan, the personal saving rate has been close to 20%, and in Germany over 14%. Even the United Kingdom saves more than the U.S. Table 3.5 shows the savings rates estimated in a recent study that corrects for conceptual differences in the measurements of different countries.

There are numerous institutional and historical factors which explain these differences in savings rates. The use of consumer credit is more highly

Table. 3.5
Savings Rates, Averages
1970 to 1980,
Six Countries

France	13.4
Germany	14.7
Italy	21.5
Japan	20.7
United Kingdom	8.0
United States	7.7

Source: Derek W. Blades and Peter H. Sturm, "The Concept and Measurement of Savings: The United States and Other Industrialized Countries," Federal Reserve Bank of Boston, Conference Series No. 25, *Saving and Government Policy*, pp. 1-30.

developed here. Until recently, government deficits represented a larger form of dissaving in the other countries and required correspondingly higher personal savings rates. Differences in private and public pension arrangements also account for some of the differences. At this time, the United States is an importer of capital, whereas Japan and Germany are exporters.

Nonetheless, the low volume of personal saving is a fundamental characteristic of the U.S. economy. With personal saving providing very little industrial capital, companies are dependent on cyclically vulnerable retained corporate earnings and on open capital markets that show large price fluctuations caused by variations in foreign and domestic flows-of-funds and in monetary policies.

THE EFFECT OF STOP-GO POLICIES: SOME ECONOMETRIC RESULTS

The American economy has experienced seven recessions since 1950. In each episode, the demand for manufacturing output dropped sharply in response to a sudden correction of the desired stocks of inventories and, in most cases, a sudden change in financial conditions. As a result, the utilization rate of manufacturing capacity was highly variable (Chart 3.9).

The timing of the recessions was a surprise to business. Usually, they were only recognized once financial conditions became extreme and sales expec-

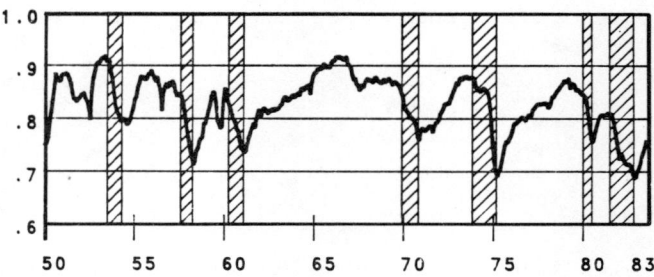

Chart 3.9
Capacity Utilization in Manufacturing
1950-July 1983
(Proportion, SA)

Note: Shaded areas denote recession periods. Extreme values are not precisely compatible across cycles because of changes in industry composition.

tations collapsed right across industry lines. Thus, the expectations on which business capital planning was based were falsified: sales were suddenly discovered to be much lower than expected, cutting the near-term need for capacity; the internal cash flow expected to finance the investment was sharply reduced; the cost of external capital and, in the earlier periods its availability, took a sudden unfavorable turn. As a result, business had no choice but to sharply curtail capital spending programs. When this process occurs 7 times in 30 years, the process of industrial capital formation and development must be expected to be seriously impaired. These disruptions reduced not only the total level of capital spending, but also may have contributed to the myopic bias often attributed to U.S. business decision making. When great uncertainty attaches to the sales, capacity needs, and profits of the next few years, it is not surprising that business adjusts to this volatile environment by insisting on quick payoffs and excessively cautious expansion plans.

The effects of the volatile postwar business cycle on manufacturing investment can be approximated by a relatively simple econometric exercise (Table 3.6). A standard equation, following the method of Dale W. Jorgenson, has been fitted to manufacturing investment data, using the actual historical record. This equation accounts for variations of investment in terms of expected output, expected rental price of capital, a debt service-liquidity variable, the existing stock of capital which produces replacement requirements, the utilization rate of capacity and surprises in this utilization rate. A second equation calculates the capital stock produced by the investment

Table 3.6
Investment and Capital Stock of U.S. Manufacturing
Two Scenarios, 1960-1980
(Billions of 1972 dollars)

	Investment		Capital Stock	
	Actual Path	"Stability" Path	Actual Path	"Stability" Path
1965	27.58	26.46	564.52	561.98
1970	35.39	36.18	645.17	639.04
1975	39.41	44.54	716.42	729.87
1980	52.36	64.03	815.03	883.09

Table 3.7
Econometric Model for Manufacturing Investment and Capital Stock

Equation for Investment

(1) $I_m = -2.78 + \sum_t \alpha_t (pq/c)_t + \sum_t \beta_t CF_t + \sum_t \lambda_t (P_E/P)_t + \sum_t \eta_t (\sigma_{pq/c})_t$
         (-0.7) (2.0) (2.2) (2.5) (-2.0)
   $+ .21 (UCAP) * (K_m) - .15 K_m$
      (7.0) (-6.3)

$\bar{R}^2$: .99   Note: t-statistics are in parentheses under coefficients

Definition of Capital Stock

(2) $K = K_{-1} - D_m + I_m$

where I_m = investment in manufacturing
       pq/c = Jorgenson term, including price, output and the rental price of capital
       CF = cash flow
       P_E/P = relative price of energy
       $\sigma_{pq/c}$ = volatility of Jorgenson term
       $UCAP$ = utilization rate of industrial capacity
       K_m = capital stock
       D_m = depreciation

To derive investment levels that would have been achieved in a more stable economy, these assumptions were made to evaluate equation (1):

1) UCAP was set at 0.85;
2) $\sigma_{pq/c}$ was set at its 1960s value for the years 1970-80;
3) The Jorgenson term was set to grow at its average rate for the 1960s in the years 1970-80.

estimates and the government's technical estimates of depreciation. Table 3.7 shows the two equations and defines the variables.

In a simulation exercise, this two-equation model is evaluated on the assumption that the economy was substantially more stable since 1960. The utilization rate of industry is held to a near-normal value. The cost of capital is near its average level; and, therefore, the liquidity variable also remains normal. The two-equation model shows what would have happened under these conditions both to the investment levels and to the growth of the capital stock. Investment would have been somewhat higher, by an average of 10.6% a year. This extra investment would have produced a more rapid expansion of the capital stock, which in turn would have provided the vehicle for modernization and replacement, and would have contributed to further increases of investment levels in a virtuous circle of expansion and modernization. By 1980, the manufacturing capital stock would have been 8.4% larger, a significant step-up which would have left American industry in a more competitive position. Thus, business paid a price for the instability of the postwar U.S. economy and for the policies which were the main causes of this instability.

To summarize our discussion of manufacturing investment: the total level of outlays in recent decades was in line with the volume of sales, and was not particularly low judged by historical standards. The problem has to be viewed differently: the United States invested less than other countries; it did not rise to the challenge of the new competition from abroad. Further, within the investment totals there was a major shift away from traditional industries toward high technology firms and high technology equipment. Given the challenge offered by new competitors and new technological opportunities, U.S. industry did not invest enough. A substantial step-up of investment levels would have been required to preserve U.S. industrial leadership, and such a step-up could not be achieved in the context of the actual policy environment in which U.S. industry functioned and in the context of the corporate structure in which investment decisions were made. The high cost of capital—higher than in other sectors and higher than in Japan—was a major cause of the inadequacy of our manufacturing investment efforts.

DID OUR TECHNOLOGICAL EFFORTS SLACKEN?

The United States was the world's technological leader throughout the postwar period. A preponderant share of Nobel prizes was won by scientists working in this country. More scientists were actively at work than anywhere else. The number of engineers was large, though not dramatically different in relation to the labor force than in other advanced countries. The American contribution to the principal technological innovations was very great. Indeed, a large percentage of all new products originated in the American economy.

American leadership in high technology industries continues to this day, with only Japan a serious challenge. Yet questions are being raised about our ability to retain our technological position; indeed, it seems almost inevitable that our leadership will, at best, be shared.

The American effort in technology has been devoted heavily to particular goals and industries. The development of missiles, nuclear weapons and other defense products, as well as the space program, particularly the all-out effort to put a man on the moon, attracted some of the best engineering and scientific talent.

If these particular programs had occurred in a setting of a rapidly expanding supply of scientific and engineering manpower, these forward thrusts would not have come at the expense of other industries that also have important scientific and engineering tasks. But the supply of engineers did not keep pace with the new demands. For example, the United States graduated 69,300 bachelor degree-level engineers in 1980 while Japan graduated slightly more, 73,500, with a population about half of ours (National Science Foundation data). In the absence of a large increase in supply, engineering industries could not compete either in terms of pay or job challenge for the scarce talent. As a result, the United States declined in some of the more traditional engineering industries and suffered a slowdown of technical advance and competitive position in other industries. Three well-known cases illustrate these points.

Thirty years ago, the United States was a leading producer of textile machinery. During the 1950s, the industry declined sharply, and today domestic production is a small part of available supply. American textile mills purchase their equipment from manufacturers in Germany, Austria, Holland, Switzerland, Japan and elsewhere. There are numerous reasons for the decline of this particular industry, but probably one of the contributing factors was the inability of the industry to compete for engineering talent. At the engineering salaries set by the defense and other high-growth sectors, American textile machinery firms could not design the rapidly advancing equipment at competitive costs.

An efficient chemical industry building state-of-the-art plants requires a sufficient supply of highly trained chemical engineers, including some with advanced degrees. The U.S. has trained very few graduate chemical engineers in recent years, making it more difficult to build chemical plants. While we have always shared our lead in this industry with Germany, the

Japanese chemical industry is now posing a major challenge, a challenge partly made possible by an abundant supply of trained specialists.

Differences in the supply of engineers can be seen in the rate of progress of various consumer products. In fields such as consumer electronics, photographic equipment and even appliances, Japanese manufacturers have been able to apply much larger design and engineering efforts than their American counterparts. While exchange rates and comparative labor costs may be the fundamental reasons for their ability to outcompete American producers, their greater ability to improve their products is also due to a more abundant supply of engineers available to work in these industries.

The total research and development effort of the major industrial countries can be seen from Table 3.8, prepared by Abram Bergson from various sources.[11] It shows that the total level of research and development effort is little different in the United States from the other major industrial countries, and in 1975 was about 2.2% of GNP. But, when the outlays for defense and space are taken out of the figures, the remaining percentage is smaller than in West Germany and Japan. Thus, the overall statistics on research and development confirm the picture of a large-scale, overall effort on the part of the United States, but a lesser effort available for civilian purposes.

Table 3.8
Expenditures on R & D, Selected Countries
(Percent of GNP)

Country	All Outlays		All Outlays Excluding Those for Defense and Space	
	ca. 1967	1975	ca. 1967	1975
United States	2.9	2.2	1.2	1.4
France	2.2	1.5	1.5	1.1
West Germany	1.8	2.2	1.6	2.1
United Kingdom	2.7	2.1[a]	1.9	1.6[a]
Japan	1.8	2.0[b]	1.8	2.0[b]
Italy	0.6	.9-1.0[a]	n.a.[c]	n.a.
USSR	2.9	3.7	1.4	n.a.

[a] R & D as a share of GDP
[b] 1974
[c] n.a.: not available

Source: Bergson, op. cit.

[11] Abram Bergson, "Technological Progress," Chapter 2 in Abram Bergson and Herbert S. Levine, eds., *The Soviet Economy: Toward the Year 2000*, p. 54.

There are both economic and philosophical explanations for the insufficiency of the supply of engineers in this country. The compensation offered has been good in relation to some occupations such as teaching, but has fallen far short of the rewards for management, marketing and finance. Some of the most talented engineering school graduates go on to advanced training in schools of business administration. Others make the switch from the technical to the administrative or marketing functions at other stages of their careers. The compensation and opportunity patterns are partly due to the changing structure of the economy: engineering industries lost their ability to pay because of their declining role in foreign markets and domestic instability.

Changing educational philosophies also reduced the supply of engineers by limiting the percentage of college students with an adequate background in mathematics. An affluent society has fewer youngsters willing to take enough mathematics and science in high school to become candidates for an engineering education. Japan still operates under a value system which tends to produce more engineers.

THE ROLE OF REGULATORY POLICY

Over the last 20 years, the scope of government regulation of business expanded considerably, as a number of policy goals came into focus. They include equal access to job opportunities for all potential workers, regardless of race, sex or age; application of minimum standards to assure occupational safety in places of work; safety standards for automobiles; and reduction of man-made damage to the physical environment, including air, earth and water.

These policies and concerns were not peculiar to the United States, but became integral parts of policy in all advanced industrial countries, although not to the same degree. Nor is there any serious disagreement that these goals must be pursued to promote a just society and to preserve the natural heritage for future generations. Nonetheless, the policies of regulation designed to assure these goals were particularly costly to certain manufacturing industries, and compounded their difficulties of adjusting to a more competitive international situation.

Environmental policies required major investments in pollution control equipment. The Department of Commerce conducts a survey and provides estimates of the total investment made for pollution abatement, at least to the extent that the equipment can clearly be identified as installed principally for this purpose. Table 3.9 shows the percentage of all investment that can be identified as of the pollution abatement type for various industries. In the last ten years they averaged 6.2%. The cost was particularly large for process industries. The chemical industry spent 9.1% of its investment dollars on pollution abatement, primary metals spent 14.9%. In a period of insufficient capital supply, some of these outlays came at the expense of investment for modernization, productivity improvement and expansion. In addition, because industry also had to modify some of its production processes, the total cost of pollution control was larger than the indicated percentage.

Pollution abatement efforts were similar in the more mature industrial countries. In Japan, where the pollution control standards are at least as high as in the United States, costs were probably somewhat more moderate because more of the capacity was new and could therefore embody high pollution control standards in its basic design. In the United States, a large part of the outlays consisted of retrofit improvements in older capacity, which are less efficient and more costly than an adequate initial process design. In the newly industrialized countries, pollution control standards are usually lower, and the requisite costs are thereby held down.

The costs of meeting other goals, such as equal opportunity and occupational safety, are harder to identify; and, indeed, there are probably substantial benefits. To give all our people access to jobs improves the supply of

Table 3.9
Pollution Abatement Expenditures as a Percent
of Investment in Plant and Equipment, 1973-1982

	1973	1974	1975	1976	1977	1978	1979	1980	1981	1982
Manufacturing	7.3	7.1	9.0	8.1	6.8	5.6	4.9	4.8	4.3	3.9
Nondurables Manufacturing	8.3	8.3	10.6	9.7	8.2	6.9	5.9	5.7	5.3	4.7
Food and Products	6.7	6.2	7.2	6.3	5.1	5.7	4.1	3.7	3.7	4.9
Textile Mill Products	3.9	4.6	5.5	3.8	3.2	2.9	4.0	4.3	3.2	2.3
Paper and Products	15.7	13.3	16.8	15.6	12.0	7.3	7.2	5.7	5.7	5.0
Chemicals	10.2	8.8	10.7	12.0	11.5	8.6	5.8	5.8	6.5	5.0
Petroleum Products	11.8	10.8	13.2	11.0	8.8	8.6	8.5	8.3	6.6	5.6
Rubber and Plastics	2.6	3.2	4.3	3.1	3.7	3.3	2.3	1.7	2.3	2.3
Durables Manufacturing	6.4	5.9	7.2	6.3	5.2	4.3	3.9	3.9	3.2	3.1
Stone, Clay, and Glass	9.5	12.9	13.3	8.1	7.2	7.4	5.3	6.5	5.1	3.1
Primary Metals	21.2	16.6	17.6	17.3	16.5	13.8	13.6	12.7	9.6	10.2
Fabricated Metals	5.0	5.2	6.5	3.6	3.6	2.1	2.3	2.4	2.4	1.5
Nonelectrical Machinery	2.3	1.7	1.8	1.6	1.8	1.8	1.3	1.3	1.1	1.4
Electrical Machinery	3.5	3.1	2.9	2.5	2.4	1.8	1.5	1.7	1.7	1.4
Transportation Equipment	3.9	2.8	2.7	2.7	2.5	2.3	2.7	2.9	2.5	2.6

labor and ultimately leads to reduced unit labor costs. Occupational safety standards reduce medical costs, though some of these cost savings will not be realized for some decades. Automotive safety reduces medical care and auto repair costs.

Other government regulations also left their imprint on the manufacturing industries in recent years. The wage-price controls imposed by President Nixon from 1971 to 1974 seriously distorted decision making. Industrial materials tended to be exported where price controls were effective, depriving our own manufacturing industries of sufficient material supplies during a worldwide boom. The profitability of some of the basic industries was also hurt by the price controls, particularly since the wage side of the program never became meaningful.

Perhaps more important than the measurable costs of regulation were the indirect costs associated with them. While business learned how to operate in an environment of expanded government authority over business decisions, its attentions and energies were diverted from business decisions themselves. The traditional hostility between business and government made the learning process particularly costly. In countries with a tradition of business-government collaboration, the amount of regulation was probably just as great; but the damage to business was less. Enforcement of the numerous old and new regulatory statutes was often unpredictable, introducing uncertainties into business decisions and delays into investment programs. It was during the years of new government regulation, 1966 to 1980, that U.S. industry lost much of its traditional strength, and this coincidence in timing is not entirely accidental.

CONCLUDING COMMENTS TO CHAPTERS 2 AND 3

A chronicle of the data of U.S. manufacturing of the last 20 years is not a happy story. Mistakes were made in private and public policies that proved to be damaging. The challenge of the new foreign competition was not met; and the domestic economic and business climates were, to a considerable degree, at fault.

But these internal problems would not have created the serious situation that we confront today if they had not occurred in the context of seriously damaging international economic policies. In the next chapter, we therefore turn to these matters in more detail.

CHAPTER 4

THE LOSS OF OUR COMPETITIVE POSITION

Diffusion of manufacturing know-how and development of new suppliers of industrial goods made some sharing of market positions inevitable, and retention of our dominant position after World War II would have been undesirable. But our decline has gone further than was necessary or desirable, and its causes should be identified. The loss of America's competitive position in world markets had many causes.

Perhaps the most fundamental cause of our loss of position was a foreign exchange rate which overvalued the dollar for much of the last 34 years. The importance of this factor cannot be understood without careful analysis of the relative cost position created for U.S. industry by the exchange rate and of the reasons for the persistence of the overvaluation.

U.S. trade policy also contributed to the decline. In the early postwar years, we deliberately encouraged recovery and growth of other countries, closing our eyes to the protectionist elements in the goals of the European Economic Community. While supporting the General Agreement of Tariffs and Trade which served to reduce tariffs, we did not take meaningful action to slow the proliferation of nontariff barriers.

U.S. industry also paid insufficient attention to the potential of foreign markets. Because of the size of our domestic market, some companies felt less urgency about opportunities abroad, and failed to make the sustained investments needed to develop overseas markets.

THE OVERVALUATION OF THE DOLLAR

Table 4.1 and Charts 4.1 to 4.3 illustrate some of the results of a recent DRI study[12] which examined the international competitive cost position of seven

---

[12]Roger Brinner and Nigel Gault, "U.S. Manufacturing Costs and International Competition," *Data Resources Review*, October 1983, pp. 1.13-1.23.

major countries. Table 4.1 shows the levels of unit labor costs for selected years, including a 1975 benchmark, for each nation and for a trade-weighted foreign composite, expressed in relation to U.S. cost levels. The benchmark was created by converting OECD measures of hourly compensation and productivity in manufacturing to dollar equivalents using purchasing-power-parity relatives for manufacturing gross product.[13]

Table 4.1
Unit Labor Costs
Multiples of U.S. Levels

	1968	1975 (Base)	1982
United States	1.00	1.00	1.00
Canada	0.90	1.03	0.94
France	0.60	0.85	0.63
United Kingdom	0.56	0.88	0.96
Germany	0.52	0.98	0.78
Italy	0.50	0.88	0.62
Japan	0.40	0.66	0.49
Foreign Composite	0.56	0.85	0.70

Chart 4.1 shows productivity, measured by output per hour in manufacturing, for the same countries in relation to U.S. productivity. It can be seen that output per manhour in West Germany surpassed U.S. productivity in 1978, and that productivity in Italy, Japan, France and Canada is now as high as or only slightly below our own. Productivity in the United Kingdom is little more than half of that in the other countries.

Chart 4.2 shows the changing pattern of wages corrected for movements in exchange rates. Average compensation per hour, after the exchange rate correction, is highest in the United States and West Germany and lowest in Japan and the United Kingdom. The chart shows clearly the effect of the recent appreciation of the dollar on U.S. competitiveness. For example, German labor compensation costs have moved from about 25% above U.S. costs in 1980 to about 20% below U.S. costs in 1982. Bringing together the wage costs with the productivity levels yields estimates of unit labor costs across countries (Chart 4.3), indicating a large disadvantage for the U.S. in

---

[13]The purchasing-power-parity relatives were taken from the study by Irving Kravis, Alan Heston and Robert Summers, *International Comparisons of Real Product and Purchasing Power,* (Johns Hopkins, Baltimore, 1978).

Chart 4.1
Productivity: Six Countries Versus
the United States, 1968-1986
(Output per manhour as a multiple of
U.S. output per manhour)

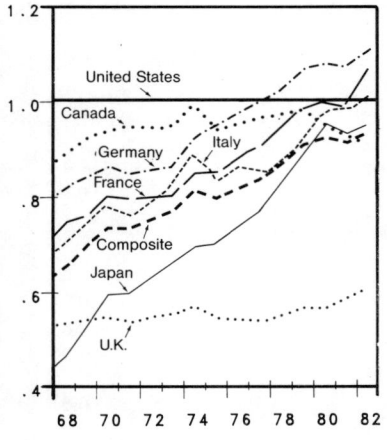

Chart 4.2
Labor Compensation: Six Countries Versus
the United States, 1968-1986
(Hourly compensation as a multiple of U.S.
hourly compensation and adjusted for
exchange rate shifts)

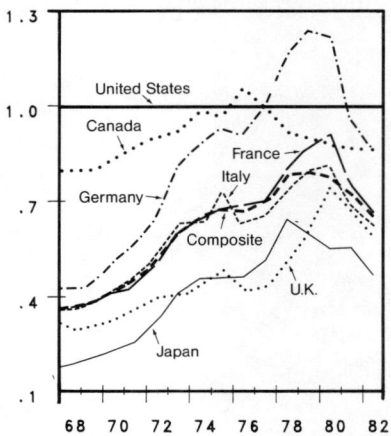

Chart 4.3
Unit Labor Costs: Six Countries Versus
the United States, 1968-1982
(Unit labor costs as a multiple of U.S.
unit labor costs)

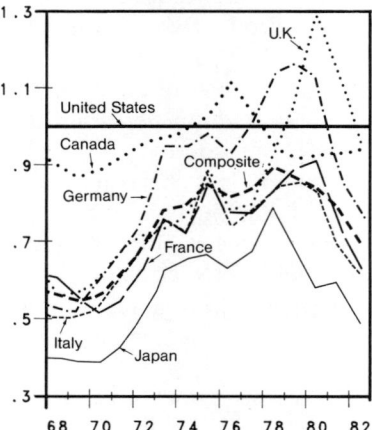

1968, the first year of the study, against all countries except Canada. Since then the figures for the United Kingdom and West Germany have moved near to, and at times above, U.S. levels. There has been a clear, continuing disadvantage against France and Italy and a very large disadvantage against Japan. In 1968 Japanese unit labor costs were little more than one-third of our own and, though rising during the 1970s to about two-thirds of our level, have now dropped back to about half the current U.S. level.

The preceding DRI analysis begins in 1968, but the overvaluation of the dollar began much earlier. In September 1949, when the major realignment of exchange rates after World War II occurred with the encouragement of the United States, the United Kingdom devalued by 30.5%, West Germany by 20.6%, and France by 21.5%. It was generally recognized that these changes were probably an overcorrection and were part of the strategy of the European Recovery Program designed to restore Western European prosperity. Exchange rates were held relatively fixed from 1949 until 1970, with just a few exceptions. France devalued several times, particularly in the late 1950s, in reflection of her higher inflation rate. The United Kingdom devalued in the mid-1960s; West Germany appreciated her currency during the 1960s in response to her good inflation record, strong export performance and the piling up of very large international reserves.

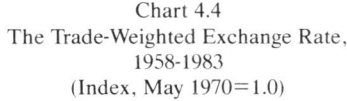

Chart 4.4
The Trade-Weighted Exchange Rate,
1958-1983
(Index, May 1970=1.0)

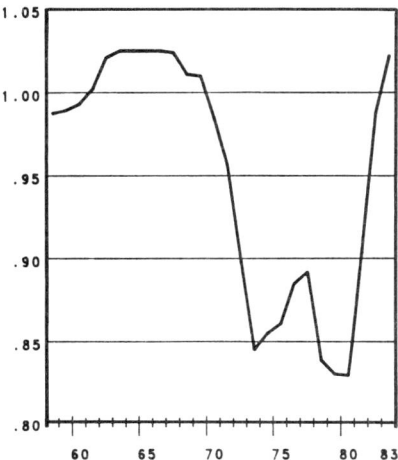

The overvaluation of the dollar was manifested in several ways. First, there were repeated episodes of losses of gold and other international reserves to which the United States responded by raising interest rates and lowering aggregate demand and economic activity. Indeed, the balance of payments was one of the major influences determining economic policy. Second, the overvaluation of the dollar was also manifested by the decline of the relative position of U.S. industries in international markets. If the exchange rate had been in equilibrium, such a decline would have been much less severe.

To be sure, equilibrium in a country's balance of payments does not require equilibrium in the balance of merchandise trade. A deficit on goods account could be offset by a surplus on services account, and a deficit on goods and services account could be offset by a surplus on capital account. But a closer look at the data leaves little doubt that there was no healthy offsetting factor to the imbalance in U.S. trade.

In the years prior to 1971, the United States experienced a series of balance of payments crises which were marked by sizable gold outflows. The government and the Federal Reserve usually responded to these gold crises by adopting somewhat more conservative budget policies and by raising interest rates. Indeed, this international factor in financial policy was one of the reasons for the credit squeezes of 1957, 1959, 1965 and 1968.

Chart 4.5
The United States Trade
Balance, Goods, Services, and
Total, 1950-1982
(Billions of dollars)

Table 4.2
U.S. International Balance of Payments, 1963-1982
(Billions of dollars, flows, annual rates, SA)

	1963	1964	1965	1966	1967	1968	1969	1970	1971	1972
Current Account										
Balance	4.4	6.8	5.4	3.0	2.6	0.6	0.4	2.3	−1.4	−5.8
Merchandise	5.2	6.8	5.0	3.8	3.8	0.6	0.6	2.6	−2.3	−6.4
Services	1.9	2.8	3.3	2.1	1.9	2.9	2.8	3.0	4.5	4.5
Net Transfers, excl. Military	−2.8	−2.8	−2.9	−2.9	−3.1	−3.0	−3.0	−3.3	−3.7	−3.9
Capital Account										
Balance	−4.1	−5.9	−5.0	−3.7	−2.4	−1.0	−1.1	−3.0	10.5	7.0
Official	0.3	0.0	−1.5	−2.2	1.0	−3.1	−3.5	5.3	25.0	8.9
Private	−4.8	−6.1	−4.7	−2.0	−3.5	2.9	5.8	−10.8	−16.8	−1.9
U.S. Assets Abroad*	−7.3	−9.6	−5.7	−7.3	−9.8	−11.0	−11.6	−9.3	−12.5	−14.5
Federal Govt. Assets	−1.7	−1.7	−1.6	−1.5	−2.4	−2.3	−2.2	−1.6	−1.9	−1.6
U.S. Private Assets	−6.0	−8.0	−5.3	−6.3	−7.4	−7.8	−8.2	−10.2	−12.9	−12.9
Foreign Assets in U.S.	3.2	3.6	0.7	3.7	7.4	9.9	12.7	6.4	23.0	21.5
Official Assets	2.0	1.7	0.1	−0.7	3.5	−0.8	−1.3	6.9	26.9	10.5
Other	1.2	2.0	0.6	4.3	3.9	10.7	14.0	−0.5	−3.9	11.0
Allocation of SDRs							0.0	0.9	0.7	0.7
Statistical Discrepancy	−0.4	−0.9	−0.5	0.6	−0.2	0.4	−1.5	−0.2	−9.8	−1.9

	1973	1974	1975	1976	1977	1978	1989	1980	1981	1982
Current Account										
Balance	7.1	2.1	18.3	4.2	−14.5	−15.4	−1.0	0.4	4.6	−11.2
Merchandise	0.9	−5.3	9.0	−9.5	−31.1	−34.0	−27.6	−25.5	−28.1	−36.4
Services	10.1	14.7	13.8	18.7	21.2	23.6	32.2	33.0	39.6	33.2
Net Transfers, excl. Military	−3.9	−7.2	−4.6	−5.0	−4.6	−5.1	−5.7	−7.1	−6.9	−8.0
Capital Account										
Balance	−4.5	−0.5	−24.0	−14.8	16.5	2.9	−25.6	−31.1	−29.9	−30.2
Official	3.4	10.9	3.6	13.5	33.1	29.0	−17.4	10.4	0.4	−2.6
Private	−8.0	−9.9	−26.7	−25.7	−16.2	−26.8	−7.0	−33.4	−25.1	−22.7
U.S. Assets Abroad*	−22.9	−34.7	−39.7	−51.3	−34.8	−61.1	−64.3	−86.1	−110.6	−118.0
Federal Govt. Assets	−2.6	0.4	−3.5	−4.2	−3.7	−4.7	−3.7	−5.1	−5.1	−5.7
U.S. Private Assets	−20.4	−33.6	−35.4	−44.5	−30.7	−57.2	−59.5	−72.8	−100.3	−107.3
Foreign Assets in U.S.	18.4	34.2	15.7	36.5	51.3	64.0	38.8	54.9	80.7	87.9
Official Assets	6.0	10.5	7.0	17.7	36.8	33.7	−13.7	15.6	5.4	3.2
Other	12.4	23.7	8.6	18.8	14.5	30.4	52.4	39.4	75.2	84.7
Allocation of SDRs	0.0	0.0	0.0	0.0	0.0	0.0	1.1	1.2	1.1	0.0
Statistical Discrepancy	−2.7	−1.6	5.8	10.5	−2.0	12.5	25.4	29.6	24.2	41.4

* Negative value indicates an increase in asset holdings.

In essence, the United States regulated its international payments by sporadically accepting the discipline of this vestigial gold standard. Aggregate demand was held down after international payments had gotten out of order. In this policy regime, excessive imports were converted into a restraint on domestic aggregate demand.

At the end of the 1960s, as the fixed exchange rate regime began to collapse, the United States no longer made any pretense of playing by the gold standard rules. Under the guise of providing the world with a sufficient supply of liquidity, we ran large deficits on capital account and diminishing surpluses on current account. As the world was flooded with liquidity, the world monetary system lost its self-equilibrating character, producing the worldwide boom of the early 1970s. In August 1971, the United States abandoned fixed exchange rates, yet the adjustment of the dollar to our deteriorated cost position was short lived. There were two reasons: first, the United States gradually developed an enormous surplus on services account; and, second, we became a major importer of capital.

Chart 4.5 shows a decomposition of the goods and services balance into its two components. Since 1976 our merchandise trade shows a rapidly enlarging deficit, but it is virtually offset by a growing surplus on services account. Thus the goods and services balance as a whole stayed near equilibrium.

The striking data of Chart 4.5 may suggest the domestic shift from goods to services associated with a post-industrial society. But "services" has a quite different meaning in international trade than in domestic activity. As Table 4.3 shows,[14] the rapid service growth is almost entirely limited to income from investments abroad, including earnings on past investments of U.S. industrial corporations and interest earnings on debt owed by foreigners to American official and private institutions. Because of the enormous rise of world debt and high rates, the United States earns enough interest to almost fully offset the decline of her trade in goods.

Some of this extraordinary service income is a delusion. Much of the foreign debt which is earning interest is in de facto default. The interest reported as earned is either postponed, or is paid by additional loans which have to be granted to stave off formal default with all of its ramifications for the world financial system. This "income" is actually an involuntary capital movement, and does not represent real purchasing power. Thus, the deficit on current account is worse than reported because the "service" income is overstated.

---

[14]For a more detailed discussion of these matters see Robert A. Feldman and Allen J. Proctor, "U.S. International Trade in Services, *Quarterly Review,* Federal Reserve Bank of New York, Spring 1983, pp. 30-36.

Table 4.3
A Decomposition of Services Exports

	Annual Growth 1970-1982	Contribution to Total Increase
Income From Investment Abroad	17.9%	77.3%
Other Services	10.2%	22.7%
Total Services	16.1%	100.0%

The other reason for the continued strength of the dollar in the face of the weak trade performance is the large volume of capital inflows into the United States. Capital has been moving to this country both because the rate of return has been high and because the United States is considered to be the safest haven. Flight capital from Asia, South America, the Middle East and Central Europe is flowing into the United States, adding to the foreign demand for dollars and offsetting the shortfalls of dollars earned by trade.

In summary, the slowdown in the growth of U.S. manufacturing activity must be partly traced to the declining share of U.S. goods, both in American and world markets. This decline in manufacturing trade was associated with relatively high unit labor costs created by unfavorable U.S. productivity and wage trends compared to those of competing nations. Capital costs also were relatively high. But where one might ordinarily expect that the dollar would cheapen as a result of this relative cost performance, policy shortcircuited such adjustment and kept the dollar in its overvalued state. In earlier postwar years, policy curtailed domestic activity in response to payments deficits, creating recessions with their disruption of capital formation. More recently, high interest rates yielded high interest income and attracted capital inflows that kept the dollar in an overvalued state.

A recent DRI study analyzed the effects of the extraordinarily strong dollar of the last three years.[15] This study simulated the DRI Model of the U.S. Economy from the third quarter of 1980 to the first quarter of 1983, assuming that the dollar's trade weighted value remained unchanged at its summer of 1980 level. The results were then contrasted with the actual path of the economy. By July 1983, the dollar's value was 23% above the 1980

---

[15]Sara Johnson, "The Cost of a Strong Dollar," *The Data Resources Review of the U.S. Economy,* July 1983, pp. 1.29-1.32.

average, rising 82% against a French franc, 78% against the Italian lira, 52% against the British pound, 41% against the West German mark, and 6.1%

Chart 4.6
The Economy's Path With the Dollar Held Stable at Its Summer 1980 Level
(Real GNP, billions of 1972 dollars)

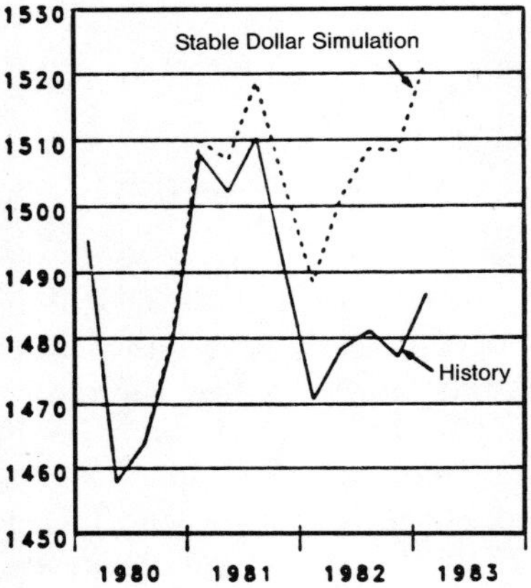

Chart 4.7
Job Losses Caused by the Dollar's Rise: Differences Comparing History With Stable Dollar Simulation
(Millions of persons)

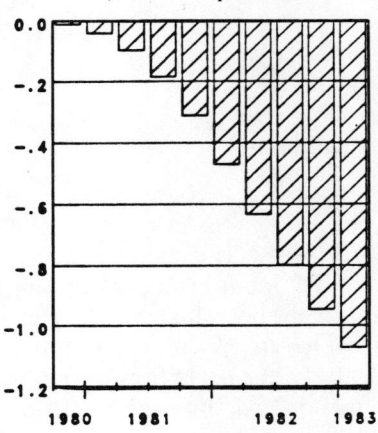

Chart 4.8
The Impact of the Dollar's Appreciation on the Goods and Services Trade Balance
(Difference comparing history with stable dollar simulation, billions of dollars)

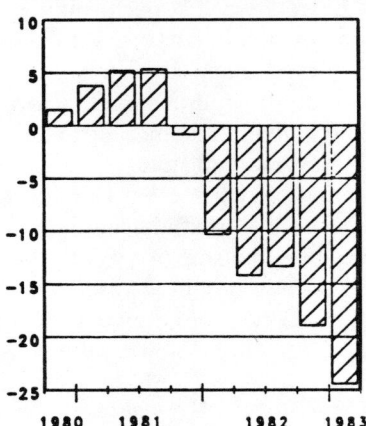

Table. 4.4
The Economic Impact of the Dollar's 1980-1982 Appreciation
(Comparison of actual performance with potential if the dollar had stayed at 1980 third-quarter levels)

	Years		Quarters	
	1981	1982	1982:4	1983:1
(Percent Difference in Levels)				
Trade-Weighted Dollars	10.9	21.3	25.1	22.4
Real GNP	−0.5	−1.7	−2.1	−2.3
Consumption	−0.1	−0.5	−0.6	−0.7
Business Investment	−0.1	−0.8	−1.3	−1.7
Residential Investment	−0.5	−1.3	−1.5	−1.8
Federal Government	0.3	0.7	1.0	1.1
State and Local Government	−0.1	−0.4	−0.6	−0.7
Exports	−1.8	−6.2	−7.8	−8.5
Imports	1.8	6.1	7.9	8.6
Consumer Price Index	−0.3	−0.9	−1.1	−1.3
Wholesale Industrial Prices	−0.7	−2.0	−2.6	−2.9
Merchandise Import Prices*	−7.4	−14.0	−16.9	−16.5
Merchandise Export Prices	−0.5	−2.1	−2.9	−3.4
Real Disposable Income	−0.1	−0.7	−0.9	−1.1
Real Profits after Tax	−0.9	−4.1	−5.0	−5.6
Industrial Production	−1.3	−4.0	−4.9	−5.3
(Difference, Units)				
Net Exports ($Bil.)	3.4	−14.2	−18.9	−24.4
Unemployment Rate (%)	0.1	0.6	0.8	0.9
Employment (Millions)	−0.2	−0.7	−0.9	−1.1
High-Grade Corp. Bond Rate (%)	−0.1	−0.4	−0.5	−0.6
Car Sales (Millions)	−0.1	−0.3	−0.4	−0.4
Federal Budget Surplus ($Bil.)	−4.9	−20.2	−26.4	−30.3

*Excluding oil import prices, which are held at historical levels in both cases

against the Japanese yen. The difference between the simulation and the actual record identifies the effects of the appreciation of the dollar. Charts 4.6-4.8 and Table 4.4 summarize this solution. Real GNP would have been 2.3% higher in early 1983 and industrial production would have been higher by 5.3% if the dollar had remained stable. The trade balance would initially have been somewhat weaker because a cheaper dollar would have yielded less immediate revenue per unit; but, after a few quarters, the trade balance would have been substantially stronger (this is the well-known J-curve effect). The economy would have multiplied this impulse created by the change in the trade balance to produce the increases in the various domestic demands, including consumption and investment. Total jobs by early 1983 would have been about 1.1 million higher, a very sizable and significant figure. Of this job effect, nearly 800,000 would have been in manufacturing with particularly large impacts in steel, autos, textiles, machinery and chemicals. Ripple effects outside of manufacturing were still growing.

To be weighed against these costs is the benefit of lessened inflation. The strong dollar lowered wholesale prices by 2.9% and consumer prices by 1.3% by the first quarter of 1983. Also, the relative decline of exchange rates in Europe and elsewhere cushioned the impact of the worldwide recession on those economies.

UNITED STATES AND FOREIGN TRADE POLICIES

All countries engage in international trade policy, defined to be government intervention designed to alter the flow of goods and services across borders. Tariffs have been the traditional instrument of trade policy, but in the postwar years tariffs have been reduced very substantially in a series of multinational negotiations, leaving them a significant force in relatively few industries. These tariff reductions have applied to the developed, industrial countries. Economies that have not yet reached full development are free to pursue more restrictive tariff policies.

In place of tariffs, nations have been developing "nontariff" barriers. These include product requirements not easily met by foreign suppliers, and entry rules which are very costly and time consuming. Domestic regulations of products have also been designed to make it difficult for foreign suppliers to compete. Government procurement policies usually follow rules designed to avoid purchases from abroad. Import licenses granting government permission to bring certain goods into the country may also be required. Certificates of the country of origin may also be needed. The documents accompanying the imports may have to be written in the native language, and the goods may also be required to carry labels and documentation in the native language. Trade may be confined to licensed traders, who are given a monopoly of trading activities. Quotas, limiting the number of units to be imported per year, may be applied formally, or may be negotiated under government pressure by a private industry in the form of voluntary marketing agreements or other mechanisms.

The General Agreement on Tariffs and Trade has been important in producing the gradual reductions of tariffs, but has been relatively ineffective in coping with the "nontariff" barriers.

One hundred and forty developing nations benefit from the Generalized System of Preferences. These preferences exempt many of their products from U.S. import duties. This system is designed to help foreign nations get started in the development process. Among the 140 countries are the newly industrialized countries such as South Korea, Taiwan, Hong Kong, Singapore, Mexico and Brazil; and they have been the principal beneficiaries of these preferences. The General System of Preferences is up for renewal by the U.S. Congress by January 3, 1985.

While it is difficult to measure the impact of trade policies on the flow of goods across borders, it is generally believed that a large part of our trade is affected very substantially. The development of manufacturing industries is partly determined by each government's trade policy objectives and the effectiveness with which it pursues them.

The United States has a trade policy, like every other nation. We limit the importation of agricultural products, steel, automobiles, textiles, apparel, and other products. We also engage in negotiations with many countries to promote their importation of our goods. The day-to-day conduct of trade policy is in the hands of the Office of the Trade Representative, with the bigger issues usually settled by the President. U.S. trade policy is conducted on a case-by-case basis, typically without coherence or consistency.

American trade policy has not been conducted with the skill and vigor shown by our principal competitors. As a result, the growth of U.S. manufacturing output has been reduced both by loss of domestic markets and by inability to enter various foreign markets.

There are many reasons for the weakness of American trade policy. We list only the highlights.

1. The United States does not really believe in an active trade policy and considers it counter to the basic philosophy of free markets. For the last fifty years, the United States government has endorsed free trade to achieve world-wide specialization of production, to promote efficiency and raise living standards around the world. The United States has not accepted the viewpoint that effective performance in foreign trade is an important ingredient for successful economic development. Consequently, policy measures designed to favor American producers are considered to be no more than political necessities which probably run counter to the long-run national interest. Countries such as Japan, France, and Korea have not taken this viewpoint and are therefore more enthusiastic about promoting the welfare of their own industries.

2. The organization of trade policies is peculiarly weak. The United States does not have the bureaucracy of a Japanese Ministry of Industry and Trade (MITI) to perform the necessary analytical work and to assert the viewpoint of industry on a broad range of issues, including trade policy. Turnover of personnel is very high, and leading officials usually work for the major importing nations upon leaving government service.
3. The United States usually places considerations of trade second to the goals of more general foreign policy. Because of our predominant concern with our struggle with the Soviet Union, we attach only secondary importance to economic questions and usually decide issues of trade policy on political grounds. This factor can be seen clearly in our patience with Japanese trade policies and in the recent textile negotiations with China. It can also be seen in the various embargoes on shipments of goods to the Soviet Union and the limitations of exports of high technology products considered to be of strategic value.
4. The agreements that we have negotiated to limit the imports of such products as television sets, textiles, steel, and autos have usually been of very partial effectiveness. The rules have usually allowed the suppliers to gradually circumvent the limitations; and, given their lack of enthusiasm, the government authorities have been less than vigilant in renegotiating the agreements or administering them so that they would achieve their goals.
5. The world debt problem places new constraints on U.S. trade policy. If the major debtor nations are to ease their debt service costs through exports, they must have access to the markets of the developed countries, including our own.

A more active international trade policy can only make a modest contribution to the renewal of American manufacturing industry, but it is an essential contribution. More general economic conditions, including exchange rates, capital costs, and instability of output, have done us more harm. All trade policy can hope to do is to make sure that the game of international trade is played by fair rules, and that the inevitable adjustments caused by shifts in comparative advantage are managed to hold the human costs to tolerable levels.

U.S. trade policy has failed to recognize the strategic importance of exports and imports in the development process. This is a particularly serious matter because several of our principal competitors have made foreign trade the centerpiece of their development strategies. They have aimed to protect their domestic manufacturing markets and promoted their exports, particularly to the very large American market. While our government grudgingly granted a bit of protection here or there to industries sinking into deep trouble, countries such as Japan and Korea have helped their industries to expand their share of world trade in order to reap the economies-to-scale and to achieve the technological progress which made their rapid economic development possible.

CONCLUDING COMMENTS TO CHAPTERS 1 TO 4

This overview of the basic facts and causes of the decline of U.S. manufacturing industries shows some of the reasons for the decline of American industry. Although manufacturing investment was "normal," given the slowly growing volume of sales and output, it did not meet the challenge of increased foreign competition or of accelerating technology. The loss of markets to import competition was a major factor in the relatively modest total growth of domestic manufacturing output. Overvaluation of the dollar, at least in terms of international relative cost differences, was a contributing factor to the growing import shares and to the declining share in world markets. International trade policies, which encouraged the development of new competitors without assuring access to their markets for our goods, also hurt our own development. The instability of the U.S. economy, which was partly created by the attempts to defend the dollar, created a business and financial environment which created further setbacks to the investment and output levels of American industry. Tax and regulatory policies were also damaging.

These forces were at work in most industries, yet have received little attention in the literature on our industrial problems. Until a more realistic view is taken of these important economic and financial policies and conditions, industry-specific solutions have little prospect of success. No degree of cleverness on the part of management, no new-found cooperation between employers and workers, no industrial policies by the federal government can overcome the handicaps of an overvalued dollar and a domestic economy disrupted by credit crunches and recession every three or four years. Better national economic and financial policies will not solve our industrial problems, but without them the more specific solutions cannot prove successful.

CHAPTER 5

ANALYSIS OF INDIVIDUAL INDUSTRIES

While the basic factors underlying the problems of U.S. manufacturing were identified in the previous chapters from data for manufacturing as a whole, additional insights are gained by examining individual industries. To be sure, specific events and decisions served an important role in determining each industry's performance, and these are generally beyond the scope of this study. Also, competitive positions differ substantially among industries, with some preserving high growth rates and world leadership, and others already substantially shrunken. These differences are partly explainable by objective factors such as labor costs, productivity, capital intensity, and the importance of technology.

This chapter examines a standard set of statistics for 20 two-digit manufacturing industries, and draws some general conclusions from a cross-section comparison.

Eight concepts are examined for each industry for the last 30 years. (In some cases the data exist only for a shorter time span.) The concepts are:

Industrial Production. The Federal Reserve Board's Index of Industrial Production and its trend are shown. The effect of changing international trade patterns on industrial production is measured by a "constant share" analysis.

Productivity – Output per Manhour. Productivity is measured as the ratio of the index of industrial production (FRB data) to total manhours worked (BLS data).

Industry Employment. Each industry's payroll employment, as measured by the Bureau of Labor Statistics, is shown historically. This measure is an indicator of the industry's importance to the labor force and its changing role.

Profits as a Margin on Sales. Data from the Federal Trade Commission on after-tax profits and Bureau of Economic Analysis sales data are employed as a measure of industry profitability. Cash flow as a margin on sales is also examined. For most industries the two measures show virtually identical results. Cash flow shows a somewhat more favorable trend for three industries, nonelectrical machinery, electrical machinery and instruments.

Investment. The Bureau of Economic Analysis data on plant and equipment expenditures for each industry are used on a deflated basis. These data are also expressed as a ratio to sales to indicate the changing effort for capital formation.

Research and Development Expenditures. The National Science Foundation provides estimates for R&D expenditures expressed as a percent of sales.

Exports and Imports. OECD and Census Bureau sources are used to compile trade balances for industry groups.

Relative Wages. Hourly earnings of the industry, divided by average hourly earnings of the nonagricultural private economy, show whether the industry is a high- or low-wage employer, and also show whether the relative wages have helped or hindered to maintain the industry's competitive position (BLS data).

Some of the concepts are not available for a particular industry. It would have been desirable to analyze numerous other concepts, such as the tax burdens of various industries, the costs of capital, total employment costs, changing balance sheet conditions, and across-country comparisons for the various costs and productivity components for each industry. However, comparable data for these concepts generally do not exist, and it would take a major research undertaking to develop them. The data that are shown generally are sufficient to account for the changing position of the industry.

Table 5.1 provides a numerical capsule summary of the industry data. The succeeding tables show time profiles for each concept by industry. In the Appendix, the data for each industry are assembled and briefly discussed.

Growth of Industrial Production. The trend line of industrial production, as measured by a logarithmic least squares regression, shows a rate of increase of 3.9% for total manufacturing for 1960-1982, and a retardation to 2.5% for 1975-1982. While both 1975 and 1982 were recession years, with

60   *Analysis of Individual Industries*

Table 5.1
Key Concepts—U.S. Manufacturing Industries
(Percent unless otherwise specified)

	Production Growth (1960-82)	Productivity Growth (1955-81)	Employment Level (Thous, 1982)	Trade Balance ($Mil 1982)	Investment Share of Shipments	Relative Wages (1982)
Total Manufacturing	3.9	3.5	18,853.2	11,991.3	6.3	110.8
Food and Products	3.2	3.7	1,638.4	−2,779.7	2.8	102.9
Tobacco Manufactures	1.3	3.6	67.7	2,075.9	—	127.8
Textile Mill Products	3.2	4.1	750.1	370.9	2.8	76.0
Apparel	2.0	2.2	1,163.6	−7,156.6	—	67.8
Lumber and Wood Products	2.2	2.5	603.5	269.5	—	97.2
Furniture and Fixtures	3.8	2.8	433.4	350.9	—	82.3
Paper and Products	3.7	3.5	662.1	−930.0	7.6	121.5
Printing and Publishing	3.3	2.2	1,268.8	711.0	—	114.0
Chemicals	6.4	5.5	1,078.9	13,268.7	7.7	129.9
Petroleum Products	2.7	3.5	201.2	−8,766.1	12.9	162.4
Rubber and Plastics	8.2	5.4	700.8	−1,172.3	3.4	99.7
Leather Products	−1.8	1.0	221.4	−1,915.1	—	69.4
Stone, Clay, and Glass	3.1	2.8	578.0	−523.4	5.9	115.5
Primary Metals	1.3	2.2	921.9	−11,278.6	7.0	147.8
Steel Mill Products	0.6	—	394.3	−9,292.5	7.4	174.6
Fabricated Metals	3.1	2.2	1,435.1	−904.9	2.3	114.4
Nonelectrical Machinery	5.0	3.0	2,266.4	31,369.8	7.1	121.2
Electrical Machinery	5.6	4.5	2,015.4	7,950.7	7.5	107.1
Transportation Equipment	2.6	3.0	1,744.7	−8,571.6	7.7	145.0
Motor Vehicles and Parts	2.8	—	704.7	−17,578.5	7.0	151.4
Instruments	5.5	3.5	715.9	1,929.5	—	105.7
Miscellaneous Manufacturing	3.7	3.7	385.8	−2,307.3	—	83.8

Note: Figures exclude crude oil and are therefore not directly comparable to standard government data.

1982 a deeper trough, the retardation in the slopes of these trend lines is more due to fundamental factors than the business cycle.

There were major differences among industries. For the longer period, the highest growth industries were rubber and plastics (8.2%), chemicals (6.4%), electrical machinery (5.6%), instruments (5.5%), and nonelectrical machinery (5.0%). At the low end, leather and its products shrank at a 1.8% rate, steel mill products showed a trend of 0.6%, and tobacco of 1.3%.

During the period 1975-1982 there were more dramatic disparities among industries. The electrical machinery industry continued to grow at a 5.7% rate and rubber and plastics remained strong at 6.0%, whereas the steel trend shows a 4% rate of decline, leather and its products minus 2.8%, motor vehicles minus 2.2%, with petroleum products, apparel and lumber also showing small declines.

Table 5.2
Manufacturing Production by Industry,
1960 to 1982

	Annual Percent Growth Trend		Difference
	1960-1982	1975-1982	
Total Manufacturing	3.9	2.5	−1.3
Food and Products	3.2	2.8	−0.4
Tobacco Manufactures	1.3	0.9	−0.4
Textile Mill Products	3.2	0.4	−2.9
Apparel	2.0	−0.4	−2.4
Lumber and Wood Products	2.2	−0.2	−2.4
Furniture and Fixtures	3.8	3.1	−0.6
Paper and Products	3.7	3.5	−0.2
Printing and Publishing	3.3	3.4	0.1
Chemicals	6.4	4.3	−2.1
Petroleum Products	2.7	−0.6	−3.3
Rubber and Plastics	8.2	6.0	−2.3
Leather Products	−1.8	−2.8	−1.0
Stone, Clay, and Glass	3.1	1.3	−1.8
Primary Metals	1.3	−2.5	−3.8
Steel Mill Products	0.6	−4.0	−4.6
Fabricated Metals	3.1	1.1	−2.0
Nonelectrical Machinery	5.0	3.5	−1.6
Electrical Machinery	5.6	5.7	0.1
Transportation Equipment	2.6	0.7	−1.9
Motor Vehicles and Parts	2.8	−2.2	−5.0
Instruments	5.5	3.0	−2.5
Miscellaneous Manufacturing	3.7	1.0	−2.7

Constant Share Production. Data in this table were created by adjusting industrial production to account for changes in import and export shares since 1965. While total production was cut by only 4.1% in 1981, many industries were severely damaged by shifting trade patterns. Among these industries are: leather (-33.1%), electrical machinery (-20.5%), petroleum products (-15.1%), and apparel (-12.2%). Tobacco (7.5%) and food (2.5%) were benefitted by the changes in trade.

Table 5.3
Constant Export and Import Share Production
(Percent, 1965 to 1981)

	Trend Production Growth			Loss(−) or Gain(+) In Output Level Due to Changing Trade Shares 1981
	Actual	Constant Share	Difference	
Total Manufacturing	3.2	3.4	0.2	−4.1
Food and Products	3.2	3.0	−0.2	2.5
Tobacco Manufactures	1.5	1.0	−0.5	7.5
Textile Mill Products	2.5	2.7	0.1	−4.3
Apparel	2.0	2.8	0.7	−12.2
Lumber and Wood Products	1.8	1.7	−0.1	1.7
Furniture and Fixtures	3.3	3.5	0.2	−3.5
Paper and Products	3.0	3.0	−0.1	1.1
Printing and Publishing	2.7	2.8	0.1	−1.4
Chemicals	5.9	5.8	−0.1	1.4
Petroleum Products	2.6	3.7	1.1	−15.1
Rubber and Plastics	7.6	7.8	0.2	−3.6
Leather Products	−2.6	−0.7	2.0	−33.1
Stone, Clay, and Glass	3.2	3.3	0.1	−2.0
Primary Metals	0.5	0.9	0.4	−8.7
Steel Mill Products	0.0	0.5	0.6	−11.0
Fabricated Metals	2.7	2.9	0.2	−2.6
Nonelectrical Machinery	4.1	3.9	−0.2	1.7
Electrical Machinery	4.4	5.2	0.8	−20.5
Transportation Equipment	1.6	1.8	0.2	−4.1
Motor Vehicles and Parts	1.9	2.3	0.4	−7.4
Instruments	4.6	4.8	0.2	−3.1
Miscellaneous Manufacturing	3.4	4.4	1.0	−17.7

Productivity. Productivity in manufacturing, or output per manhour, shows a least squares growth trend of 3.5% a year, 1954-1981, retreating to 2.3% for the period 1975-1981. For the longer period, the productivity trends of individual industries are clustered near the manufacturing average, with only chemicals and rubber products substantially higher at 5.6% and 5.4% respectively, and only the declining leather and products industry dramatically lower at 1.1%.

The period 1975-1981 saw a greater variation of productivity experience among industries, though virtually all industries experienced some retardation. The slowdown was greatest for petroleum products and instruments, both of whom showed negative productivity trends. Strong productivity growth performance was maintained by chemicals and rubber products at 4.6%.

Table 5.4
Manufacturing Productivity by Industry,
1954 to 1981

	Annual Percent Growth Trend		Difference
	1954-1981	1975-1981	
Total Manufacturing	3.5	2.3	−1.2
Food and Products	3.8	3.4	−0.4
Tobacco Manufactures	3.6	2.0	−1.6
Textile Mill Products	4.2	2.6	−1.6
Apparel	2.2	1.4	−0.8
Lumber and Wood Products	2.6	0.0	−2.6
Furniture and Fixtures	2.8	2.3	−0.5
Paper and Products	3.5	3.4	−0.1
Printing and Publishing	2.2	1.0	−1.2
Chemicals	5.6	4.6	−1.0
Petroleum Products	3.6	−0.9	−4.5
Rubber and Plastics	5.4	4.6	−0.8
Leather Products	1.1	−0.2	−1.2
Stone, Clay, and Glass	2.8	3.0	0.2
Primary Metals	2.2	1.1	−1.1
Fabricated Metals	2.2	1.9	−0.3
Nonelectrical Machinery	3.0	1.3	−1.7
Electrical Machinery	4.5	3.3	−1.2
Transportation Equipment	3.0	0.7	−2.2
Instruments	3.5	−0.8	−4.3
Miscellaneous Manufacturing	3.8	2.4	−1.4

Employment. Employment showed a small 0.8% growth trend for total manufacturing for the years 1950-1982, with seven of the 20 two-digit industries showing negative employment trends. Six industries experienced their peak employment before 1960, and another two industries experienced their peak job levels in the 1960s. Only four industries enjoyed employment growth of 2% a year or more: rubber and products (3.1%), instruments (2.4%), electrical machinery (2.1%), and nonelectrical machinery (2.0%).

Table 5.5
Manufacturing Employment by Industry,
1950 to 1982

	Year of Peak	Level at Peak (Thousands)	1982 Level (Thousands)	Percent Change	Trend Annual Growth (Percent)
Total Manufacturing	1979	21,044	18,853.2	−10.4	0.8
Food and Products	1956	1,842	1,638.4	−11.0	−0.3
Tobacco Manufactures	1952	106	67.7	−35.9	−1.4
Textile Mill Products	1950	1,256	750.1	−40.3	−0.8
Apparel	1973	1,438	1,163.6	−19.1	0.3
Lumber and Wood Products	1951	871	603.5	−30.7	−0.4
Furniture and Fixtures	1973	507	433.4	−14.5	1.3
Paper and Products	1969	711	662.1	−6.9	1.1
Printing and Publishing	1982	1,269	1,268.8	0.0	1.6
Chemicals	1979	1,109	1,078.9	−2.7	1.6
Petroleum Products	1953	242	201.2	−16.7	−0.5
Rubber and Plastics	1979	782	700.8	−10.4	3.1
Leather and Products	1950	394	221.4	−43.9	−1.7
Stone, Clay, and Glass	1973	716	578.0	−19.2	0.6
Primary Metals	1953	1,325	921.9	−30.4	−0.3
Steel Mill Products	1953	620	292.5	−52.9	−1.3
Fabricated Metals	1979	1,718	1,435.1	−16.5	1.3
Nonelectrical Machinery	1981	2,498	2,266.4	−9.3	2.0
Electrical Machinery	1979	2,117	2,015.4	−4.8	2.1
Transportation Equipment	1968	2,155	1,744.7	−19.0	0.4
Motor Vehicles and Parts	1978	1,008	707.0	−29.9	0.4
Instruments	1981	730	715.9	−1.9	2.4
Miscellaneous Manufacturing	1973	454	385.8	−15.1	0.3

Profit Margins. Profits as a percent of sales averaged 3.6% for all manufacturing for the years 1960-1979, but retreated to 2.6% for 1980-1982. The highest profit margins were experienced in petroleum products, where the reported profits are dominated by the earnings from exploration and production of crude oil and include large foreign earnings. Above average profits were also experienced by instruments, chemicals and the machinery industries, industries in which reported profits include the return on large outlays for research and development and technical know-how.

The declines in profit margins were most acute in transportation equipment, primary metals and textiles, all industries impacted by international competition.

Table 5.6
Profits as a Percent of Sales by Industry,
1960 to 1982

	Average 1960-1979	Average 1980-1982	Difference
Total Manufacturing	3.6	2.6	−1.0
Food and Products	2.5	3.6	1.1
Textile Mill Products	2.6	2.1	−0.5
Paper and Products	4.0	3.2	−0.8
Chemicals	7.7	6.8	−0.9
Petroleum Products	7.8	6.5	−1.3
Rubber and Plastics	3.8	2.7	−1.0
Stone, Clay, and Glass	4.9	2.9	−2.0
Primary Metals	4.1	1.3	−2.8
Fabricated Metals	3.1	3.0	−0.1
Nonelectrical Machinery	5.7	5.7	0.0
Electrical Machinery	5.0	5.4	0.3
Transportation Equipment	4.7	1.1	−3.5
Instruments	4.8	2.5	−2.2

Investment in Plant and Equipment. Real outlays for plant and equipment show a growth trend of 4.1% for all manufacturing, 1950-1982, with some acceleration, to 5.7%, for the years 1975-1982. The acceleration in investment was led by the machinery and transportation equipment industries.

Investment outlays as a percent of sales also show an increase from the period 1965-1967 to 1980-1982. These increases were largest in transportation equipment and the paper industry. Declines in investment in relation to sales were particularly notable in textiles and steel, but were also seen in chemicals and fabricated metals.

Table 5.7
Real Plant and Equipment Investment by Industry,
1950 to 1982

	Annual Percent Growth Trend		
	1950-1982	1975-1982	Difference
Total Manufacturing	4.1	5.7	1.6
Food and Products	3.5	3.0	−0.5
Textile Mill Products	1.5	−0.4	−1.9
Paper and Products	5.3	6.5	1.2
Chemicals	4.6	2.3	−2.4
Petroleum Products	2.5	5.3	2.8
Rubber and Plastics	4.5	−1.5	−6.0
Stone, Clay, and Glass	2.7	1.3	−1.5
Primary Metals	2.3	−2.4	−4.7
Steel Mill Products	0.9	−5.9	−6.8
Fabricated Metals	3.3	−2.2	−5.5
Nonelectrical Machinery	6.6	10.1	3.5
Electrical Machinery	7.5	14.5	7.0
Transportation Equipment	4.5	10.5	6.0
Motor Vehicles and Parts	2.8	8.1	5.3

Research and Development Expenditures as a Percent of Sales. The percentage of sales revenue spent on research and development in all manufacturing declined from 4.2% in the period 1965-1967 to 3.1% for 1978-1980. R&D expenditures are very large in the nonelectrical and electrical machinery industries, instruments, chemicals and transportation equipment.

Table 5.8
R&D Expenditures as a Percent of Sales by Industry,
1960 to 1982

	Average 1960-1979	Average 1980-1982	Difference
Total Manufacturing	4.23	3.10	−1.13
Food and Products	0.43	0.40	−0.03
Paper and Products	0.87	1.03	0.17
Chemicals	4.43	3.50	−0.93
Petroleum Products	0.90	0.70	−0.20
Rubber and Plastics	1.90	2.00	0.10
Stone, Clay, and Glass	1.63	1.27	−0.37
Primary Metals	0.77	0.60	−0.17
Fabricated Metals	1.30	1.17	−0.13
Nonelectrical Machinery	4.03	5.23	1.20
Electrical Machinery	8.73	6.40	−2.33
Instruments	5.60	6.10	0.50

Merchandise Trade Balance. The merchandise trade balance for the manufacturing industry, which historically had been substantially positive, showed a $2.6 billion rate of deficit in the first half of 1983. The United States showed an $11.4 billion rate of surplus for chemicals, $22.6 billion for nonelectrical machinery, and $7.6 billion for electrical machinery. The non-automotive components of the transportation equipment industry—principally airplanes—showed a surplus of $11.7 billion. On the deficit side, motor vehicles and parts showed net imports of $22.7 billion; refined petroleum products, $9.2 billion; primary metals, $9.7 billion, including $5.2 billion of steel mill products; and $7.9 billion of apparel.

Table 5.9
Table Balances by Industry
(Millions of dollars; annual rates)

	Average 1970-1979	Average 1980-1982	1983
Total Manufacturing	11,084.2	27,371.7	−2,650.2
Food and Products	−2,513.7	−1,086.9	474.6
Tobacco Manufactures	1,056.8	2,045.2	1,534.4
Textile Mill Products	14.7	1,030.0	−274.0
Apparel	−2,378.5	−6,142.1	−7,946.0
Lumber and Wood Products	−268.9	222.6	−681.4
Furniture and Fixtures	84.3	436.1	108.4
Paper and Products	−659.6	−620.5	−1,056.2
Printing and Publishing	304.1	675.7	561.4
Chemicals	5,437.8	13,948.3	11,382.2
Petroleum Products	−4,765.0	−10,131.8	−9,220.4
Rubber and Plastics	−611.7	−1,046.6	−1,320.4
Leather Products	−716.5	−1,559.6	−2,211.8
Stone, Clay, and Glass	−158.1	−452.0	−790.0
Primary Metals	−4,765.0	−8,659.6	−9,721.4
Steel Mill Products	−4,540.0	−8,572.6	−5,162.8
Fabricated Metals	−177.9	−473.2	−940.2
Nonelectrical Machinery	14,479.2	33,448.1	22,558.2
Electrical Machinery	4,321.6	8,138.1	7,574.0
Transportation Equipment	1,500.3	−3,165.6	−10,930.0
Motor Vehicles and Parts	−3,869.3	−13,511.4	−22,658.4
Instruments	1,396.9	2,033.6	1,148.0
Miscellaneous Manufacturing	−496.5	−1,268.2	−2,109.6

Relative Wages. The relative wage position of manufacturing compared to the total economy showed small changes over the last 15 years, with the average relative wage improving from a 6% to a 10% premium. This small updrift is the result of very large relative wage gains by primary metals, transportation equipment, tobacco and petroleum products, partly offset by declining wage positions in apparel, furniture, printing and publishing, rubber products and instruments. Several manufacturing industries show substantially higher wages than the economy-wide average, led by steel wages with a 73% premium, followed by the auto industry with a 50% premium. The apparel, leather and textile industries show relative wages which are 24 to 32% below the economy-wide averages.

Table 5.10
Industry Wage Levels Relative to the Total Economy

	Average 1965-1967	Average 1980-1982	Difference
Total Manufacturing	1.06	1.10	0.04
Food and Products	0.99	1.03	0.04
Tobacco Manufactures	0.85	1.22	0.37
Textile Mill Products	0.76	0.76	0.00
Apparel	0.75	0.68	−0.06
Lumber and Wood Products	0.88	0.97	0.09
Furniture and Fixtures	0.86	0.82	−0.04
Paper and Products	1.08	1.19	0.12
Printing and Publishing	1.23	1.13	−0.10
Chemicals	1.17	1.27	0.10
Petroleum Products	1.33	1.57	0.23
Rubber and Plastics	1.04	0.99	−0.05
Leather Products	0.76	0.69	−0.07
Stone, Clay, and Glass	1.06	1.14	0.08
Primary Metals	1.27	1.48	0.21
Steel Mill Products	1.37	1.73	0.37
Fabricated Metals	1.12	1.13	0.01
Nonelectrical Machinery	1.20	1.21	0.01
Electrical Machinery	1.04	1.06	0.02
Transportation Equipment	1.30	1.43	0.13
Motor Vehicles and Parts	1.34	1.50	0.16
Instruments	1.07	1.03	−0.03
Miscellaneous Manufacturing	0.87	0.83	−0.04

RECENT DEVELOPMENTS IN INTERNATIONAL TRADE

The most striking change in industry data is the accelerated decline of our trade. Merchandise trade began to show large deficits in 1977 which remained relatively constant until 1982. They averaged $27.6 billion for 1980 to 1982. In 1983 the trade deficit will exceed $50 billion (Table 5.11), and, according to the DRI forecast, will rise to $72.1 billion in 1984 and to $82.2 billion in 1985. The government projects a deficit of $100 billion in 1984, but conceptual differences account for most of the larger figure.

Table 5.11
A Breakdown of the U.S. Current Account Balance
(Exports minus imports, billions of dollars)

	History			Forecast		
	1980	1981	1982	1983	1984	1985
Census Basis:						
Merchandise Trade	−24.3	−27.5	−31.6	−56.7	−72.1	−82.2
Surplus Categories:						
Capital Goods	43.0	43.5	34.5	26.3	22.2	24.0
Foods, Feeds, and Beverages	17.2	19.8	14.2	12.9	15.8	17.6
Reexports, Military, nec	5.6	8.5	10.0	9.3	9.8	10.9
Nonfuel Industrial Materials	15.4	7.6	6.8	0.2	−3.0	−4.7
Deficit Categories:						
Fuels and Lubricants	−75.8	−71.7	−53.5	−50.7	−54.7	−58.5
(Exports)	7.9	10.3	12.8	10.0	11.2	12.4
(Imports)	−83.8	−82.1	−66.4	−60.7	−65.9	−70.9
Consumer Goods except Autos	−18.2	−22.8	−25.4	−31.2	−36.0	−41.0
Automotive Vehicles and Parts	−11.2	−12.5	−18.4	−23.7	−26.1	−30.4

The trade deficit deteriorates so sharply over the next few years because the U.S. economy is in a much stronger recovery than our trading partners. The United States experienced a sharp recession in the last few years, probably somewhat sharper than those of most of our trading partners other than Canada. Under those conditions, our merchandise trade should have been in surplus rather than in sizable deficit. The disparity in cyclical conditions, with the U.S. growing much more rapidly than other countries, now produces a sharp deterioration in our trade. We will be importing material to restock our inventories; the inflow of capital goods will expand while exports will barely rise; consumer goods imports will surge along with consumption generally; and our fuel bill will increase, now that the drawdown of oil inventories is completed.

The pattern of exports and imports by country shows further reasons for expanding prospective deficits (Table 5.12). In the first six months of 1983, exports were 10.5% lower than a year earlier. Exports to developed countries were down only moderately, by 4.4%; and this figure should turn positive as they join the recovery. But exports to developing countries (including OPEC) were down by 16.1% and to the Communist countries by 42.3%. Both these groups will not be able to resume heavy purchases because their ability to obtain credit has been lost for several years because of their excessive debts.

Table 5.12
A Geographic Breakdown of U.S.
Merchandise Exports, January-June 1983
(Annual rates, free alongside ship, NSA)

	Billions of Dollars	Percent Change*	Percent of Total
All Countries	201.16	−10.5	100.0
Developed	123.06	−4.4	61.2
Western Europe	58.57	−8.3	29.1
Developing	72.82	−16.1	36.2
Latin America	21.85	−34.3	10.9
East Asia	22.95	1.7	11.4
Mideast Asia	14.41	−10.0	7.2
Africa	9.19	−20.3	4.6
Communist	5.03	−42.3	2.5
Canada	37.79	7.4	18.8
Japan	20.08	−4.1	10.0
United Kingdom	10.97	−1.2	5.5
Germany	8.79	−11.6	4.4
Mexico	8.79	−38.9	4.4
Saudi Arabia	8.44	−4.2	4.2
Netherlands	8.27	−11.5	4.1
France	6.62	−10.1	3.3
South Korea	5.92	13.3	2.9
Italy	4.35	−14.1	2.2

*First six months of 1983 compared with first six months of 1982.

Source: Bureau of the Census, U.S. Department of Commerce

Examining the export decline by product, we see (Table 5.13) that exports of nonelectrical machinery, tobacco, apparel, and textile products fell sharply.

Table 5.13
U.S. Merchandise Exports: 1980-1983
(Estimates for two-digit industries)

	Millions of dollars				Percent change		
	1980	1981	1982	1983*	1981	1982	1983*
Total Merchandise Exports	220,782.5	233,739.1	212,274.6	201,159.4	5.9	−9.2	−5.2
Food and Products	17,310.1	18,448.1	14,338.3	18,597.6	6.6	−22.3	29.7
Tobacco Manufactures	2,425.6	2,722.8	2,815.5	2,366.0	12.3	3.4	−16.0
Textile Mill Products	3,818.7	3,832.6	2,800.2	2,400.4	0.4	−26.9	−14.3
Apparel	1,469.2	1,542.5	1,252.9	1,128.2	5.0	−18.8	−10.0
Lumber and Wood Products	3,225.1	2,644.7	2,528.2	2,543.0	−18.0	−4.4	0.6
Furniture and Fixtures	1,527.6	1,608.1	1,496.1	1,347.6	5.3	−7.0	−9.9
Paper and Products	4,973.3	4,967.5	4,340.8	4,195.2	−0.1	−12.6	−3.4
Printing and Publishing	1,060.0	1,248.2	1,289.0	1,224.2	17.8	3.3	−-5.0
Chemicals	19,815.7	20,274.0	19,386.9	18,601.4	2.3	−4.4	−4.1
Petroleum Products	2,846.7	3,768.9	6,217.3	5,760.6	32.4	65.0	−7.3
Rubber and Plastics	1,539.7	1,589.0	1,250.7	1,182.4	3.2	−21.3	−5.5
Leather Products	1,429.5	1,429.6	1,441.9	1,358.2	0.0	0.9	−5.8
Stone, Clay, and Glass	1,622.6	1,747.7	1,527.7	1,404.4	7.7	−12.6	−8.1
Primary Metals	16,366.1	11,821.9	7,841.8	7,551.2	−27.8	−33.7	−3.7
Steel Mill Products	1,495.7	889.8	778.6	738.0	−39.8	−13.5	−5.2
Fabricated Metals	2,214.6	2,387.8	1,968.7	1,817.8	7.8	−17.6	−7.7
Nonelectrical Machinery	48,785.7	55,649.4	51,467.9	44,271.0	14.1	−7.5	−14.0
Electric Machinery	21,938.1	24,370.3	24,267.9	24,806.4	11.1	−0.4	2.2
Transportation Equipment	32,507.0	35,514.0	30,699.3	34,260.3	9.3	−13.6	11.6
Motor Vehicles and Parts	15,856.5	17,987.2	15,671.5	17,011.6	13.4	−12.9	8.6
Instruments	5,130.7	5,767.1	5,363.6	4,983.0	12.4	−7.0	−7.1
Miscellaneous Manufactures	4,100.6	4,208.1	3,794.7	3,538.4	2.6	−9.8	−6.8
All other	8,675.9	8,756.8	9,185.2	3,456.3	0.9	4.9	−62.4

* Data through June at annual rates

Based on "Highlights of U.S. Export and Import Trade," published monthly by the Census Bureau. Classification into 2-digit SIC categories by DRI.

Among the gainers were the exports of transportation equipment, particularly aircraft.

On the import side (Table 5.14), there was little change in the total so far this year; but large declines in iron and steel imports masked increases in nonferrous metals, chemicals, foods, textiles and apparel, machinery, and autos and trucks. Viewed over three years, the iron and steel drop can be seen to be a major correction of the earlier surge, and the nonferrous metals

Table 5.14
U.S. Merchandise Imports: 1980-1983
(Estimates for two-digit industries)

	Millions of dollars				Percent change		
	1980	1981	1982	1983*	1981	1982	1983*
Total Merchandise Imports	244,870.6	261,304.9	243,951.9	243.113.0	6.7	−6.6	0.3
Food and Products**	18,126.4	18,112.8	17,118.0	18,123.0	−0.1	−5.5	5.9
Tobacco Manufactures	455.3	633.3	739.6	831.6	39.1	16.8	12.4
Textile Mill Products	2,225.4	2,706.7	2,429.3	2,674.4	21.6	−10.2	10.1
Apparel	6,507.9	7,773.6	8,409.5	9,074.2	19.4	8.2	7.9
Lumber and Wood Products	2,746.0	2,725.4	2,258.7	3,224.4	−0.8	−17.1	42.8
Furniture and Fixtures	1,055.1	1,123.3	1,145.2	1,239.2	6.5	1.9	8.2
Paper and Products	5,268.9	5,603.3	5,270.8	5,251.4	6.3	−5.9	−0.4
Chemicals	5,346.3	6,167.2	6,118.2	7,219.2	15.4	−0.8	18.0
Petroleum Products	13,078.2	15,166.7	14,983.4	14,981.0	16.0	−1.2	0.0
Rubber and Plastics	2,443.7	2,652.5	2,423.0	2,502.8	8.5	−8.7	3.3
Leather Products	2,579.9	3,042.9	3,357.0	3,570.0	17.9	10.3	6.3
Stone, Clay, and Glass	2,039.7	2,163.2	2,051.1	2,194.4	6.1	−5.2	7.0
Primary Metals	20,315.7	22,572.5	19,120.4	17,272.6	11.1	−15.3	−9.7
Iron and Steel	7,559.2	11,261.7	10,071.1	5,900.8	49.0	−10.6	−41.4
Fabricated Metals	2,369.9	2,747.1	2,873.6	2,758.0	15.9	4.6	−4.0
Nonelectrical Machinery	15,823.2	19,637.3	20,098.1	21,712.8	24.1	2.3	8.0
Electrical Machinery	14,055.6	15,789.1	16,317.2	17,232.4	12.3	3.3	5.6
Transportation Equipment	32,568.3	36,378.0	39,270.9	45,190.0	11.7	8.0	15.1
Motor Vehicles and Parts	27,062.3	29,737.0	33,250.0	39,670.0	9.9	11.8	19.3
Instruments	3,120.0	3,606.6	3,434.1	3,835.0	15.6	−4.8	11.7
Miscellaneous Manufactures	5,069.8	5,728.4	6,680.0	6,310.8	13.0	16.6	−5.5
All Other, Including Crude Petroleum	89,675.3	86,975.0	69,853.8	57,915.8	−3.0	−19.7	−17.1

* Data through June at annual rates
** Food includes raw farm products as well as processed foods (SIC 20).

Based on "Highlights of U.S. Export and Import Trade," published monthly by the Census Bureau. Classification into 2-digit SIC categories by DRI.

are a correction in the opposite direction. It is particularly striking that imports of textiles and apparel, machinery and automobiles kept right on advancing through the recession despite poor market conditions.

From the long-term point of view, it is reassuring that the peak trade deficits of $70 to $100 billion of the next year or two will probably be temporary because they are partly due to the disparity between the recovery of the U.S. economy and our trading partners. But this is only of limited comfort. The trade deficits are real and will lead to further damage to our industries. The capital flows that will be needed to offset these trade deficits will generate future interest payments that will be a burden. And, if one takes the data of the early 1980s as a whole, they imply that the United States now experiences a "structural" trade deficit in the $40 to $60 billion range.

CONCLUSIONS

The review of particular statistical measurements for each of 20 manufacturing industries yields some conclusions that cannot be derived from aggregate data. They include:

1) In a number of industries, U.S. manufacturing performance has been outstanding, and leadership has been preserved, despite the handicaps under which all manufacturing industries have been operating. These industries are principally the capital goods industries: nonelectrical and electrical machinery, and instruments. They are still producing a large positive trade balance and show relatively high production trends. The relative wages in these industries are only moderately above the economy-wide averages, and productivity performance is exceptionally favorable. These industries include many of the high technology products, including computers, word processors, electronic instruments, etc. But they also include older lines in which American technology is strong.

    The rise of Japan and of other suppliers is cutting into some of these markets, and will continue to do so at the current exchange rates.

2) The relative wage changes in manufacturing have been strongly perverse over the last ten years. The biggest wage gains have been received by the workers of industries that are showing the sharpest declines. These tend to be industries that possess a relatively concentrated market structure, and where strong industrial unions, partly through the workings of escalator clauses, have obtained extraordinarily large wage gains, though at the expense of sharp employment cutbacks.

3) The productivity trends of the various industries generally do not show major slowdowns. To be sure, there are temporary deviations from trend due to the recessions, but it appears that most of these industries will

return to their long-run productivity trend once the economy returns to normal. Apparently the industries were able to adjust their employment levels to the diminished growth of production.

4) The import penetration ratio is up sharply for all industries. Thus, it is not an isolated phenomenon that can be related to specific cases, but is an all-pervasive symptom of the changed basic economic conditions. The import penetration ratios are up both because of the general internationalization of manufacturing activity, with trade growing much more rapidly than world output, and because of the decline in the U.S. relative competitive position at the prevailing exchange rates.

5) The U.S. share of world exports also shows large declines for virtually all industries. This is partly the result of the development of other countries who have joined the ranks of major suppliers of industrial goods, and partly due to the declining U.S. competitive position.

CHAPTER 6

IS MANUFACTURING INDUSTRY NEEDED?

The American economy will continue the rapid expansion of the production of services and the retardation of its manufacturing industries if recent trends are allowed to continue. Consumers will keep shifting their outlays toward services as their incomes rise and their average age increases. The U.S. role on the international scene will be that of a diminishing supplier and increasing buyer of goods in world markets, an increasing earner of interest and profits earned on capital, and an increasing borrower to help finance her budget deficits. What is wrong with this scenario which would be produced by free market forces governed by the laws of comparative advantage, though admittedly affected by the large budget deficits and the role of the dollar as a reserve currency? This chapter explores the case for altering this scenario, for working to retain a strong U.S. manufacturing sector.

HIGHER PRODUCTIVITY LEVELS IN MANUFACTURING

Traditionally, manufacturing jobs have created greater growth in output per worker than jobs in other sectors (Chart 6.1). This stronger productivity trend has been recognized since Adam Smith, who, in his *Wealth of Nations* published in 1776, identified manufacturing as the sector most beneficial to economic development. He argued that the division of labor has more scope in manufacturing, and permits the greater use of capital. The data in the succeeding 200 years leave little doubt that manufacturing jobs offer the opportunity to produce more output per worker.

Since wages will reflect productivity, manufacturing wages are higher than the average for other sectors (Chart 6.2). Workers recognize the attractiveness of manufacturing jobs; and, particularly in the high wage industries, there is usually an excess of workers seeking positions.

Chart 6.1
Output Per Worker Per Year in the Manufacturing
and Nonmanufacturing Sectors, 1948-1982
(Thousands of 1967 dollars)

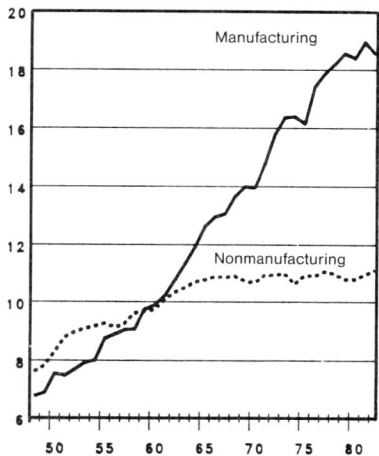

Chart 6.2
Relative Wages: Manufacturing Compared
to Nonmanufacturing, 1940-1982

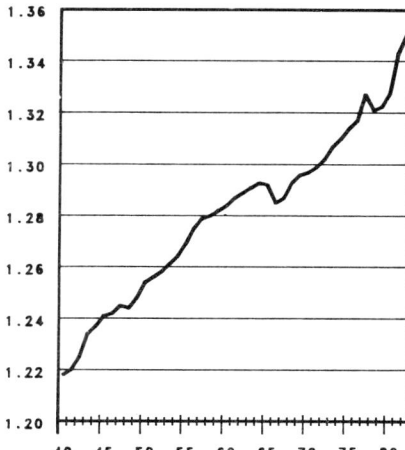

The skill levels of manufacturing jobs also tend to be somewhat higher than in such sectors as services and trade. The percentage of workers at the top of the blue collar skill hierarchy is quite small in the typical modern factory because of the division of labor, but the percentage of technical workers and of semi-skilled workers is high. Many factory jobs also require higher educational qualifications, typically a high school diploma, whereas millions of jobs in the service and trade sectors are still unskilled and have lesser educational requirements.

As a result of the above-average productivity of manufacturing, an economy in which the employment share of manufacturing is shrinking rapidly will experience a reduction in the level of productivity. Workers will be shifting out of high-wage, high-productivity manufacturing jobs into low-wage, low-productivity service jobs. This shift will come gradually, by providing few entry positions into manufacturing for new workers, and by gradually causing factory workers who have permanently lost their jobs to accept lower wage positions in the service and trade sectors or to accept early retirement or unemployment.

The United States has been experiencing a rapid decline in the manufacturing share of employment, from 34% in the early 1950s to 21% in 1982. If manufacturing had been able to maintain its 1965 share in total employment, economy-wide productivity would have been 2% higher in 1982.

A HIGHER PRODUCTIVITY TREND

Besides enjoying a permanently higher productivity level, manufacturing industries also experienced a substantially more favorable rate of advance of productivity. It is not surprising that manufacturing would have a more favorable trend: the production of goods provides more scope for increasing the division of labor and for improving the technology of production. It is striking that United States manufacturing showed a relatively favorable productivity trend in the last few decades despite its exceptionally large loss of position. Comparable data for Japan show far more dramatic differentials between manufacturing and other sectors, and in newly industrializing countries the productivity gaps would be even greater still.[16]

---

[16]Service industries also benefit from technological progress, and are particularly helped by the advances in data processing. For example, financial services are ideally suited for computerization. For evidence of technological progress in the service sector see Victor Fuchs, *The Service Economy*, National Bureau of Economic Research, Columbia University Press, 1969.

STATIC AND DYNAMIC ECONOMIES-TO-SCALE

Manufacturing industries also tend to show a greater benefit from economies-to-scale. In many lines of activity, the modern industrial enterprise operates most efficiently at a large volume of output. Optimal factory size may be large, and the overhead costs of management, marketing and innovation will be spread over more factories. The realization of economies-to-scale will produce measured productivity gains and lower costs.[17]

Such static economies are reinforced by the now well-recognized phenomenon of dynamic economies-to-scale. In the case of many products and processes, costs fall, often dramatically, as the firm learns to operate factories more effectively and adopts secondary innovations that reduce costs and improve quality. The rapid descent of costs along the learning-curve is essential to success in new products.

To be the low-cost producer in world markets frequently requires both large-scale operation and a sufficient rate of expansion. The increase in markets provides the incentive and the resources to advance the technology of production and marketing and to improve the quality of product. This situation is another example of dynamic economies-to-scale.

The importance of these factors is demonstrated by the predominance of particular firms in the world markets for many important goods. For example, the Boeing Corporation is the principal supplier of aircraft to the world. IBM produces more than half the world's large computers; and other American companies, many of them now under pressure from Japanese competitors, have played a similar role. In such fields as consumer electronics, Japanese companies play an equally leading role in world markets.

In the fields suitable for this kind of world dominance, it is very difficult to recapture market position if it is ever lost. Indeed, it is hard to find an example of a lead that was regained. There is an enormous advantage in being the number-one firm, in possessing the largest market share, the lowest costs, the market power, and the ability to finance technological and product progress. Once the lead is lost, profitability diminishes, resources shrink, and management is pressed into shortsighted, defensive cost cutting moves that soon produce a further loss of market share. A nation that casually surrenders leading industrial positions through policies of neglect will find it

---

[17]The empirical evidence on the presence of static economies-to-scale was surveyed in A.A. Walters, "Production and Cost Functions: An Econometric Survey," *Econometrica*, April 1963, Vol. 31 No. 1-2, pp. 1-66. Also see Frederick T. Moore, "Economies of Scale: Some Statistical Evidence," *Quarterly Journal of Economics*, May 1959, and Edward F. Denison, *The Sources of Economic Growth in the United States*, Committee for Economic Development, 1962, pp. 173-181, *Accounting for Slower Economic Growth*, Brookings, 1979, and *Why Growth Rates Differ*, Brookings, 1967.

INVESTMENT AND REINVESTMENT OPPORTUNITIES

It has been recognized since the earliest days of classical economics, in the writings of Adam Smith, that manufacturing produces more savings and investment than other sectors. The modern industrial enterprise distributes only a modest percentage of its profits in the form of dividends, and reinvests retained earnings and depreciation allowances, usually in further industrial investments. Some of the more passive forms of investment, such as residential construction and commercial construction are not likely to produce a comparable stream of reinvestment.[18]

While a country can pour a virtually unlimited amount of capital into investment in services, by providing ever more modern office buildings, bank branches, hotels, shopping malls, etc., these types of investments have a lesser growth potential than investment in a successful manufacturing industry. A well-executed investment plan will quickly generate further investment opportunities if the product finds its place in world markets. Economies-to-scale, improved marketing based on information obtained from actual experience, and the technological opportunities created by an active and responsive R&D effort will make the "follow-on" investments successful as well. Thus, a flourishing manufacturing sector not only creates capital available for reinvestment, but also creates the opportunities that normally will assure a good rate of return on that investment.

THE RELATION OF MANUFACTURING GROWTH TO GENERAL ECONOMIC GROWTH: SOME ECONOMETRIC RESULTS

Because industrial and general economic development are so closely intertwined, it is difficult to identify precise quantitative relationships. There is also relatively little empirical knowledge about the importance of some of the factors sketched above—the technological opportunities, static and dynamic economies-to-scale and reinvestment opportunities. As a result, it

---

[18]For a discussion of these matters see the theoretical literature on investment criteria for economic development, including Walter Galenson and Harvey Leibenstein, "Investment Criteria, Productivity, and Economic Development," *Quarterly Journal of Economics,* August 1955, pp. 343-370, and Otto Eckstein, "Investment Criteria for Economic Development and the Theory of Intertemporal Welfare Economics," *Quarterly Journal of Economics,* February 1957, pp. 56-85.

is difficult to construct a precise quantitative model which converts differences in manufacturing progress into differences in general economic progress.

Nonetheless, if manufacturing plays a special role, it should be empirically discernible in a comparison of the economic performance of the major countries. A "reduced form" statistical test has been constructed, and it does show a very strong association. Chart 6.3 shows the rate of increase of gross domestic product per capita for six major industrial countries for the period 1965-82 plotted against the rate of increase of manufacturing output per capita for the same period. The relationship is strong, with Japan showing very high growth rates both for manufacturing and the economy as a whole, the United States and Britain showing low growth rates for manufacturing, with the U.S. doing somewhat better on GDP growth, West Germany showing slightly better results than the U.S. on both variables, and Italy and France showing intermediate results. A regression equation fitted for this cross section of six countries shows highly significant statistical results, with a coefficient of determination ($\bar{R}^2$) of 0.94.

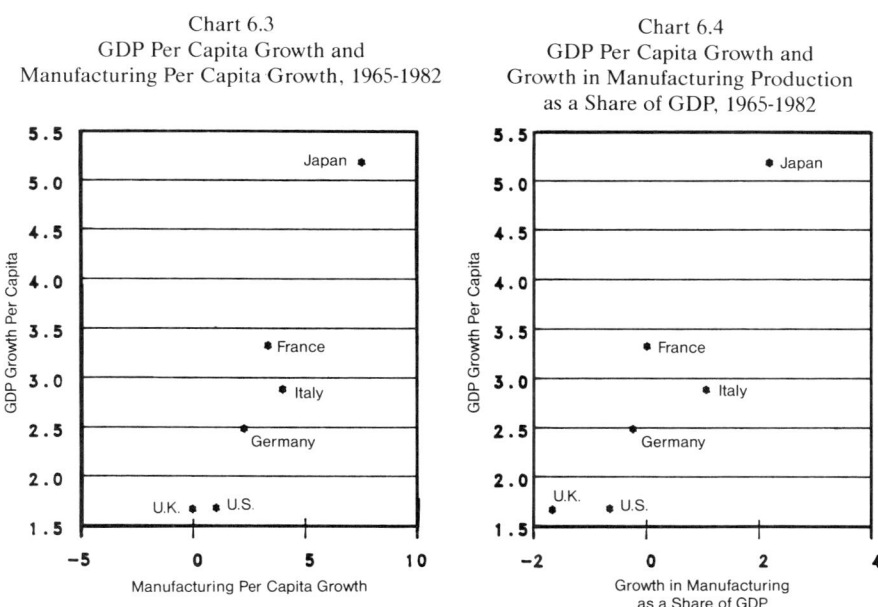

Chart 6.3
GDP Per Capita Growth and
Manufacturing Per Capita Growth, 1965-1982

Chart 6.4
GDP Per Capita Growth and
Growth in Manufacturing Production
as a Share of GDP, 1965-1982

Since a high-growth country is very likely to show strong progress for a major sector such as manufacturing, the above statistical test shows only an association, and not a particular one-directional causality. A second test is somewhat more sensitive, however. Chart 6.4 shows per capita real GDP growth plotted against the change in the share of economic activity represented by manufacturing. In the high-growth countries, manufacturing was a rapidly rising share of activity, whereas in the low-growth countries the manufacturing share did not show any comparable growth. A regression equation again produces strong statistical results with an $\bar{R}^2$ of 0.74.

The above tests cannot be taken as conclusive proof that a strong manufacturing sector is an essential component for strong economic performance of an advanced economy. But the "reduced form" equations are very suggestive: it is demonstrable that there was a close association between manufacturing success and general economic success in the observed cases of large advanced countries over an extended period of years.

Table 6.1
Cross-Sectional Analysis: Two Equations

Equation 1: Real per capita GDP growth as a function of real per capita manufacturing GDP growth.

%GR(GDP/N) = 1.42 + .48 (%GR(PRODM/N))
        (6.6)   (8.6)

$\bar{R}^2$: 0.936

Equation 2: Real per capita GDP growth as a function of change in manufacturing production's share of GDP.

%GR(GDP/N) = 2.77 + .87 (%GR(PRODM/GDP))
        (10.6) (4.16)

$\bar{R}^2$: 0.765

Note: GDP = real gross domestic product, PRODM = manufacturing production, N = population; t-statistics are in parentheses under coefficients.

Table 6.2
Manufacturing: A Cross-Sectional Analysis, 1965-1982
(Annual percent growth rates)

	Real GDP Per Capita	Manufacturing Production Per Capita	Manufacturing Production to Total GDP
Japan	5.2	7.5	2.2
France	3.3	3.3	0.0
Italy	2.9	4.0	1.1
Germany	2.5	2.2	−0.2
United States	1.7	1.0	−0.7
United Kingdom	1.7	0.0	−1.7

MANUFACTURING INDUSTRY AND THE NATIONAL DEFENSE

The link between industrial strength and military strength has surely become looser with the arrival of the nuclear age and the growth of international trade, but it has not disappeared. The United States played the decisive roles in World War I and World War II because of her enormous industrial strength. Civilian production was quickly converted to military production—autos to tanks, suits to uniforms, etc. Both wars were wars of economic attrition; and the apparently unlimited ability of the United States to produce weapons, ammunition and food ultimately wore down our enemies and produced victory.

If a nuclear war were ever to begin, the ability of the industrial base to produce weapons would be irrelevant because the war would be so short and destructive. Further, the Soviet Union has demonstrated that even a country with a limited industrial base is able to be a world power if it makes military strength its predominant national objective. Finally, the United States could, under normal peacetime circumstances, purchase those military goods or components from friendly sources that its own industrial base cannot produce.

But these considerations do not close the issue. Conventional (non-nuclear) military power is an important component of our defense posture, and one which may reduce the risk of the use of nuclear weapons. America's ability to meet the defense goals set by the present administration will depend upon the adequacy of our industrial base. It would be illusory to believe that the United States has the ability, as the Soviet Union does, to have a strong manufacturing capacity for military goods while the rest of manufacturing was in poor condition. Dependence on foreign suppliers, which is already increasing, is also not without its costs: alliances shift, politics changes, and the supplies may suddenly prove not to be available. Further, our technological leadership in the military field is interwoven with the general technological progress of U.S. industry. Production of weapons is itself one of the industries in which economies-to-scale, R&D, and learning-by-doing are important economic factors; and, if our position in this field weakens, the imports of military supplies would raise the real cost of national preparedness.

The financing of our national defense also requires good economic performance. While the current increases in the structural federal budget deficit are as much attributable to tax reduction as to the increases in military spending, and a full resolution of the budget problem will require fiscal action, the budget continues to be highly responsive to variations in economic growth. The budget problem becomes more soluble in a high-growth economy.

If the United States wishes to pursue a policy of military strength, she must preserve her industrial strength. World political leadership continues to require an industrial base sufficient to support the requisite foreign policy.

MANUFACTURING PROSPERITY AND REGIONAL DEVELOPMENT

In most nations, manufacturing industry tends to be clustered in particular geographic areas, usually near the raw materials for manufacturing in its early stages. The result is high population growth and expansion of jobs. The blue-collar workers and their families become dependent on the local industry. Should manufacturing enter a period of decline, the older industrial regions become depressed areas.

This pattern could be seen in England decades ago. In the United States, the departure of the textile and shoe industries to other parts of the United States and then to foreign nations left New England in a depressed economic condition for more than a decade. Ultimately new high technology industry developed, and today New England is one of the most prosperous regions of the country. But the transition was long and painful.

The Midwest region is now facing a similar adjustment as the older durable goods industries are experiencing a decline. Unemployment is substantially higher in the Midwestern industrial states than in the nation as a whole. Durable goods industries are always particularly cyclical, but their experience in the recent recession was a combination of the cycle with a negative trend. The recovery will be helpful; of course, and the import limitations on steel and automobiles will give American manufacturers a full share of the market growth of the next few years. But other industries will continue to suffer erosion to foreign suppliers, and the import agreements for autos and steel are on shaky ground.

The Midwestern region will have a major problem of revitalization even under the best of circumstances. Labor costs are high, discouraging new industry from locating there. The financial resources of local governments have been hurt by the decline of the economic base, making it difficult to sustain public services. Past advantages of proximity to natural resources have been diminished; and the new, high technology industries have not taken root.

If U.S. manufacturing as a whole returns to a healthier state, the Midwest could stage a comeback of its own, with some of the older industries showing good employment growth and public costs of adjustment reduced. But, if manufacturing as a whole continues its slide, the prospects for the Midwest are weak for the next decade, and perhaps for much longer.

AN EARLIER EXAMPLE OF MANUFACTURING NEGLECT: THE UNITED KINGDOM

The United Kingdom was the first country to experience the industrial revolution; and, in much of the 19th century, she was the principal supplier of manufactured goods to the world. But Britain's lead began to suffer by the end of the last century, and she was surpassed by Germany and the United States as this century opened.

In subsequent decades, British manufacturing suffered from neglect. Economic policy pursued other goals, with the restoration of the pound to an unrealistic prewar parity in 1925 ushering in an industrial depression long before the world lapsed into the Great Depression. Industry was also damaged during World War II, and the rebuilding did not proceed with the speed and thoroughness of the reconstruction in Germany, Japan and France.

The British economy did not do as badly as manufacturing. London was the financial capital of the world in the interwar years, and did not lose that position until World War II. Even thereafter, the city of London was a major world financial center, not only earning a good income for the financial industry, but also making London a great center of business and tourist travel. While the Midlands, the industrial heartland of Britain, were languishing, London was a successful metropolis with a flourishing service sector.

Without attempting a full evaluation of British economic performance, it is instructive to see whether her economy could thrive without a leading thrust from manufacturing. The answer is clear: the economy stagnated, with real GNP growing at the lowest rate of any major industrial nation (Table 6.3). By 1980, the British output per capita, and, therefore, the standard of living, was only 70% as high as in Germany and France, a loss that occurred in the last three decades.[19]

Table 6.3
Gross Income per Capita: Six Countries
1965-1980

	Income per Capita 1965 (1970 dollars)	Annual Growth 1965 to 1980 (Percent)	Income per Capita 1980 (1970 dollars)
Japan	1,168	7.7	2,964
France	2,193	4.3	3,768
Italy	1,476	4.1	2,431
West Germany	2,544	3.3	3,922
United States	4,336	3.1	5,822
United Kingdom	2,013	2.0	2,649

Of course there are many differences between the British and the American situations. Industrial relations were substantially worse there for most of the postwar period; the defense of the pound was probably even more damaging than the defense of the dollar; economic policy was even more inflationary; foreign policy was too costly in terms of military budgets and soldiers stationed abroad; and the internal political and social tensions between management and labor were more acute, and expressed themselves in programs of nationalization followed by denationalization. But while the specifics might be different and the British process of manufacturing decline has gone further, the similarities are also quite telling. If the path of manufacturing neglect leads to the economic stagnation from which Britain has suffered, it is a warning to us.

---

[19]See Sidney Pollard, *The Wasting of the British Economy: British Economic Policy 1945 to the Present,* New York: St. Martin's press, 1982, 197 pp, and Richard E. Caves and Lawrence B. Krause, eds., *Britain's Economic Performance,* Washington, D.C.: Brookings, 1980, 388 pp.

CHAPTER 7

MANUFACTURING IN 1995: SOME ALTERNATIVE SCENARIOS

So far, this study has been devoted to an historical analysis of the origins and developments of the problems of the U.S. manufacturing industry. What are the prospects for its future growth? And how can policies make a difference? This chapter presents two alternative scenarios, one assuming policies that are unfavorable to manufacturing, the other assuming an improvement in the environment which would allow manufacturing to prosper. These scenarios are calculated using the DRI Model of the U.S. Economy, including particularly its industrial sector based on an input-output table embedded in the model.

Scenario projections of this type cannot produce precise forecasts, and that is not their goal. Instead, they are designed to indicate the range of possible outcomes and the implications. They show very sizable differences in terms of employment, productivity, real income growth and other broad dimensions of performance.

The national results are also converted into regional dimensions using DRI's regional models. Because so many of the industries at issue are concentrated in the Midwest and the Southeast, the regional implications are of particular social, economic, and political importance.

THE PESSIMISTIC SCENARIO: ECONOMIC POLICY WITHOUT AN INDUSTRIAL VIEWPOINT

The pessimistic scenario projects the future of manufacturing production and employment principally on the basis of four essential assumptions. They are:

1) **The business cycle continues, triggered by "stop-go" monetary policies.**
   The base line for this scenario is the DRI long-term alternative solution,

CYCLELONG2008B, which portrays an economy that is about as cyclical as it was during the last three decades, certainly not an unreasonable assumption. Expansion is vigorous, and is followed by a period of credit restraint which triggers a recession in late 1987. The recession is not as severe as the experience of 1975 and 1982, but civilian unemployment does peak at 8.7%, real investment declines by 9.0%, and other cyclical variables move correspondingly.

2) **The federal budget deficit continues near 5% of GNP**, keeping real interest rates high. No fiscal actions are taken to cut spending, and taxes are increased too little and too late. Weak economic performance contributes to the deficit.

3) **The dollar remains grossly overvalued.** This scenario assumes the trade-weighted exchange rate to remain at its average value for August 1983. This value, using the Morgan Guaranty Bank trade-weighted index, is set at 103.5 with May 1970 equaling 100. Since the dollar was still pressing upward in 1983 under the impetus of high interest rates and capital inflows, this must be considered a reasonable assumption. It does require that the resultant current account deficit will continue to be offset by capital inflows. With concentrations of wealth in many parts of the world in nervous hands, such capital inflows are a possibility.

4) **The existing major trade agreements are terminated**, so that the imports of textiles, apparel, automobiles, and steel will be determined in an environment of an overvalued dollar, a slack world economy and widespread government protection, subsidy and ownership. No actions of reciprocity in the trade policies of others are assumed. The resultant increases in the imports of these goods produce some secondary effects within manufacturing through input-output relationships.

The results of this scenario, as seen in 1995, are summarized in Tables 7.1 to 7.5. Highlights of this solution include:

- Potential real GNP, the standard measure of aggregate supply of the economy, grows at 2.5%, 1983-1995, compared to a figure of 3.5% in the preceding two decades.
- Actual real GNP grows at a 2.8% rate to 1995. With the economy in a business cycle upswing in 1995, the estimates are affected somewhat by cyclical timing. But unemployment is also boosted by the difficulties of reemploying workers laid off in manufacturing, increasing the "natural" rate of unemployment.
- Business fixed investment for the economy as a whole averages 11.4% of GNP, a small improvement from recent depressed levels.

- Manufacturing investment is 4.0% of GNP, compared to 3.7% in the previous two decades, a figure still substantially lower than our principal competitors.
- The average inflation rate, as measured by the GNP deflator, is 5.7%, 1983-1995, and long-term interest rates, as measured by a 10-year Treasury bond, stay in the range of 9.9% to 11.3%, keeping the real cost of capital high.
- Nonfarm payroll employment grows by 1.6% a year, 1983-1995, to a level of 109 million workers.

Turning to the more specific impacts on manufacturing, the pessimistic scenario produces a growth rate of manufacturing production of 3.2% for the years 1983 to 1995, a figure which is substantially aided by the fact that the economy was in deep recession in the base year. There will still be some high-growth industries, even under this scenario, in the high technology fields. Industries such as food production will expand along with the economy and the population, and imports will remain a minor factor for them. But the more traditional durable goods industries, as well as textiles, apparel, and chemicals, will show low growth rates, some even negative figures. The deepest troubles will be found for steel, fabricated metals, autos, textiles and apparel.

In terms of employment, total job growth in manufacturing will be about 1.5 million jobs, a poor rate of growth of just 0.6%. This would represent no more than 7.9% of the total job growth of the economy in these years. Thus, manufacturing will be making a very small contribution to the total job growth of 18.9 million nonfarm jobs, almost all of which will have to be created by services and trade.

The manufacturing employment share in total employment will keep on declining, of course. Compared to the figure of 34% in the early 1950s and 22.4% in 1980, the percentage will have dropped to 19.4% by 1990 and to 18.5% by 1995. This represents some slowing in the rate of decline from that observed historically; simple extrapolation of the trend would give a 1995 share of 17%. The share remains above this downtrend mainly because the projected recessions are not as severe or frequent as those of the 1970s, and because the surge of employment in services and trade is projected to weaken with the inevitably slower labor force growth.

Manufacturing investment would also be damaged by this kind of economic environment. In real terms, the rate of growth of manufacturing investment would be just 2.5%, 1980-1995. Investment in such capital intensive industries as electrical machinery, chemicals, and airplanes is held back by low output growth, the high cost of capital, and the low rate of profitability under worsening international competition. The distortions in the pattern of investment of the last 20 years—the absence of new basic industrial capacity, the diversion of capital into such sheltered areas as real estate and oil exploration, and the inadequacy of long-term investments in overseas marketing—would continue, of course, and would worsen for the industries in deepest trouble.

The structure of unemployment would also be affected by this pattern of development. Because manufacturing industry employs a larger than proportionate share of adult males, heads of household and older workers, the unemployment rates for these categories would be particularly affected. The regional employment implications of this scenario will be discussed below.

THE OPTIMISTIC SCENARIO: AN ECONOMIC POLICY WITH AN INDUSTRIAL VIEWPOINT

What will happen to U.S. manufacturing if the general economic environment were to become more favorable? Is a revival still possible, and what would it take to accomplish? To explore these issues, the DRI Model of the U.S. Economy was used for a simulation in which the economic factors were changed for the better compared to recent history. This optimistic scenario combines more favorable assumptions on four critical macro-issues to create a more favorable environment, without attempting to show the precise effects of any one factor alone. The results should be interpreted as indicative of the improvements that could be achieved with reasonable measures, without pursuing any of them to their extremes.

A Competitive Exchange Rate. The solution assumes a 23% reduction in the value of the dollar in foreign exchange markets, setting the Morgan Guaranty trade-weighted rate at 80% of its 1970 value. This was the exchange rate that prevailed during some years in the late 1970s, when manufacturing was temporarily stemming its decline in world markets. Part of this reduction in the value of the dollar would be achieved by the reduction in the budget deficit discussed below, but this would not suffice to achieve this result. Other measures, such as a reduction of foreign restraints on capital inflows and possibly a change in exchange rate policies would be needed.

This is the most fundamental change of the solution, working its way through the model by changing exports and imports substantially over an 18-month period and considerably affecting industrial production.

A Reduced Budget Deficit. Fiscal action and the better economic environment are assumed to reduce the budget deficit to about 1 1/2% of GNP by

1995. This fiscal action takes the form primarily of increased reliance on indirect taxation with some spending cuts. Table 7.1 shows the structural budget deficits in the good and bad environments. Savings on interest payments made possible by smaller actual deficits and lower interest rates make a major contribution to the reduced structural deficit. Chart 7.2 shows the actual budget deficits.

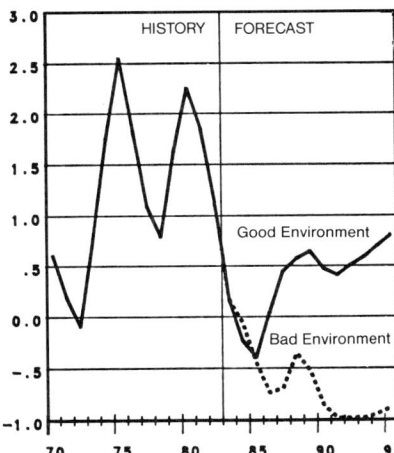

Chart 7.1
The Non-Oil Merchandise Trade Balance as a Percent of GNP, 1970-1995

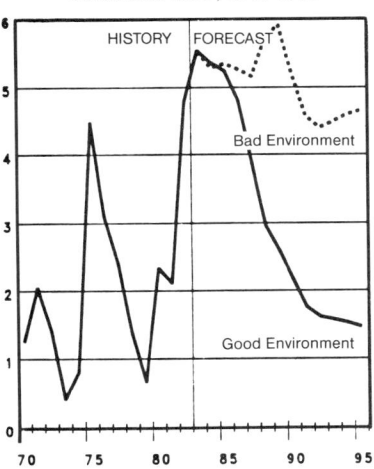

Chart 7.2
The Federal Deficit as a Percent of GNP, 1970-1995

Table 7.1
The Cyclically Corrected Budget, Selected Years
(Billions of dollars)

	1986	1988	1990	1995
Good Environment	−159.8	−123.4	−100.1	−65.9
Percent of GNP	−3.7	−2.3	−1.6	−0.7
Bad Environment	−171.3	−184.4	−206.0	−294.7
Percent of GNP	−4.0	−3.8	−3.5	−3.3

A Lower Absolute and Relative Cost of Industrial Capital. A reduction in the cost of capital for manufacturing industries is assumed. This reduction is accomplished partly by lower interest rates and partly by measures to provide capital to industry on more comparable terms with other sectors of the economy. Greater equality of capital costs could be achieved by new tax incentives for industry, or by reducing the special tax provisions open to the other sectors, including tax shelters, the privilege of issuing tax exempt bonds, and other devices. The result of these assumptions is an increase in manufacturing investment and productivity, and in total business fixed investment, while holding down the gain in house building.

A More Stable Economy. The solution also assumes that there will be no major recessions from now to 1995. Though there are smaller fluctuations, real GNP approaches its potential values in a gradual, noninflationary fashion. Such a path would free manufacturing from the periodic disappointment of its output expectations and the resultant inventory corrections, and from the spikes in capital costs created by the credit cycle. It implies that policymakers keep a steadier hand on the wheel than they have historically.

More Favorable Trade Policies. The solution assumes that the United States succeeds in opening the doors to our export markets somewhat further, while retaining the informal trade agreements which now reduce the importation of autos, steel and textiles. These assumptions have a major influence in the directly affected industries and are a significant contributor to prosperity in other industries.

The Results of the Optimistic Scenario

Both the economy as a whole and the manufacturing sector in particular would perform substantially better under this scenario. The ability of the economy's potential output, viewed from the supply side, would be enhanced by 4.8 percentage points over the pessimistic solution by 1995, as increased capital formation and the absence of cyclical losses would enhance the productivity trend. The annual growth rate of potential real GNP would be 2.9%.

The reduction of instability would improve structural balance among sectors and regions, lower the unemployment rate, draw additional people into the labor force, and thereby make possible a 2.9% boost in employment. Combining the improved productivity with the increased employment yields an increase in total real GNP of 7.0% by 1995.

Table 7.2
A Comparison of Two Projections, 1995

	Levels		Percent Difference
	Good Environment	Bad Environment	
Supply			
Employment (Millions)	112.2	109.0	2.9
Productivity Trend (Annual growth, 1983-95)	2.0	1.5	0.5*
Potential GNP (Billions of 1972 dollars)	2,410.7	2,299.5	4.8
Potential GNP Trend (Annual growth, 1983-95)	2.9	2.5	0.4*
Demand—Billions of 1972 Dollars			
Gross National Product	2,275.1	2,127.1	7.0
Consumption	1,410.1	1,381.2	2.1
Business Fixed Investment	319.8	273.9	16.8
Residential Investment	63.5	58.8	8.0
Exports	259.7	226.4	14.7
Imports	203.0	227.4	−10.7
Trade			
Exchange Rate (May 1970=1.0)	0.800	1.035	−22.8
Trade Balance (Billions of dollars)	−22.1	−158.4	136.3*
Other			
Deflator for GNP (1972=1.0)	4.289	4.214	1.8
Civilian Unemployment Rate (Percent)	6.2	7.4	−1.2*
Aftertax Corporate Profits (Billions of dollars)	350.1	303.6	15.3
Hourly Wage Index (1967=1.0)	7.04	6.51	8.0
95-Day T-Bill Yield (Percent)	6.4	7.7	−1.3*
New Issue Rate, AAA Corp Bonds (Percent)	9.2	11.4	−2.1*
Federal Deficit (Billions of dollars)	−142.6	−416.4	273.8*

* Absolute difference.

Inflation performance would be somewhat worse because the economy would be busier, and continued restrictions on foreign trade would have an inflationary influence. The cheaper exchange rate would raise the price of imported goods, and the reduced volume of imports would ease the competitive pressure which foreign suppliers exercise on our producers.

By the end of the decade, the larger volume of investment and the improved productivity performance would gradually offset the initial inflationary impulses. The price level would be up an extra 1.8% by 1995, but the rate of inflation in the later years would be little changed.

To a considerable extent, the outcome of the solution depends on the assumptions made about monetary policy. The simulations were run so that interest rates would be lower in the optimistic scenario. If a monetarist regime had been modeled, with its assumption of an unchanged growth in the money supply under the two solutions, the variations in the price level would have forced a partial compensating adjustment in real activity.

Turning to the specifics of the manufacturing industries, the optimistic scenario shows a significantly higher growth rate for the total of manufacturing production as well as particularly large increases for textiles and apparel, transportation, capital goods, and primary metals industries (Table 7.3). By 1995, manufacturing production is enlarged by an extra 17.9%, an increase in the growth rate from 3.3% to 4.7%.

Chart 7.3
Real Value of Manufacturing Production
as a Percent of GNP, 1970-1995

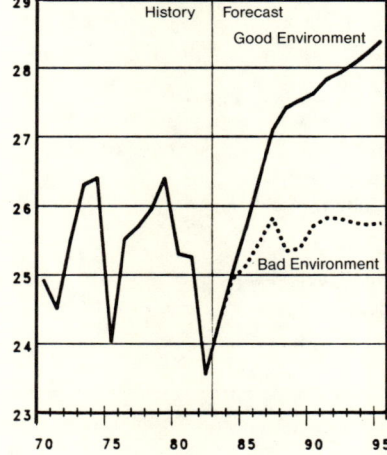

Table 7.3
Production by Industry in Two
Projections, 1995

	Percent Difference
Total Production	16.5
Manufacturing	17.9
Ordnance	3.3
Food and Products	2.9
Tobacco Manufactures	6.0
Textile Mill Products	69.0
Apparel	84.6
Lumber and Wood Products	14.8
Furniture and Fixtures	12.6
Paper and Products	6.5
Printing and Publishing	4.6
Chemicals	14.7
Petroleum Products	1.3
Rubber and Plastics	15.4
Leather Products	25.3
Stone, Clay, and Glass	12.3
Primary Metals	21.8
Steel Mill Products	29.6
Nonferrous Metals	14.2
Fabricated Metals	18.9
Nonelectrical Machinery	21.5
Electrical Machinery	22.6
Transportation Equipment	25.0
Motor Vehicles and Parts	41.2
Trucks, Buses, and Trailers	34.0
Aircraft and Parts	8.9
Instruments	24.8
Miscellaneous Manufacturing	24.8

The increase in manufacturing employment would be somewhat less than the increase in manufacturing output because productivity performance would be enhanced. The total gain in manufacturing employment would be an extra 9.3% by 1995. Because there would be more manufacturing jobs, the average real wage would be higher. The stronger economy would also create jobs in other sectors, particularly in construction. The total job gain is boosted by 3.2 million workers.

Table 7.4
Employment by Industry in Two Projections, 1995
(Thousands of workers)

	Good Environment	Bad Environment	Difference
Nonagricultural Establishments	112,168	109,004	3,165
Manufacturing			
Manufacturing	22,006	20,141	1,866
Nondurables Manufacturing	8,417	7,672	744
Food and Products	1,479	1,454	25
Tobacco Manufactures	70	69	1
Textile Mill Products	770	585	185
Apparel	1,338	980	358
Paper and Products	730	724	6
Printing and Publishing	1,512	1,474	38
Chemicals	1,190	1,135	55
Petroleum Products	204	199	5
Rubber and Plastics	904	843	61
Leather Products	221	210	11
Durables Manufacturing	13,590	12,469	1,121
Lumber and Wood Products	687	634	54
Furniture and Fixtures	568	528	41
Stone, Clay, and Glass	671	643	28
Primary Metals	1,116	986	130
Fabricated Metals	1,605	1,473	133
Nonelectrical Machinery	3,307	3,082	226
Electrical Machinery	2,340	2,190	149
Transportation Equipment	1,943	1,694	248
Instruments	907	842	66
Miscellaneous Manufacturing	444	396	48
Nonmanufacturing			
Contract Construction	5,711	5,348	362
Finance, Insurance & Real Estate	7,225	7,149	76
Mining	1,032	1,006	26
Transportation and Public Utilities	5,280	5,345	−64
Services	26,250	26,010	240
Wholesale and Retail Trade	25,195	24,951	244
Federal Government	3,462	3,462	0
State and Local Governments	16,008	15,592	416

The pattern of employment gains would still show a preponderant share of new jobs created in the services and trade sectors, but the rate at which the manufacturing employment share declines would be reduced. Whereas only 18.5% of employment would be in manufacturing by 1995 under the negative scenario, 19.6% of workers would be holding manufacturing jobs under the optimistic scenario. Of total job growth, manufacturing would be providing 15.1%.

Table 7.5
Real Investment in Plant
and Equipment by Industry:
a Comparison of Two Projections, 1995

	Percent Difference
All Industries	15.0
Manufacturing	23.7
Durable Goods	24.3
Stone, Clay, and Glass	5.5
Primary Metals	26.7
Blast Furnace, Steel Works	61.1
Nonferrous	10.7
Fabricated Metals	10.7
Electrical Machinery	29.7
Nonelectrical Machinery	25.8
Transportation Equipment	31.0
Motor Vehicles	43.1
Aircraft	19.0
Other Durables	5.5
Nondurable Goods	23.1
Food and Products	12.3
Textile Mill Products	86.4
Paper and Products	5.9
Chemicals	22.6
Petroleum Products*	29.9
Rubber and Plastics	55.3
Other Nondurables	18.3
Nonmanufacturing	9.9

* Includes some investment in oil and gas drilling.

Chart 7.4
Manufacturing Employment,
1970-1995
(Millions)

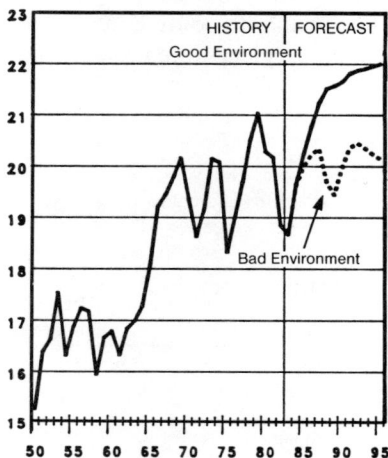

The profitability of the manufacturing industries would, of course, be raised substantially by the larger output and stronger market position. For the economy as a whole, profits would be up an additional 15.3% by 1995, and much of this gain would accrue in manufacturing.

Real investment in the manufacturing industries would be 23.7% larger by 1995 under this more favorable environment, producing a growth rate of investment of 6.2% a year, 1983 to 1995, compared to the 4.3% under the alternative scenario (Chart 7.5). The growth of the sector's capital stock would be accelerated. The larger capital stock would include more modernization, a more rapid introduction of new technology and some expansion of capacity. Worker productivity growth would be boosted by approximately 0.5 percentage points a year.

In summary, the "good" and "bad" environments portrayed in these scenarios show large differences in the performance levels of industry and of the economy. They are illustrative, even representative of the futures that may await us. But they do not represent the outer bounds of what is possible. Some of the assumptions could have been pushed much further, such as much larger budget deficits (or balanced budgets). Only the exchange rate assumptions may be strained toward the extreme—it is hard to believe that the current very high exchange rate could persist, or that the rest of the world would let us return to the favorable parity of 1980.

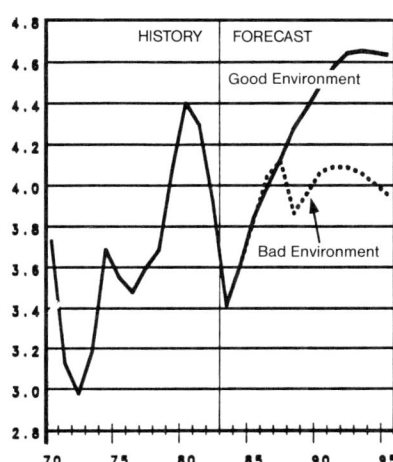

Chart 7.5
Real Manufacturing Investment as a
Percent of Real GNP, 1970-1995

Both scenarios are more favorable than recent history in the mildness of the business cycles that are shown. There is no OPEC III in either future, nor any other comparable shock to our economy. There is no war, no hyperinflation, just historically observed differences in routine macroeconomic policy parameters. Yet even these differences suffice to produce dramatically different patterns of industrial development.

REGIONAL IMPLICATIONS OF THE TWO SCENARIOS

Because manufacturing industry, especially those industries most subject to foreign competition, are concentrated in particular regions, the employment effects are particularly concentrated. To calculate these effects, the industry employment results of the two macroeconomic scenarios have been disaggregated according to the industry composition of each state in the nonrecession year of 1979. Table 7.6 summarizes these results.

Several Southeastern states heavily dependent on textile and apparel production show the biggest favorable effects from the healthier manufacturing scenario. Older durable goods industries, including steel and automobiles, are also heavily affected.

Table 7.6
Manufacturing Employment, Effects by State—1995

	Good Environment (Thousands)	Bad Environment (Thousands)	Difference	Percent Difference
Alabama	348.7	307.5	41.2	13.4
Alaska	8.8	8.6	0.2	2.6
Arizona	115.3	107.0	8.3	7.8
Arkansas	221.6	204.7	16.9	8.2
California	2,117.3	1,947.7	169.6	8.7
Colorado	193.8	180.9	12.9	7.1
Connecticut	441.3	403.9	37.4	9.3
Delaware	63.7	59.6	4.1	6.9
District of Columbia	15.6	15.2	0.4	2.5
Florida	435.1	401.3	33.8	8.4
Georgia	495.3	430.6	64.7	15.0
Hawaii	10.0	9.8	0.2	1.7
Idaho	53.4	50.6	2.8	5.6
Illinois	1,372.1	1,279.5	92.7	7.2
Indiana	762.0	701.9	60.2	8.6
Iowa	279.9	262.2	17.7	6.8
Kansas	181.3	167.3	13.9	8.3
Kentucky	303.7	278.1	25.6	9.2
Louisiana	206.1	191.8	14.3	7.5
Maine	112.3	104.0	8.3	8.0
Maryland	256.2	236.4	19.8	8.4
Massachusetts	734.7	674.4	60.3	8.9
Michigan	1,187.2	1,079.7	107.5	10.0
Minnesota	418.9	393.0	25.9	6.6
Mississippi	239.7	214.3	25.5	11.9
Missouri	464.1	427.0	37.1	8.7
Montana	20.2	19.0	1.3	6.7
Nebraska	95.6	89.7	5.9	6.5
Nevada	9.2	8.9	0.4	4.5
New Hampshire	127.2	117.8	9.4	7.9
New Jersey	854.8	789.5	65.3	8.3
New Mexico	18.1	16.1	2.0	12.7
New York	1,619.2	1,475.2	143.9	9.8
North Carolina	829.3	721.4	107.9	15.0
North Dakota	15.8	15.0	0.8	5.1
Ohio	1,458.6	1,349.1	109.4	8.1
Oklahoma	171.6	157.5	14.0	8.9
Oregon	228.8	212.4	16.4	7.7
Pennsylvania	1,430.3	1,298.6	131.7	10.1
Rhode Island	136.9	123.6	13.3	10.8
South Carolina	377.7	322.9	54.9	17.0
South Dakota	21.3	20.2	1.1	5.4
Tennessee	542.3	490.5	51.9	10.6
Texas	1,077.9	993.8	84.1	8.5
Utah	61.9	55.9	6.0	10.8
Vermont	43.7	41.0	2.8	6.7
Virginia	418.8	379.2	39.6	10.4
Washington	297.7	272.9	24.8	9.1
West Virginia	118.9	109.9	9.0	8.2
Wisconsin	636.0	593.8	42.2	7.1
Wyoming	4.4	4.2	0.2	3.9

The regional effects are of particular importance from a social point of view because recent years have seen a sharp divergence in the economic performance of the newer and the older regions. Both the decline of our industrial position in the world and the severity of the recent recessions have imposed damaging blows on the economies of the highly industrialized states. During the recent recession employment declined particularly in Ohio, Michigan, Pennsylvania, and Illinois. Unemployment reached such high figures as 17% in West Virginia, 15% in Michigan, 13% in Pennsylvania and Ohio, and 12% in Illinois, Alabama and Mississippi. This weak economic performance has made it difficult for these states to preserve the quality of their public services, has threatened the finances of their governments, and has created large pockets of unemployment which will make adjustment particularly difficult.

The problems of the older industrial regions would not be solved entirely by a more favorable national environment for industrial development. Some of them go too deep and some of the changes are irreversible. Several industries will never return to previous peak outputs, even in the optimistic case. But the difference in the economic performance of these regions is very large between the two scenarios. An industrial renaissance would go a considerable distance toward restoring them to economic viability.

CONCLUDING COMMENTS

While the two scenarios can be only suggestive of the impact of different policies on the fate of American industry and of the economy as a whole, they do show some startling results. There can be little question that, if we stay on the path of the last two decades, with an exchange rate which makes our goods noncompetitive, an economy which disrupts industrial capital formation every few years, a cost of industrial capital which is far higher than in Japan, and trade policies that sacrifice our industries for the benefit of our allies, the outlook for all of our industries is clouded, and grim for our older industries. On the other hand, if we can create a more favorable general economic environment and consider the industrial viewpoint more strongly in our macro- and microeconomic policy decisions, the slide of U.S. manufacturing can be stemmed and the stage set for a reassertion of our leadership.

The current problems of industry are generally understood by economists, but there is a belief that the normal forces of adjustment will ultimately solve them, whether policies are changed or not. It is believed that real interest rates will come down, the dollar will weaken, the budget deficit will be dealt with in a few years, and workers will shift into service occupations. Then, it is believed, manufacturing will resume a stronger position, and the present troubles will be viewed as just another historical episode.

The danger lies in too slow an adjustment process. If the present macro-situation is allowed to continue, more markets will be lost and the damage to our trade position will become irretrievable. The present problems will not keep: in the absence of improvement in the current decade, they will become insoluble by the next one.

CHAPTER 8

CONCLUSIONS

The data gathered in this study and the analytical conclusions that have been drawn do not point to simple policy prescriptions. The sources of our problems are clear, though there may be disagreement about their relative importance. But how vigorously we should pursue these problems will remain a matter of dispute.

In essence, the conclusions of this study are as follows: a prosperous manufacturing industry continues to be important to America. Good general economic development and rising living standards require industrial participation in the growth process. Our political leadership in the world cannot be sustained without strong U.S. industrial performance. Nor can we support the necessary military effort without a solid industrial base.

The demand for services will grow more rapidly than the demand for goods in the decades ahead because of our high income levels and aging population. International competition in the manufacture of mass-produced goods is also inevitable at the current juncture of world economic development. But these trends do not negate the hypothesis that a flourishing manufacturing sector is essential to general economic growth. The demand for many of the services originates, directly or indirectly, in manufacturing activity; the production of goods is the principal component of the economic base of most communities and regions. The historical situation requires special efforts to promote the success of U.S. manufacturing industry. It would be unfounded optimism to believe that the service sector will somehow sustain our economic progress on its own. A predominantly service economy would lack forward thrust and would fail to provide adequate job opportunities for large segments of our population and for major regions of our country.

Nor should the problems of manufacturing be blamed principally on inevitable historical forces. U.S. manufacturing has lost much ground because the general economic environment was particularly unfavorable in recent decades. The economy was managed in a highly unstable fashion, creating seven business cycles which disrupted the capital formation process. Capital costs were kept too high and policies of taxation and regulation raised costs further. The expensive dollar placed American products at a handicap in world markets and made imports unduly attractive to our own consumers. International trade policy was without focus and suffered from weak execution.

Exchange Rates and the Federal Budget Deficit. The dollar must be brought to a more realistic value through vigorous reduction of the deficits in the federal budget. If the deficit could be reduced to the historical range of 1-2% of GNP, interest rates would be lower, reducing capital inflows, assuring a reduction in the demand for dollars and thereby lowering the exchange rate. There is no other practical way to significantly reduce the overvaluation of the dollar. Direct government intervention in exchange markets would require enormous resources in the face of the much enlarged private dollar balances. Even if a reduction in the dollar could be accomplished without budget reform, the indirect effect would be a reduction in the trade deficit which, in turn, would reduce capital inflows and reduce the total resources available for domestic investment. It is the high interest rates and the foreign capital they attract which permit our economy to continue to invest, albeit at a subnormal rate, given the federal government's absorption of the larger part of all domestic saving.

There are some limited steps that would bring the dollar closer to competitive levels. If Japanese authorities were to appreciate the value of the yen, perhaps by a further opening of the capital markets of Japan, this would help some particularly threatened industries. International coordination of monetary and budget policies might also help to move exchange rates closer to an equilibrium pattern.

Capital Costs. The 1981 corporate tax changes have helped to bring capital costs down, but they are still higher than in some of our principal competitor countries. There are further across-the-board tax incentives that could be granted, including devices to facilitate long-term debt financing. Selective capital subsidies or tax incentives are also possibilities. But, given the position of the federal budget, the total outlays of any new initiatives would be severely limited.

Industrial capital costs can be lowered substantially at this time by a reduction in the federal budget deficit. Interest rates would be lowered, by 1-3% according to DRI estimates; and the supply of long-term capital would be more abundant, thereby facilitating a larger volume of new bond issues by industrial corporations and lowering cut-off rates for investment projects.

Economic Stability. The economy has just passed through a 4-year disinflation process which was costly in terms of lost output and unemployment, but was successful in terms of lowering the inflation rate from double digits to low single-digit rates. This progress could set the stage for an exceptionally sustainable recovery. Oil price shocks are hardly likely to be repeated on the scale of the 1970s, and the rate of wage increase has slowed substantially. Productivity should be aided by the recovery and by the extra capital formation made possible by the 1981 tax incentives.

Whether the economy will realize this potential of a sustained recovery will depend, more than any other single issue, on our ability to reduce the budget deficit. It is the single biggest uncertainty for the recovery, with its danger of a collision between private and public borrowing needs. The search for appropriate expenditure savings and new revenue sources will pose a major challenge to the political process.

Improved economic stability will also require a better stabilizing strategy for monetary policy. In previous business cycles, real interest rates typically were near zero or negative during the early stages of the business cycle upswing, flooding the economy with excessive liquidity which could only be drained through the sharp credit restraints which proved so disruptive to capital formation. This time, the Federal Reserve has maintained real interest rates at very high levels even during the recession, and raised them as soon as the recovery appeared to have arrived. While these rates are directly damaging to capital formation, they may produce a more sustainable pattern of recovery.

This approach may well succeed. If it could be combined with substantial improvement in the budget deficit to achieve lower real interest and exchange rates, the economy would have a real chance of growing well without major disruption for the better part of the decade.

Trade Policy. The United States should strengthen the machinery of trade policy—either by making it the principal mission of the Department of Commerce or by some other reorganization. The opportunity to renegotiate the General Preference System Provisions by January 1985 should be used to put our trade relations with the newly industrialized countries on a new basis, with major emphasis on reciprocity and a sharing of responsibilities. The existing import limitation agreements should be administered more effectively, or replaced with other instruments of trade policy. Efforts to open markets to U.S. exports should be strengthened, for a world of competition and free trade flows is preferable to protected markets. But if the barriers to our goods remain high in many countries, bilateral reexamination of trade relationships becomes unavoidable.

Industrial Policy. While the general economic environment will be decisive to the future of market manufacturing, proposals to develop policies to help particular industries are also being advanced. The example of Japan's Ministry of Trade (MITI) is inspiring thoughts that the United States should follow a similar approach, identifying industries for development with a goal of predominance in world markets, encouraging firms in those fields to invest by providing cheap capital, and suggesting a division of markets among the major firms of the industry. There is no doubt that MITI is part of a very successful industrial strategy, though to what extent it was the general economic situation rather than the industrial policy efforts that created Japan's success is still a matter of controversy.

The MITI example has clearly only a very limited applicability for the United States. If a rapidly advancing country chooses to target on specific markets to dramatically increase its market share, starting from a very low base, an industrial policy may be an effective device. But an older, larger economy which already has a substantial market share in virtually every line of activity has less need for a centralized instrument for searching for opportunities and devising strategies. Existing firms should readily be able to fulfill these tasks. Japan's economy also has less of a tradition of competition than our own. Indeed, as Japan's production levels approach ours, the role of industrial policy is diminishing and is now focusing principally on the high-technology area, where government subsidy and coordination of research and development efforts may prove essential for a successful challenge to United States leadership.

Proposals for industrial policy have concentrated on two areas. The government could provide subsidized capital in selected situations. These would include companies in danger of bankruptcy or factories in danger of closing, and, at the other end of the spectrum, investments in new enterprises or in new technologies. A second proposal calls for a new agency to engage in some economic planning, particularly to coordinate international trade policy, investment in infrastructure, other government aids and government regulations. Other proposals cover such areas as expanded worker retraining and community adjustment assistance, and public works programs to rebuild infrastructure such as roads, bridges, airports and sewers. Some proposals call for a tripartite approach, led by a committee of business, labor and public members.

Industrial policy could provide logic and coherence for government's numerous policies toward industry. It might be a useful complement to the improvements in macroeconomic policy outlined above. But whether the federal government is capable of such rationality in an era of intense lobbying activity is very much an open question. The success of such a policy would surely depend upon the degree of commitment by the President, and high public visibility to assure that it would not fall into the hands of parochial interests. It will be an important political choice in the years ahead whether the United States chooses to go in the direction of an explicit industrial policy.

The Industrial Viewpoint in General Economic Policy. One policy conclusion does emerge very strongly from this study: there is need for stronger representation of an industrial viewpoint in general economic policy. The monetary and budget decisions which govern the economy's progress are made principally on macroeconomic, financial and political viewpoints. Budgets and interest rates are the result of struggles among short-term political desires, economists' technical controversies, and the perceived needs of the financial community. Industry, on the other hand, has generally remained preoccupied with smaller issues of regulation, taxation, and trade policy. Yet the overall development of industry is largely determined by the broader macroeconomic questions, by capital costs, exchange rates and the degree of stability of markets. Industrial development must become an explicit objective of economic policy.

APPENDIX

DETAILED INDUSTRY MATERIALS

The underlying material for individual industries which is used throughout this report, and particularly in Chapter 5, is presented in graphic form in this Appendix. For definitions and sources, see Chapter 5.

FOOD AND KINDRED PRODUCTS

The food industry showed good performance in the postwar period. Production rose at a 3.2% rate from 1960 to 1982, and the recent slowdown can be explained by the recession. The industry is based on the highly productive agriculture of this country, and so it is a strong participant in world markets.

The industry is a large employer, providing 1.64 million jobs in 1982. Productivity shows a trend rate of increase of 3.7%, which exceeds the growth of output. As a result, employment has been falling. As a share of all nonfarm employment, the food industry shows a decline from 4% of all workers in 1950 to less than 2% in 1982.

This industry operates on thin profit margins, but these margins have been rising. The industry's principal costs include agricultural materials and labor, and the rate of return on capital is close to the manufacturing average. Industry investment has been trending downward as a percent of the total manufacturing investment, but shows a real rate of growth of 2.7%. Research and development expenditures are low.

Wages are close to the economy-wide average and have not deviated far from that figure. Compared to other manufacturing industries, wages are low.

Imports have risen quite substantially as the food industries of other countries have developed novelty items not produced here and offered some products at lower prices. The trade balance of the food industry has been negative, but should be a positive $475 million in 1983. The U.S. share of world exports was 7% in 1977, but has dwindled to approximately 5% recently.

Agricultural products, which are not shown in the exhibits because they are not manufactured goods, have suffered a loss of share in world markets because of various government interventions, such as the grain embargoes to the Soviet Union triggered by political events and the embargo on soybean exports in 1973, which led to the development of a competing industry in Brazil. The industry benefits from some protectionist measures, such as controls on dairy imports. The U.S. loses exports because of protectionism abroad, including the aggressive measures by the European Economic Community to promote its agriculture.

FOOD AND KINDRED PRODUCTS

PRINCIPAL PRODUCTS

Foods, beverages, and animal feeds

RECENT TRADE DATA
(Millions of dollars)

	1981	1982	1983 (Est.)
Exports	18,448	14,338	18,598
Imports	18,113	17,118	18,123
Trade Balance	335	−2,780	475

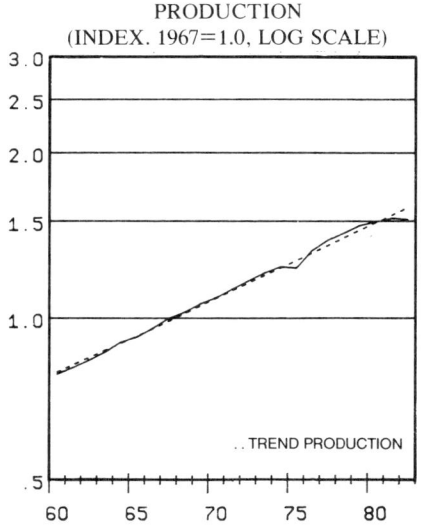

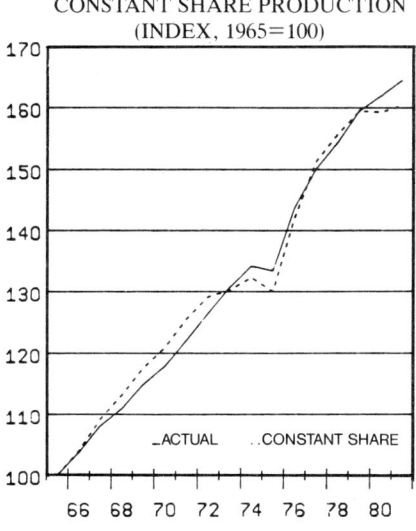

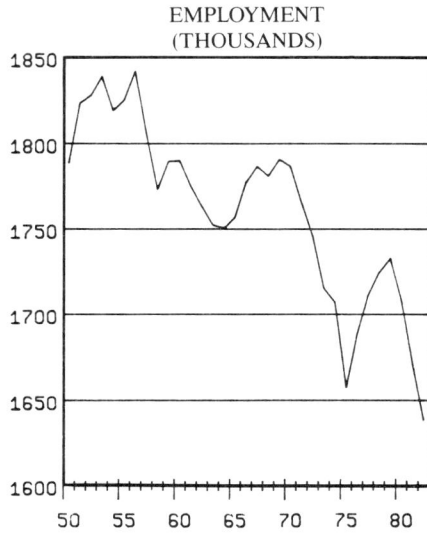

FOOD AND KINDRED PRODUCTS

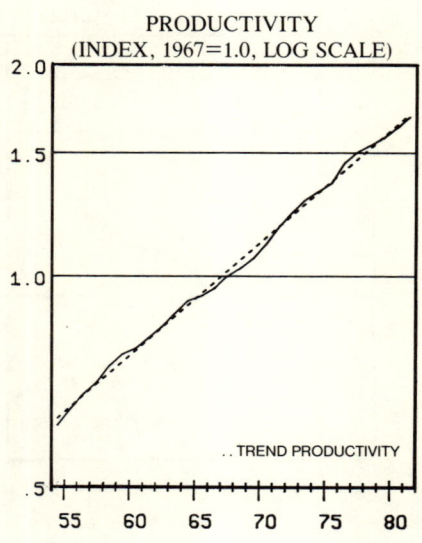

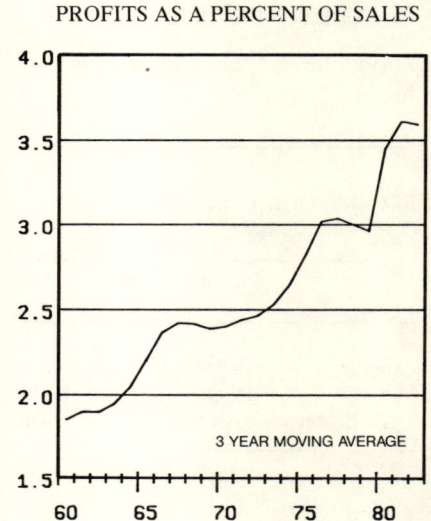

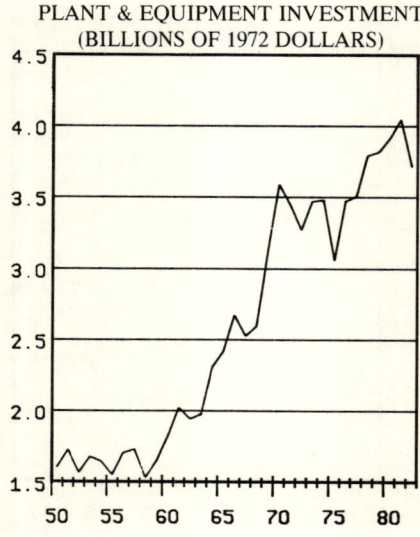

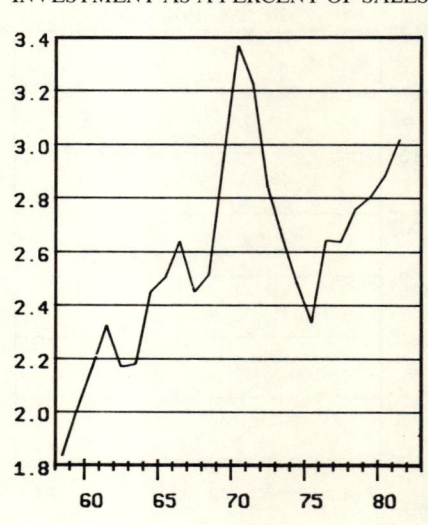

FOOD AND KINDRED PRODUCTS

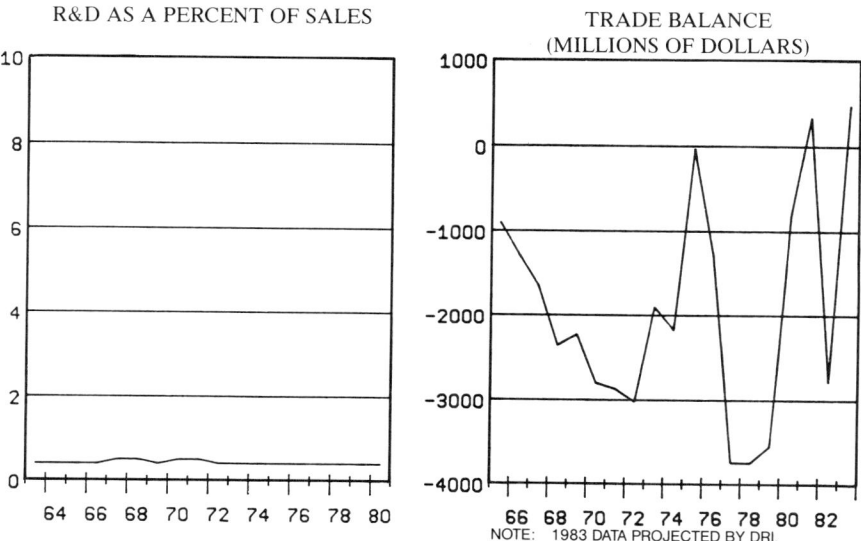

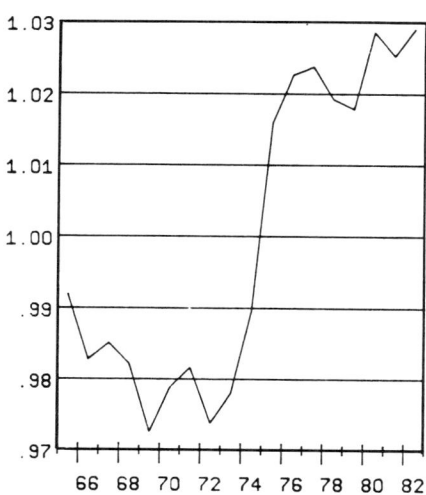

TOBACCO MANUFACTURES

The tobacco industry is highly specialized in the processing of one particular agricultural commodity, and employs only 68,000 workers. It is treated here for completeness, but only briefly.

Industrial production grew at a 1.3% rate, and the productivity trend was 3.6%. As a result, industry employment declined from 0.23% of total nonagricultural employment in 1950 to only 0.08% in 1982. Wages moved from substantially below the economy-wide average to substantially above average. Profitability is high as a margin on sales; and, while foreign tobacco products are making some inroads in the American market, the industry trade balance is both highly favorable and improving. With relatively few other sources of tobacco in the world and smoking still responding positively to rising world incomes, exports have been growing, and the industry trade surplus was $2.1 billion in 1982.

TOBACCO MANUFACTURES

PRINCIPAL PRODUCTS

Cigarettes, cigars, and other tobacco products

RECENT TRADE DATA
(Millions of dollars)

	1981	1982	1983 (Est.)
Exports	2,723	2,816	2,366
Imports	633	740	832
Trade Balance	2,090	2,076	1,534

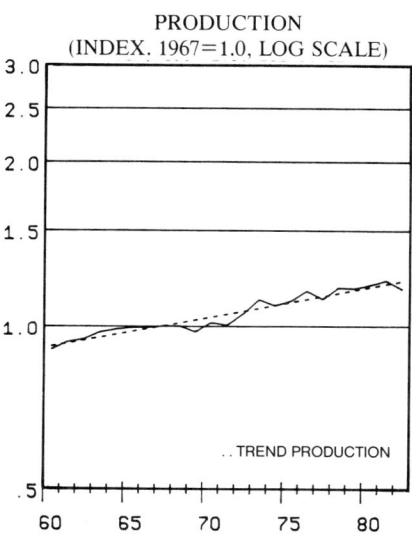

PRODUCTION (INDEX. 1967=1.0, LOG SCALE)

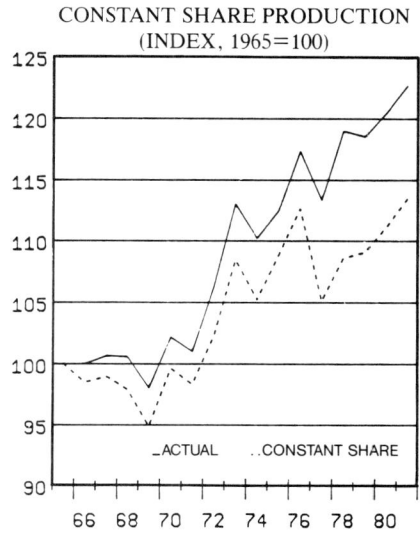

CONSTANT SHARE PRODUCTION (INDEX, 1965=100)

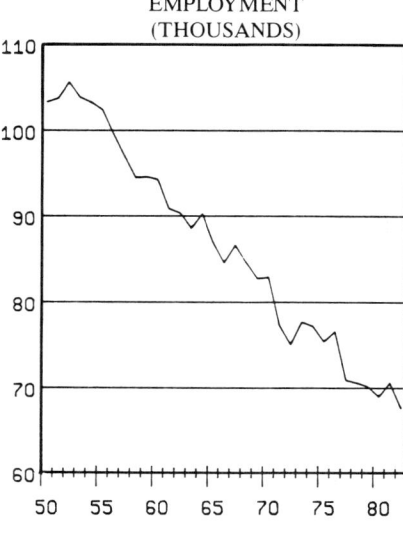

EMPLOYMENT (THOUSANDS)

TOBACCO MANUFACTURES

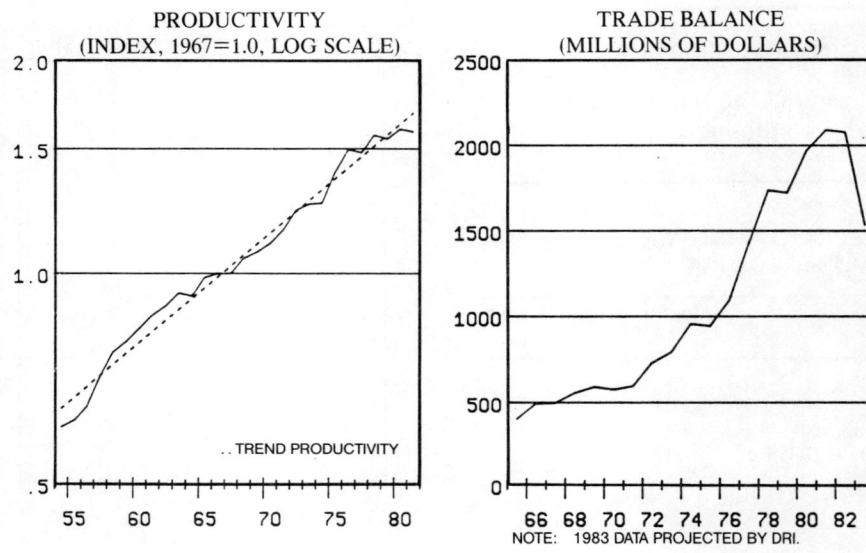

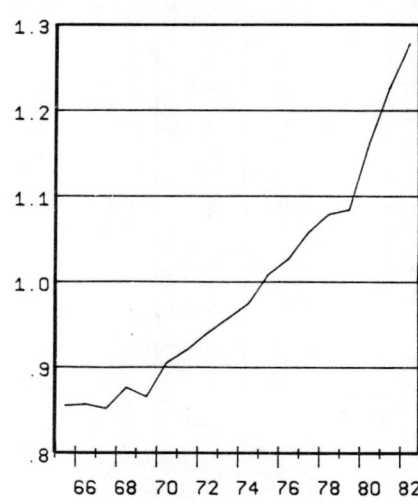

TEXTILE MILL PRODUCTS

The textile industry's production expanded until 1974 and has been stagnant since then. This lack of growth is due to the increased import penetration of foreign apparel. Also, sales to the automobile industry were hurt by reduced automobile demand during the recent recessions and by the increased share of foreign cars. Finally, home furnishing sales were hurt by high interest rates. Foreign markets, on the other hand, remain small as the principal overseas apparel producers follow protectionist policies on textiles.

The textile industry is a major employer, providing 750,000 jobs in 1982. Thirty years ago employment was much larger, providing one and one-quarter million jobs. With output growth held back by increased import penetration, and with productivity showing a healthy 4.1% a year trend, employment shrank very substantially.

Relative wages in the industry have been low, 76% of the economy-wide average in 1982. With productivity on a healthy trend, and with labor cost a smaller fraction of total cost than for apparel, the competitive difficulties of the textile industry stem less from a changing pattern of its own trade flows than from the loss of market position of the apparel industry.

Investment in the textile industry has been trending downward since the late 1960s, though manufacturers made major efforts to assure modern plant capacity. The extraordinarily weak output of the last few years has impaired profitability and has led to a reduction in the real volume of investment.

In the mid-1970s, the import penetration ratio had fallen slightly because of industry modernization, a more favorable exchange rate, some changes in taste favorable to the United States, as well as a temporary tightening in the administration of the Multi-Fiber Arrangement. More recently, import penetration has been rising sharply as the MFA proved of limited effectiveness in a less favorable market environment.

Between 1980 and the first half of 1983, imports of textiles rose 20.2% (Table 5.14) while exports fell by 37.1% (Table 5.13), leading to a projected trade deficit in 1983 of -$274 million.

TEXTILE MILL PRODUCTS

PRINCIPAL PRODUCTS

Woven and knit fabrics, knit apparel, yarn, thread, and floorcoverings

RECENT TRADE DATA
(Millions of dollars)

	1981	1982	1983 (Est.)
Exports	3,833	2,800	2,400
Imports	2,707	2,429	2,674
Trade Balance	1,126	371	−274

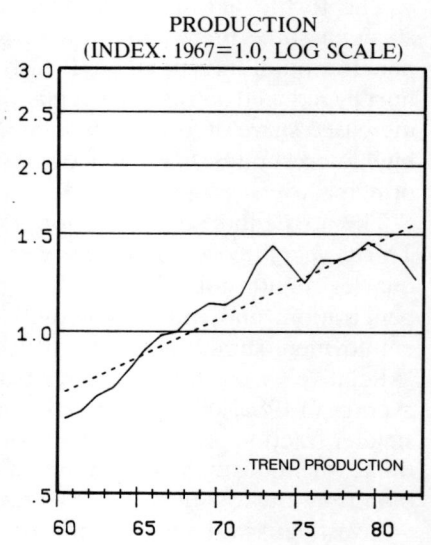

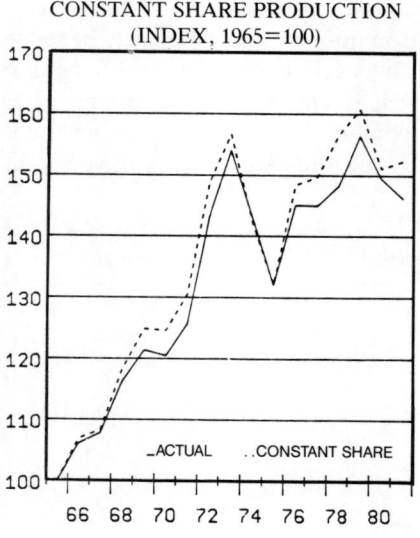

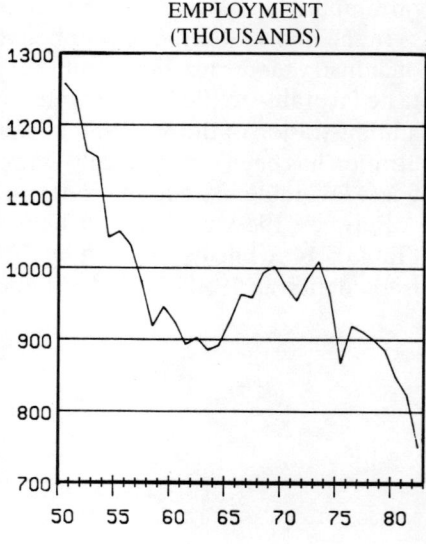

TEXTILE MILL PRODUCTS

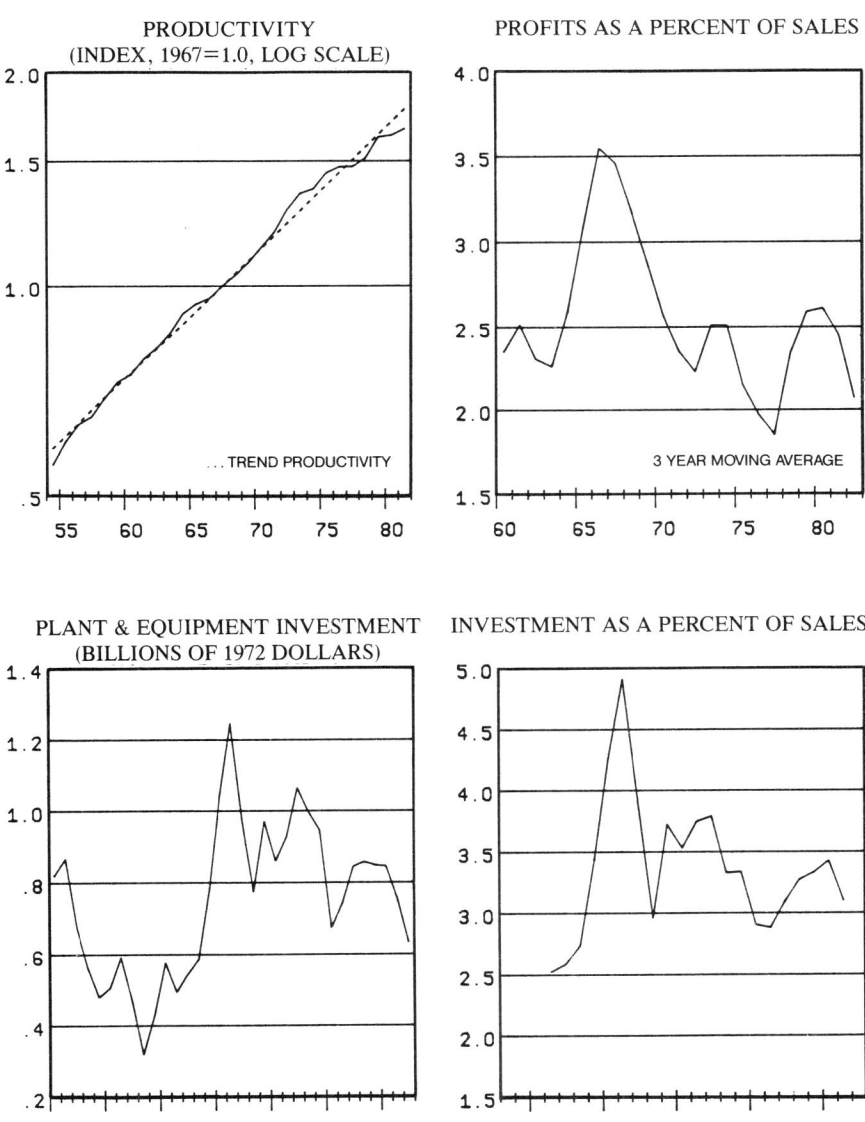

TEXTILE MILL PRODUCTS

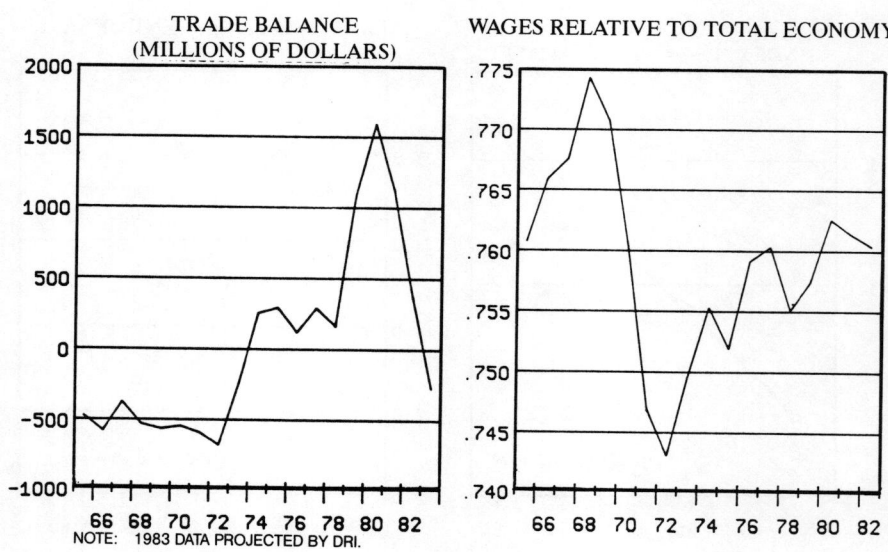

APPAREL

The apparel industry has been one of the principal victims of the changing pattern of international trade. It is a big industry, with employment of 1.16 million people in 1982. However, employment has declined by over 200,000 workers since the late 1960s.

From 1954 to 1977, production of apparel rose at a trend rate of 3.1%. But in the late 1970s and in the early 1980s, imports surged. Measured in millions of pounds, they reached 22% of the market in 1980, 28% in 1982, and an estimated 30% in 1983. Between 1980 and the first half of 1983, imports rose 39.4%, while exports fell 23.2%. It is striking that this enormous import penetration occurred despite the existence of the Multi-Fiber Arrangement which was designed to control the volume of apparel and textiles entering this country and other markets for major commodity categories from the principal supplying countries. The Arrangement has proved relatively ineffective because suppliers are able to switch product lines in the absence of a global limit on imports.

The apparel industry faces a particularly difficult problem of international competitiveness because labor content is high and the skills required to produce apparel are found in many countries where there are few other employment opportunities. Thus, even though wages in this industry are relatively low, just 68% of the economy-wide average, the wages in the principal supplier countries are much lower still. Productivity performance showed a 2.2% rate of increase, at least until the sharp production declines of recent years. Data on profits, industry investment, and R&D are not available, partly because the industry is still comprised of many small enterprises.

The negative trade balance in apparel is very large indeed, having reached $7.2 billion in 1982. The principal sources of our imports are Korea, Japan, Taiwan, and Hong Kong. The Republic of China has recently gained a role under the Multi-Fiber Arrangement and is likely to be another aggressive exporter to the United States markets.

APPAREL

PRINCIPAL PRODUCTS
Finished clothing, draperies, and home furnishings

RECENT TRADE DATA
(Millions of dollars)

	1981	1982	1983 (Est.)
Exports	1,543	1,253	1,128
Imports	7,774	8,410	9,074
Trade Balance	−6,231	−7,157	−7,946

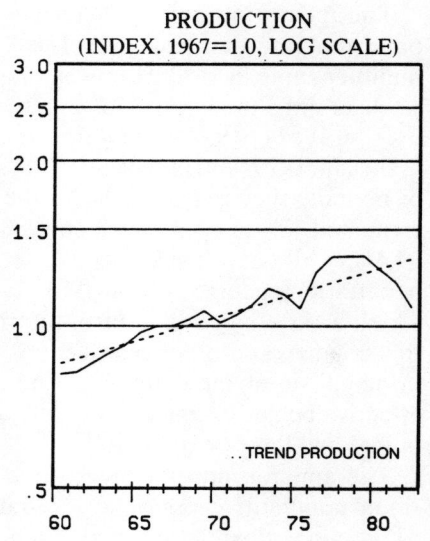

PRODUCTION (INDEX. 1967=1.0, LOG SCALE)

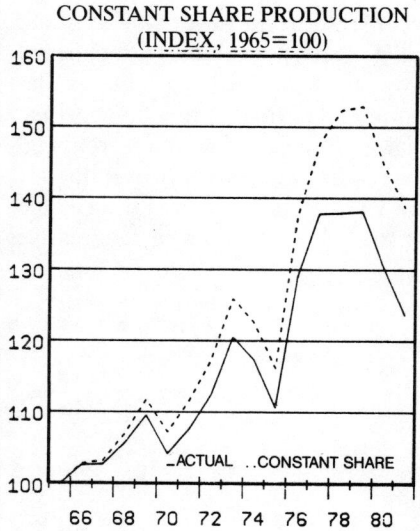

CONSTANT SHARE PRODUCTION (INDEX, 1965=100)

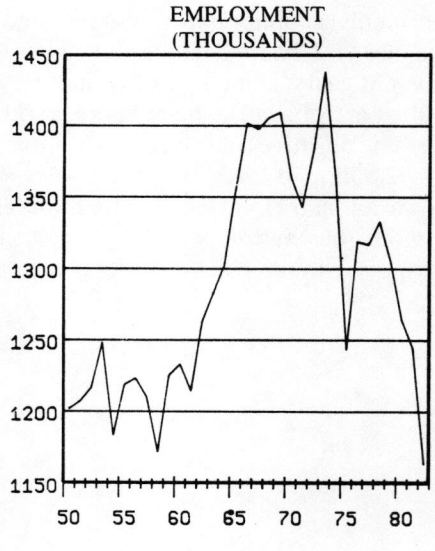

EMPLOYMENT (THOUSANDS)

APPAREL

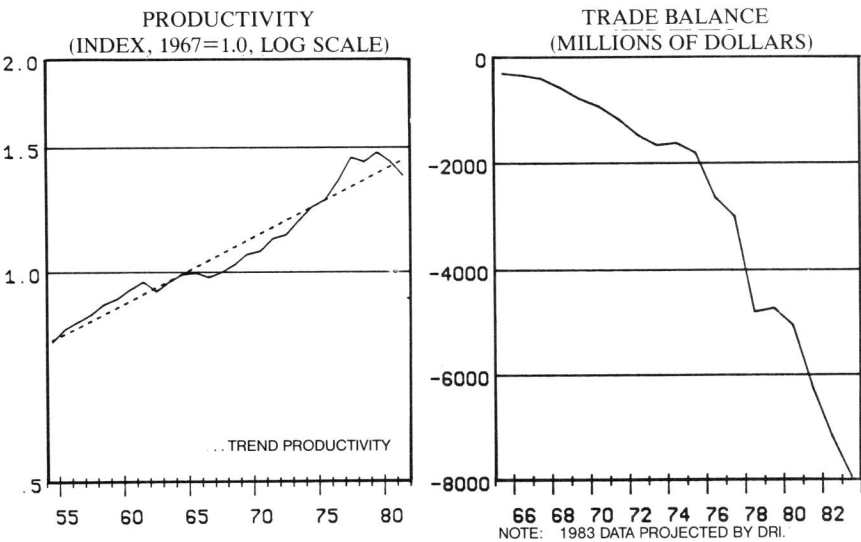

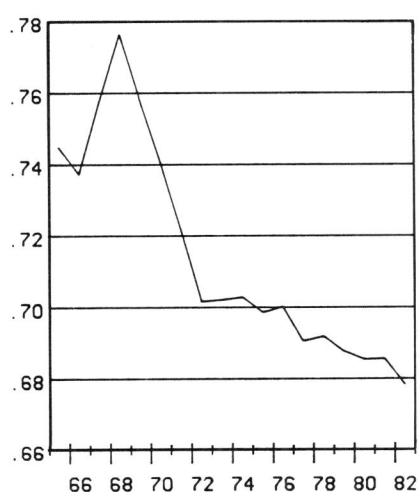

LUMBER AND WOOD PRODUCTS

The wood products industry benefits from the exceptionally favorable resource base of our forests. Our principal competitors in world markets are Canada, Sweden, and the Soviet Union.

Industrial production shows a growth trend of 2.2%, below the manufacturing average, though it has been exceptionally unstable and with lessened growth since 1974. This recent experience was mainly due to the instability of the housing industry created by high interest rates.

Employment in the lumber industry was 604,000 last year. Wages are close to the economy-wide average, after a substantial increase over the last 15 years made possible by the strong resource base. Productivity shows a 2.5% trend.

The United States is usually a net exporter of lumber and wood products, though we were a net importer in the first half of 1983. Since lumber is a commodity which is priced in world markets, the high value of the dollar is reflected in the relatively low domestic prices and diminished profitability of the industry. Capacity has been shrinking, and the U.S. share in world markets is believed to be diminishing.

LUMBER AND WOOD PRODUCTS

PRINCIPAL PRODUCTS

Timber, lumber, cabinets, and mobile homes

RECENT TRADE DATA
(Millions of dollars)

	1981	1982	1983 (Est.)
Exports	2,645	2,528	2,543
Imports	2,725	2,259	3,224
Trade Balance	−81	270	−681

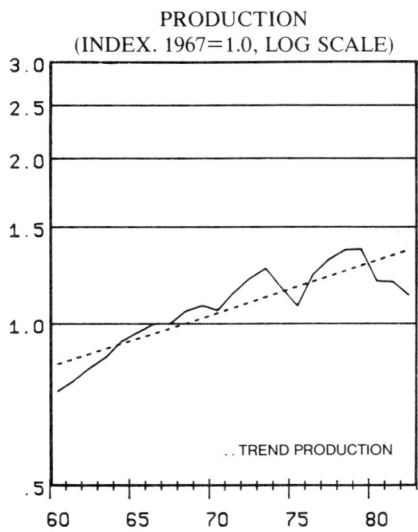

PRODUCTION (INDEX. 1967=1.0, LOG SCALE)

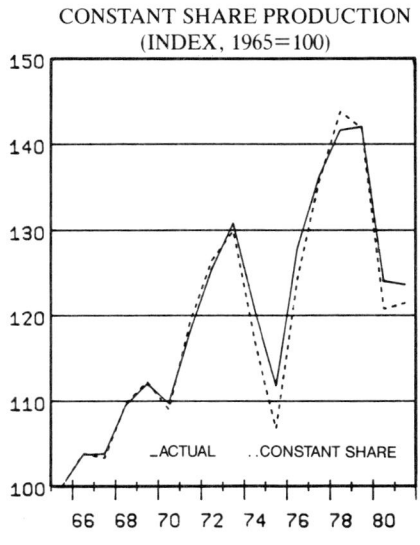

CONSTANT SHARE PRODUCTION (INDEX, 1965=100)

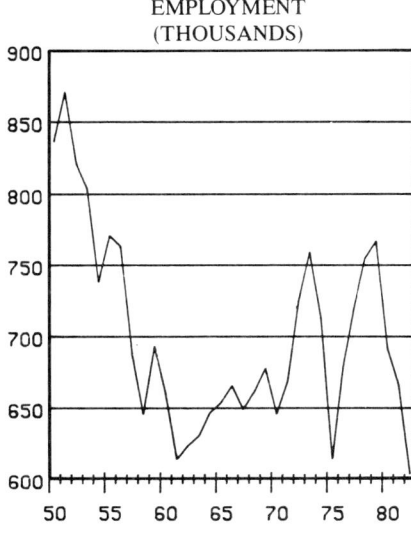

EMPLOYMENT (THOUSANDS)

LUMBER AND WOOD PRODUCTS

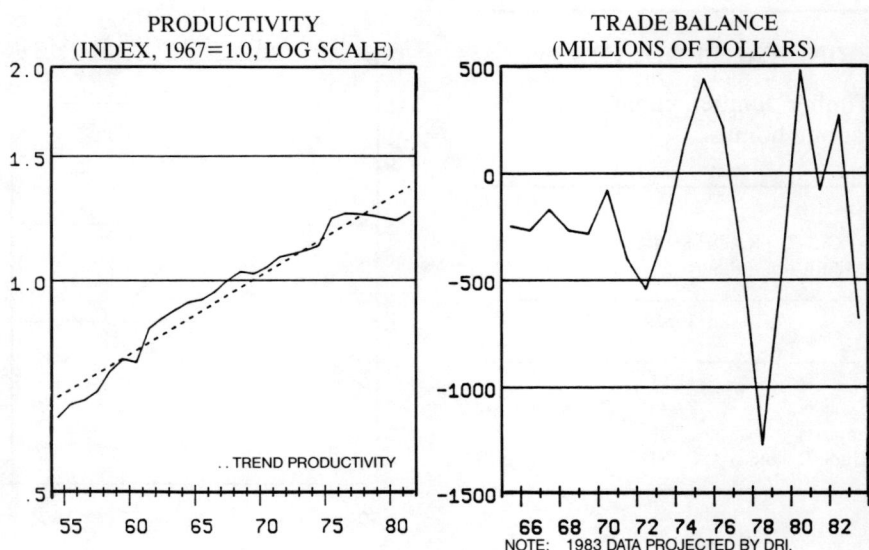

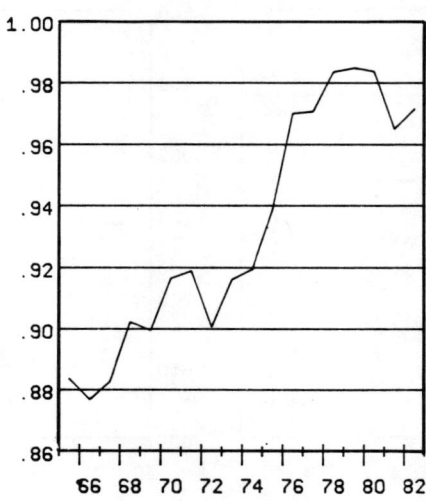

FURNITURE AND FIXTURES

The furniture industry has shown relatively stable growth at a trend rate of 3.8%. Compared to other industries, international trade is a minor element in the performance of this industry.

The industry employed 433,000 workers in 1982. Wages are only 82% of the economy-wide average and have been falling. Productivity grows at a 2.8% rate. Because the industry still has many small enterprises in it, data on profitability and investment are not available.

The data on exports and imports show that the United States is a net exporter of furniture, to the extent of $351 million in 1982. Imports have made some inroads since the 1960s; but, due to the small role of international trade, the furniture industry has still shown good output performance.

FURNITURE AND FIXTURES

PRINCIPAL PRODUCTS
Home and office furniture, shelving, drapery hardware, and display fixtures

RECENT TRADE DATA
(Millions of dollars)

	1981	1982	1983 (Est.)
Exports	1,608	1,496	1,348
Imports	1,123	1,145	1,239
Trade Balance	485	351	108

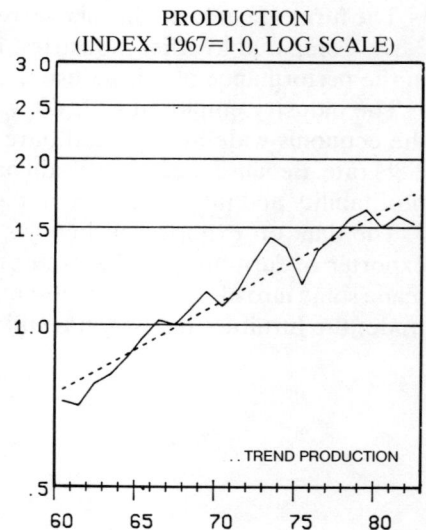

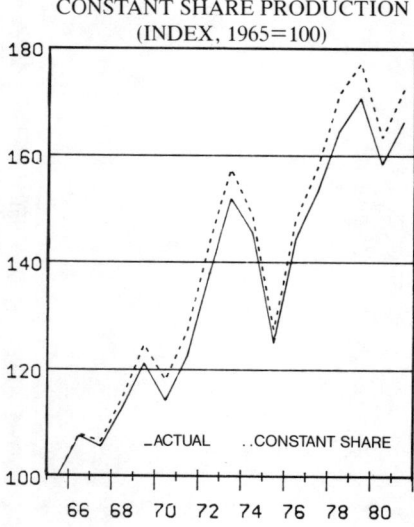

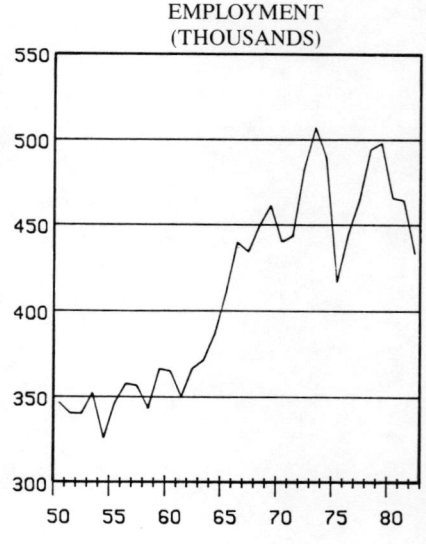

FURNITURE AND FIXTURES

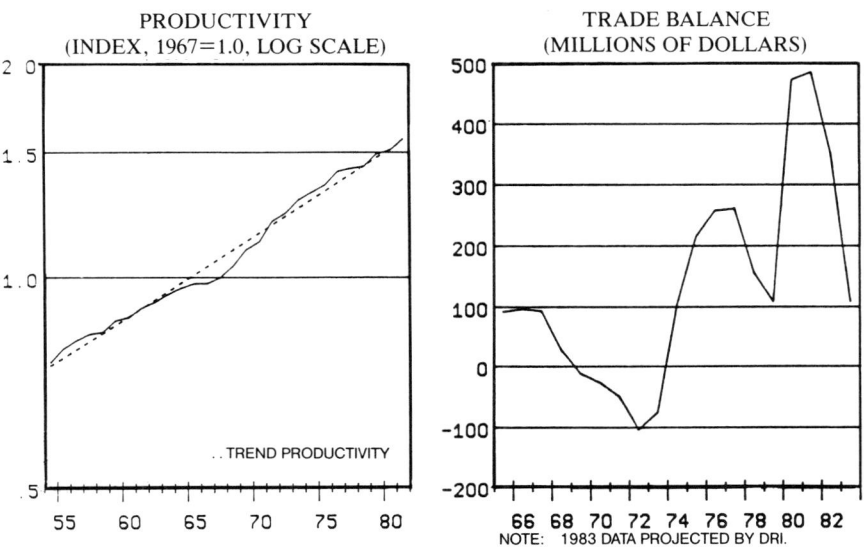

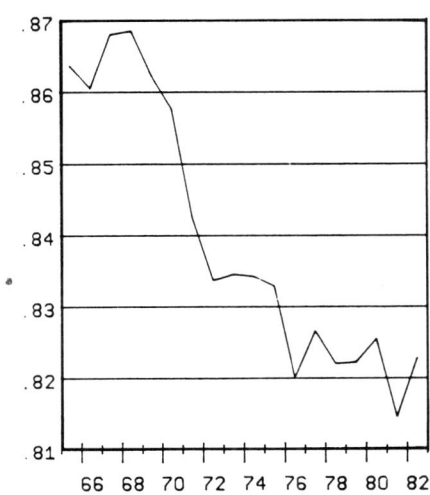

PAPER AND PRODUCTS

The paper industry is based on the strong resource base of American forests. The trend growth of production is 3.7%, and the deviations from trend have principally been due to the business cycle which varies demand for packaging materials.

The industry provides 660,000 jobs. Wages have been increasing very substantially, and are now 22% above the economy-wide average. Productivity shows a 3.5% trend. The profits of the industry are highly cyclical because of variations in the utilization rates of capacity, but do not show a downtrend. The paper industry has been one of the few manufacturing industries to show an increasing share of the country's total investment. Research and development expenditures are modest.

The import penetration ratio has been rising moderately, with imports mainly coming from Canada. U.S.-Canadian trade is governed by some informal agreements. Foreign trade in this industry used to be close to balance, but 1982 showed a deficit of $930 million.

PAPER AND PRODUCTS

PRINCIPAL PRODUCTS

Paper, pulp, paper containers, and paperboard

RECENT TRADE DATA
(Millions of dollars)

	1981	1982	1983 (Est.)
Exports	4,968	4,341	4,195
Imports	5,603	5,271	5,251
Trade Balance	−636	−930	−1,056

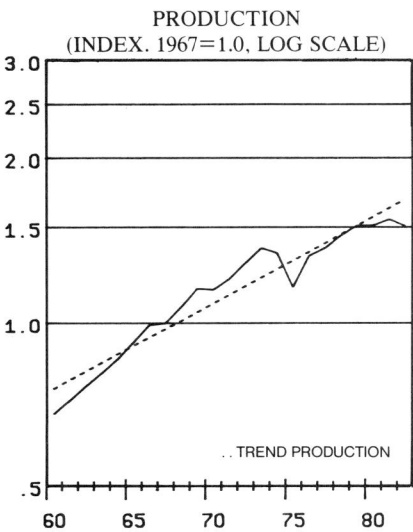
PRODUCTION (INDEX. 1967=1.0, LOG SCALE)

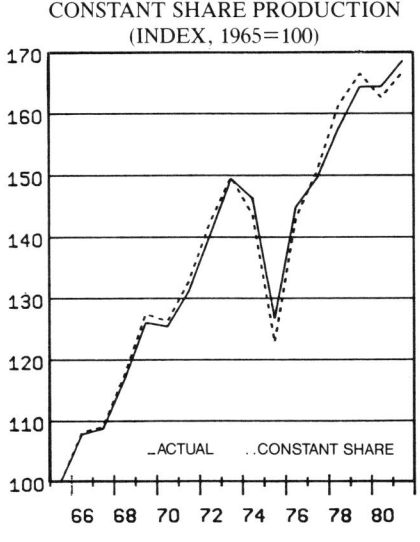
CONSTANT SHARE PRODUCTION (INDEX, 1965=100)

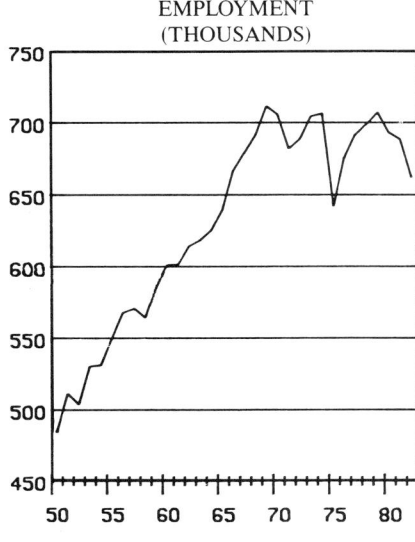
EMPLOYMENT (THOUSANDS)

PAPER AND PRODUCTS

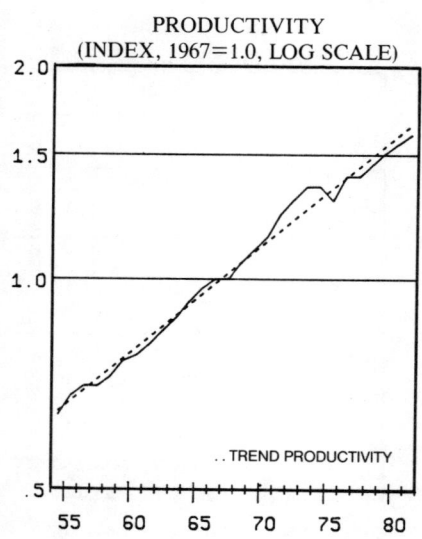

PRODUCTIVITY
(INDEX, 1967=1.0, LOG SCALE)

...TREND PRODUCTIVITY

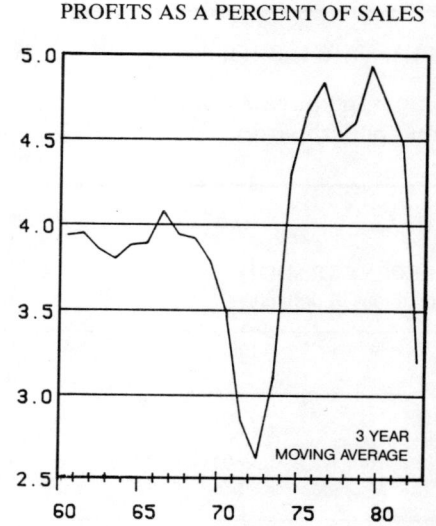

PROFITS AS A PERCENT OF SALES

3 YEAR MOVING AVERAGE

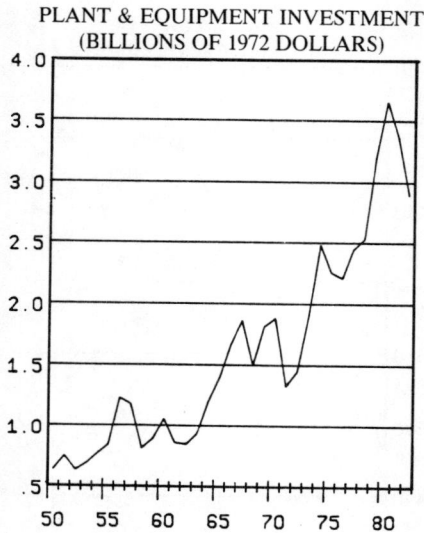

PLANT & EQUIPMENT INVESTMENT
(BILLIONS OF 1972 DOLLARS)

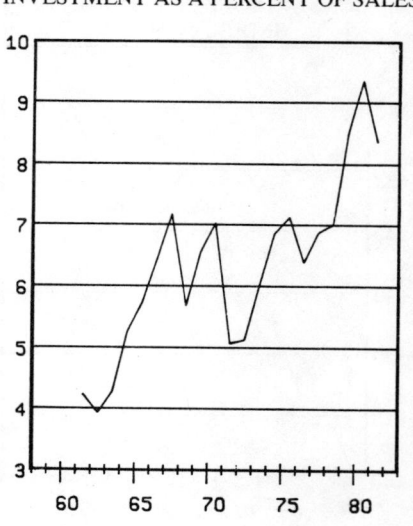

INVESTMENT AS A PERCENT OF SALES

PAPER AND PRODUCTS

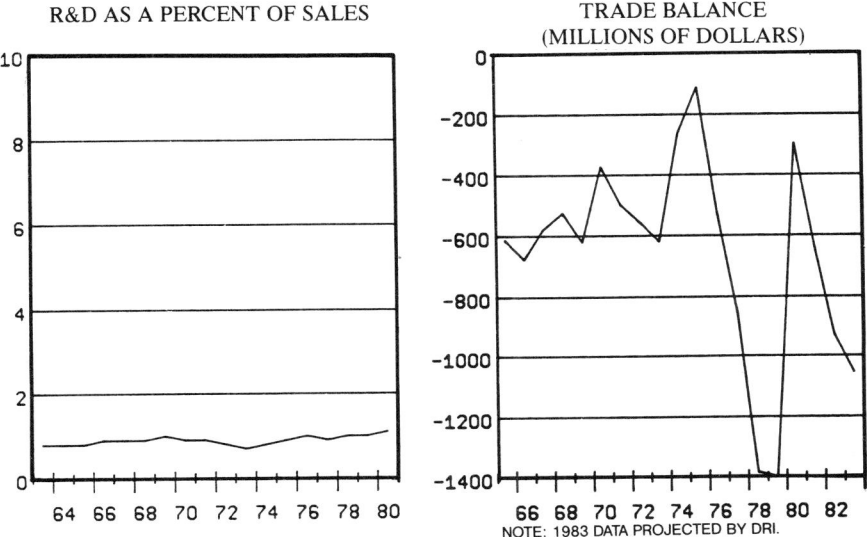

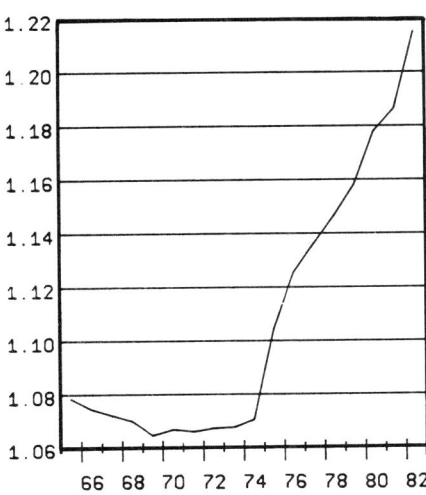

PRINTING AND PUBLISHING

Printing and publishing is partly a localized industry, coexisting with a large national market. A small share of output enters international trade. The industry provides 1.27 million jobs, so it is a major employer in the economy.

The printing and publishing industry has been growing at about 3.3% a year, with no visible signs of a slowdown. Deviations from trend are caused by the business cycle.

Employment in the industry has shown positive growth, unlike many manufacturing industries. Wages are about 14% above the economy-wide average, though relative wages were falling quite substantially until the late 1970s. Productivity shows a trend of about 2.2%.

The industry has been relatively profitable, as demand for its output is aided by the "information" revolution. Investment data are not available for the industry. Generally, the development of the information to be printed represents more of an "investment" than the purchase of physical capital.

Because of the size of the U.S. market, the cultural leadership which the United States still exercises, as well as the transfer of U.S. technology through the print medium, the printing and publishing industry is an net exporter.

PRINTING AND PUBLISHING

PRINCIPAL PRODUCTS

Newspapers, periodicals, books, and commercial printing

RECENT TRADE DATA
(Millions of dollars)

	1981	1982	1983 (Est.)
Exports	1,248	1,289	1,224
Imports	517	578	663
Trade Balance	731	711	561

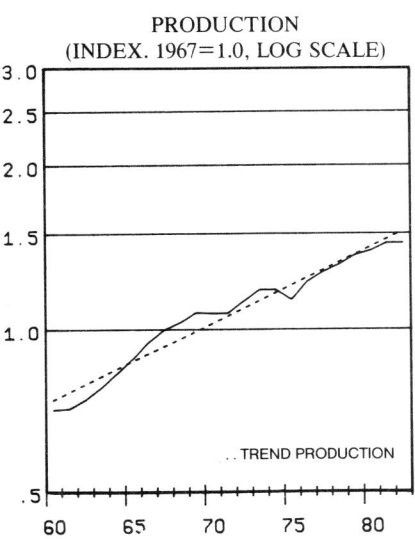

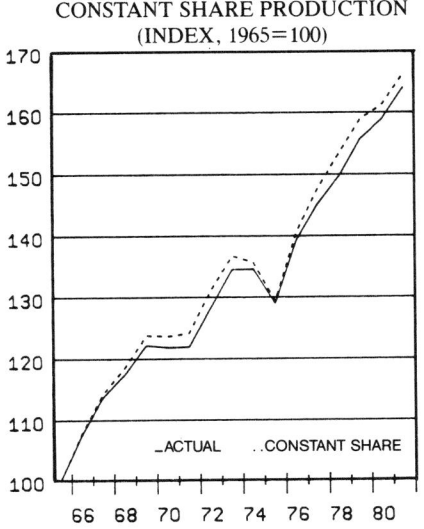

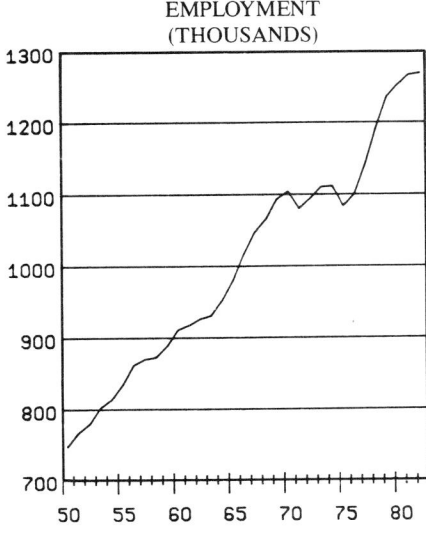

PRINTING AND PUBLISHING

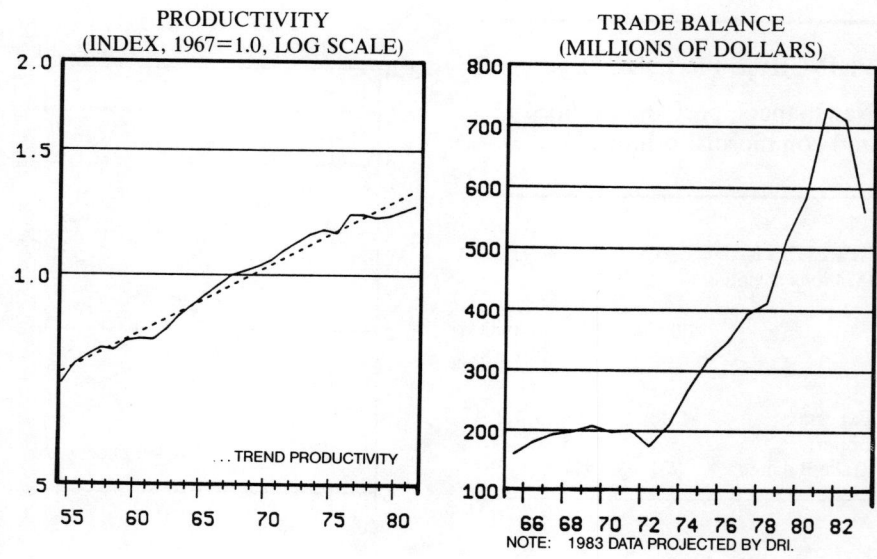

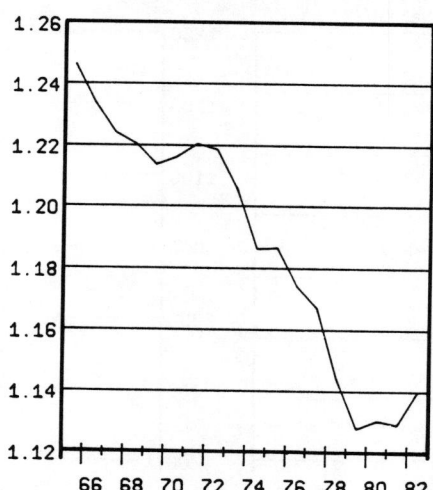

CHEMICALS

The chemical industry has traditionally been the fastest growing manufacturing industry in output, capital and productivity. The industry has been a major exporter, though the pattern of trade is currently going through major changes.

The industry is quite heterogeneous, including basic chemicals, synthetic materials, drugs, soaps and toiletries, paints and agricultural chemicals. Here the chemical and products industry is treated as a unit.

Production shows a 6.4% trend, 1960-1982. This trend has been slowing since the late 1970s, as the industry became more vulnerable to the business cycle, and, toward the end of the period, to changes in international trade.

Employment in the chemical industry was 1.08 million workers in 1982. With strong productivity increases and production slowing, the growth of employment stopped in the early 1970s, though it remained at high levels. Wages are 30% above the economy-wide average and have been rising rapidly. Investment continues to be high and is a constant share of the economy's total investment, though fluctuating with the business cycle. The industry is one of the principal performers of research and development, though the percentage of total sales devoted to R&D has fallen from 4.5 to 3.5%.

The international trade position of the chemical industry is eroding due to several factors. U.S. raw material prices are rising to reach parity with the rest of the world. In the mid-1970s, when the United States controlled her domestic price of oil and gas, U.S. petrochemical producers had a cost advantage over other countries. With the decontrol of oil and rising prices of natural gas, this advantage is gradually disappearing. Further, the chemical industry is losing markets because of the rising volume of imports of finished goods that are major chemical markets. The importation of automobiles, consumer electronics and apparel represents losses of markets for U.S. plastics, textile fibers and numerous other chemical materials. Finally, the decision of several OPEC countries, particularly Saudi Arabia, to develop basic petrochemical capacity to utilize available natural gas and oil will mean that the American chemical industry will have to surrender certain markets to these newcomers. A glut of capacity for some chemical commodities, such as methanol, ammonia, and ethylene, is a very likely prospect.

The import penetration ratio of chemical markets has been rising for two decades, although the United States remains a large net exporter. Our share of world exports was falling until the mid-1970s, when the temporary raw material cost advantage stabilized it. More recently, the export share has resumed its decline. The trade balance of the industry was still a large $13.3 billion in 1982.

CHEMICALS

PRINCIPAL PRODUCTS

Industrial chemicals, plastics materials, drugs, paints, fertilizers, and synthetic fibers

RECENT TRADE DATA
(Millions of dollars)

	1981	1982	1983 (Est.)
Exports	20,274	19,387	18,601
Imports	6,167	6,118	7,219
Trade Balance	14,107	13,269	11,382

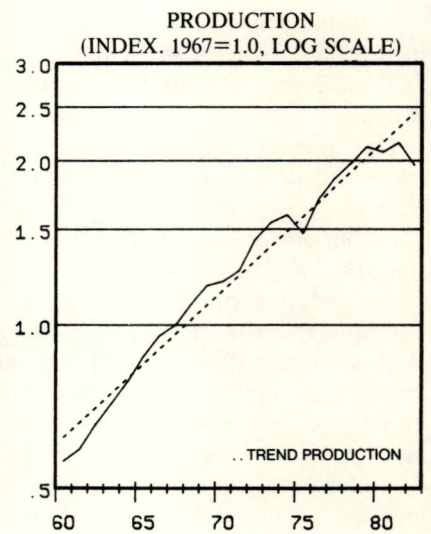

PRODUCTION (INDEX. 1967=1.0, LOG SCALE)

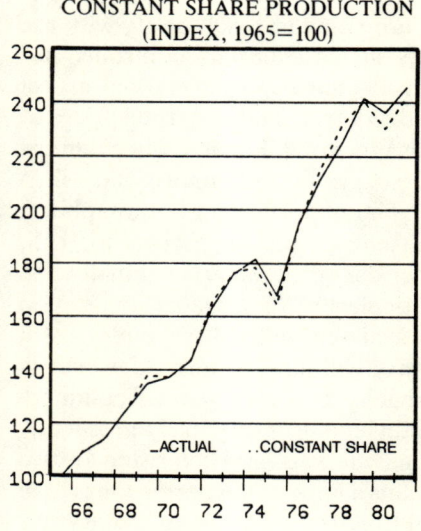

CONSTANT SHARE PRODUCTION (INDEX, 1965=100)

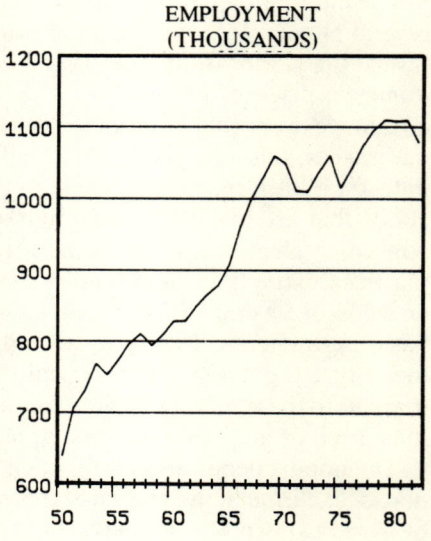

EMPLOYMENT (THOUSANDS)

CHEMICALS

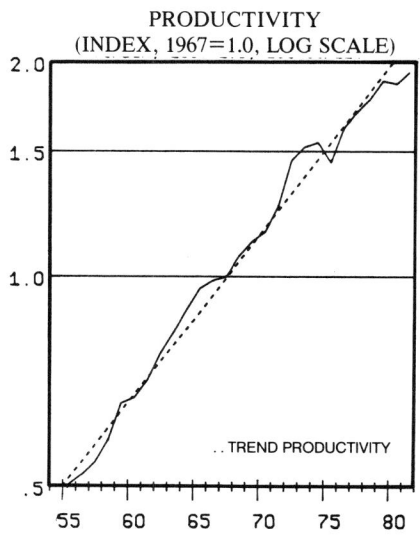

PRODUCTIVITY
(INDEX, 1967=1.0, LOG SCALE)

.. TREND PRODUCTIVITY

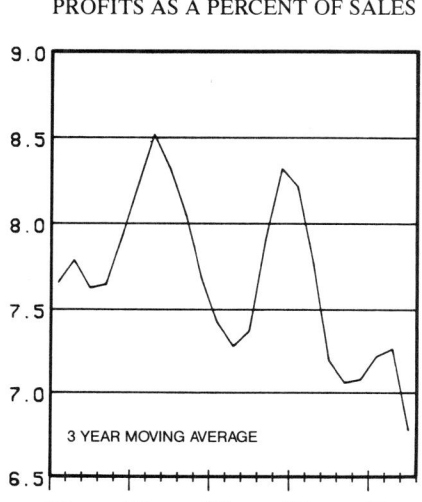

PROFITS AS A PERCENT OF SALES

3 YEAR MOVING AVERAGE

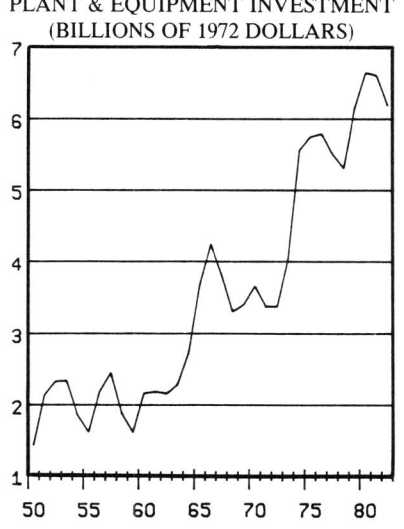

PLANT & EQUIPMENT INVESTMENT
(BILLIONS OF 1972 DOLLARS)

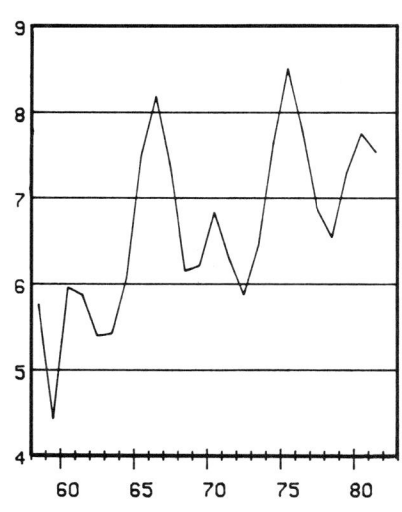

INVESTMENT AS A PERCENT OF SALES

CHEMICALS

R&D AS A PERCENT OF SALES

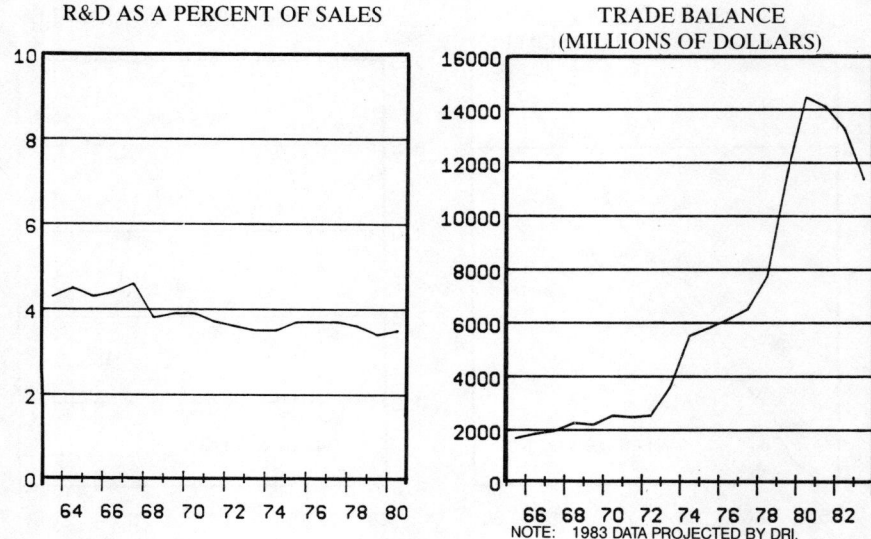

TRADE BALANCE
(MILLIONS OF DOLLARS)

NOTE: 1983 DATA PROJECTED BY DRI.

WAGES RELATIVE TO TOTAL ECONOMY

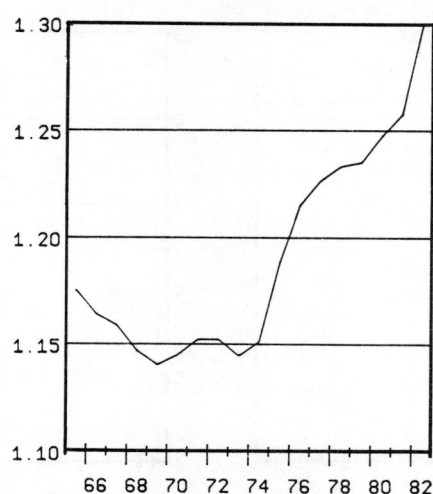

PETROLEUM PRODUCTS

The growth of output of the petroleum refining industry was 4.0% a year until the world oil price explosion in 1974. After two years of declining output, production surged once more with the stabilization of the real price of oil. But with the second OPEC wave of price increases, the output of the industry declined very sharply; and it is hardly likely to recover fully for many years because of greater efficiency in the use of energy.

The industry employs only 200,000 workers but vast amounts of capital. Wages are 62% above the economy-wide average, and have been rising very rapidly relative to other wages, despite the declining volume of output. Productivity shows a 3.5% trend for the period 1953-1982, but all of the increases were prior to 1974.

PETROLEUM PRODUCTS

PRINCIPAL PRODUCTS

Petroleum refining, paving materials, and lubricating oils

RECENT TRADE DATA
(Millions of dollars)

	1981	1982	1983 (Est.)
Exports	3,769	6,217	5,761
Imports	15,167	14,983	14,981
Trade Balance	−11,398	−8,766	−9,220

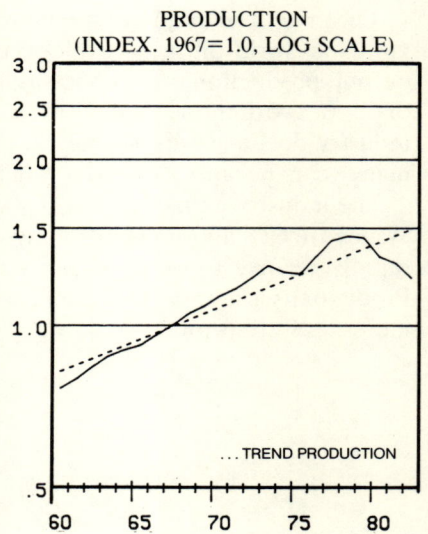

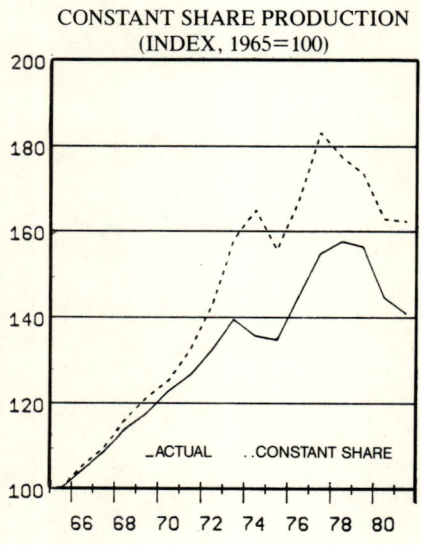

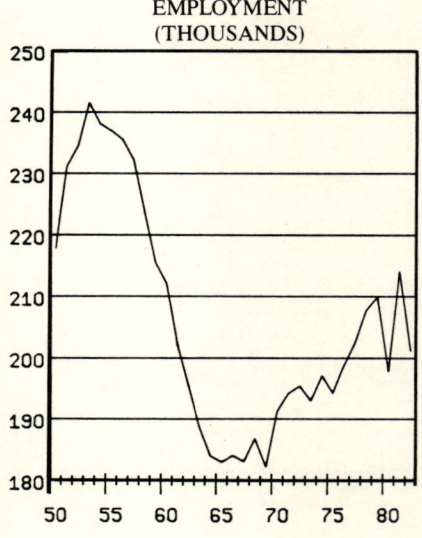

PETROLEUM PRODUCTS

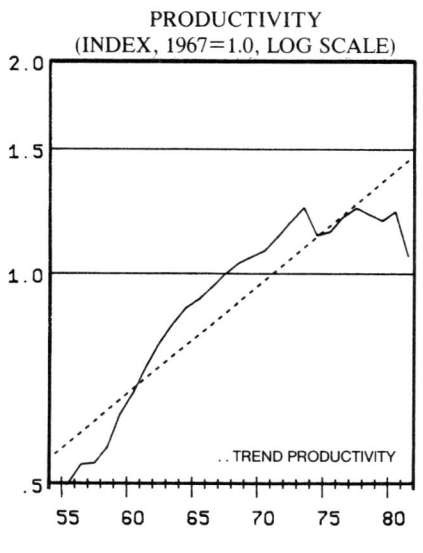

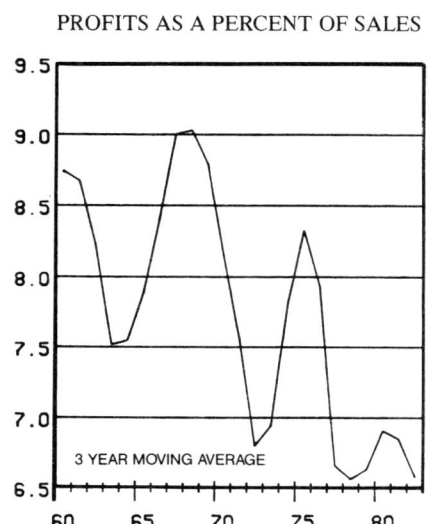

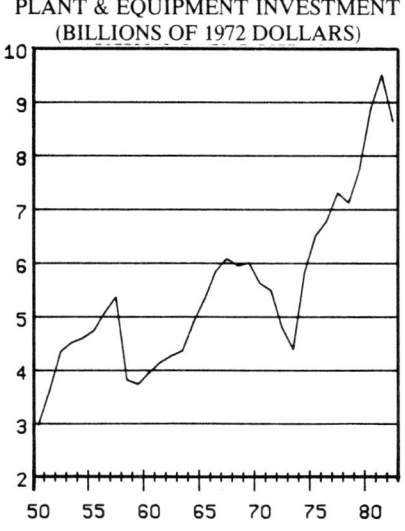

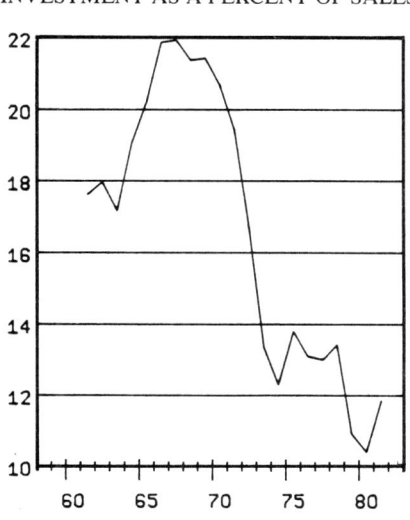

Appendix

PETROLEUM PRODUCTS

R&D AS A PERCENT OF SALES

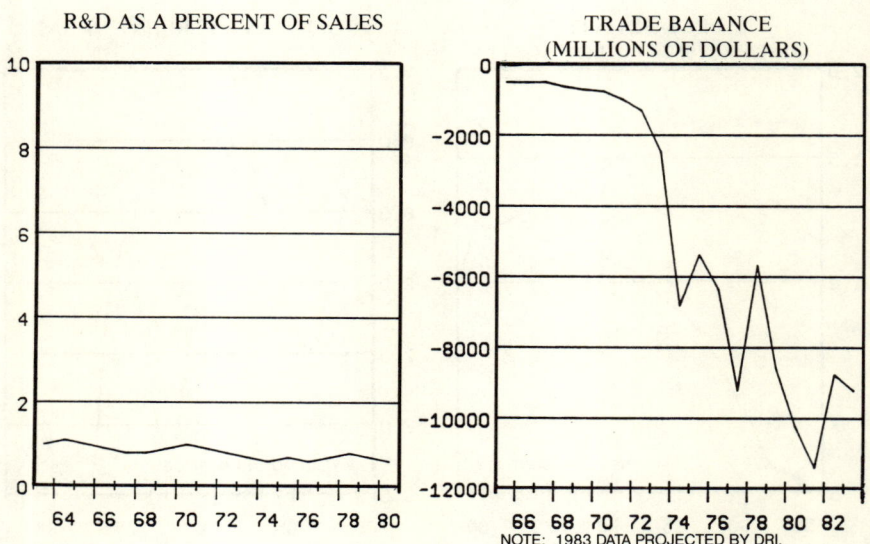

TRADE BALANCE
(MILLIONS OF DOLLARS)

NOTE: 1983 DATA PROJECTED BY DRI.

WAGES RELATIVE TO TOTAL ECONOMY

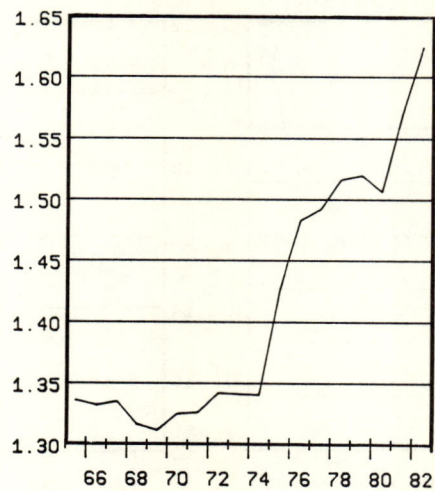

RUBBER AND PLASTICS

The rubber and plastics products industry has shown a high historical growth, some increase of instability, and a slowing of a previously high employment growth. The products of the industry consist principally of tires, other rubber products, and plastic products.

Employment in the rubber and plastics products industry is 700,000 workers. Wages are close to the economy-wide average, a decline from previous figures. This average hides major variations within the industry, however: tire workers receive relatively high wages, workers making plastic products, relatively low wages.

The productivity trend has been 5.4% a year and shows some acceleration. Investment was unstable but remained high until 1978, when it began to drop.

Import penetration has been rising rapidly since the mid-1960s. The U.S. share of world export markets has also been falling. The trade deficit was $1.2 billion in 1982.

RUBBER AND PLASTICS

PRINCIPAL PRODUCTS
Tires, hoses, and plastic articles

RECENT TRADE DATA
(Millions of dollars)

	1981	1982	1983 (Est.)
Exports	1,589	1,251	1,182
Imports	2,653	2,423	2,503
Trade Balance	−1,064	−1,172	−1,320

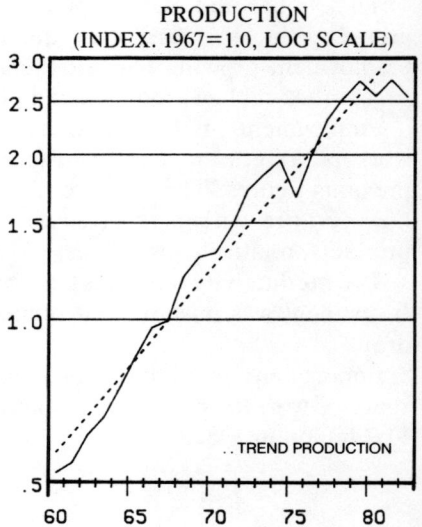
PRODUCTION
(INDEX. 1967=1.0, LOG SCALE)

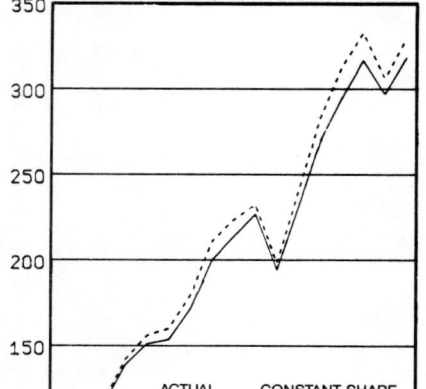
CONSTANT SHARE PRODUCTION
(INDEX, 1965=100)

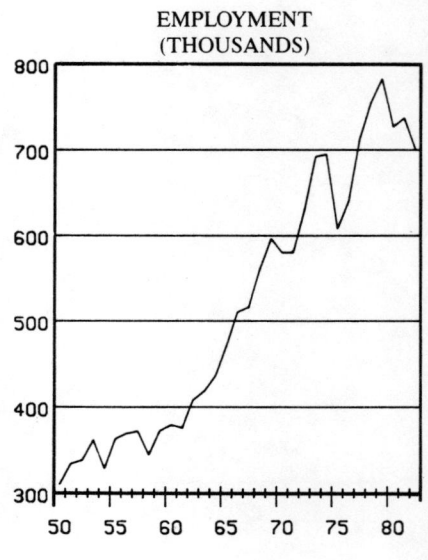
EMPLOYMENT
(THOUSANDS)

RUBBER AND PLASTICS

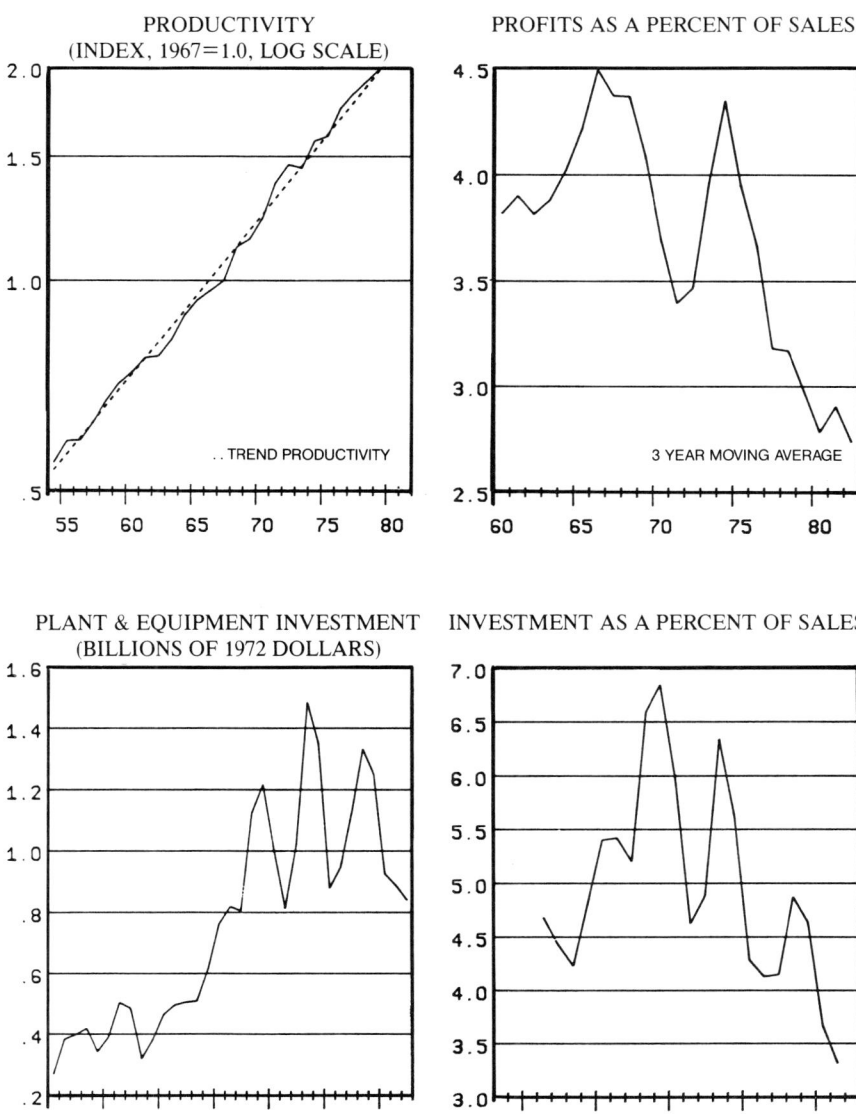

RUBBER AND PLASTICS

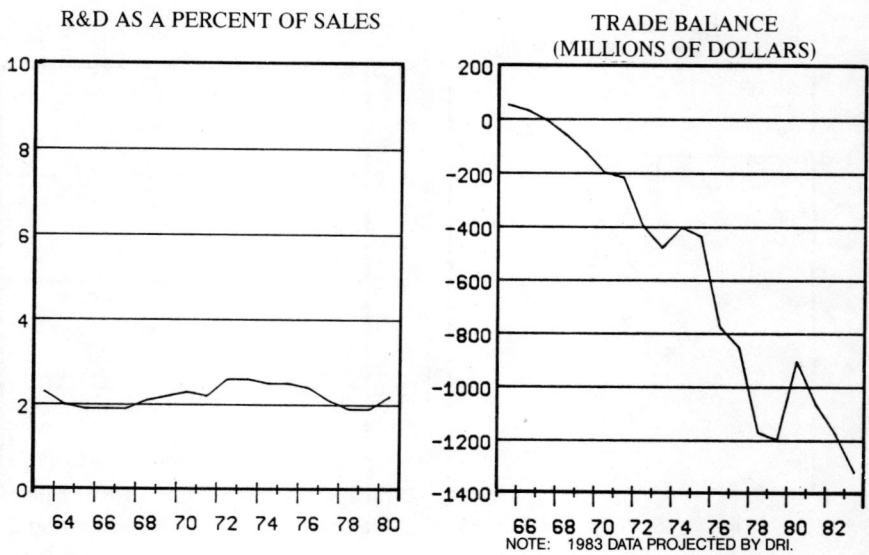

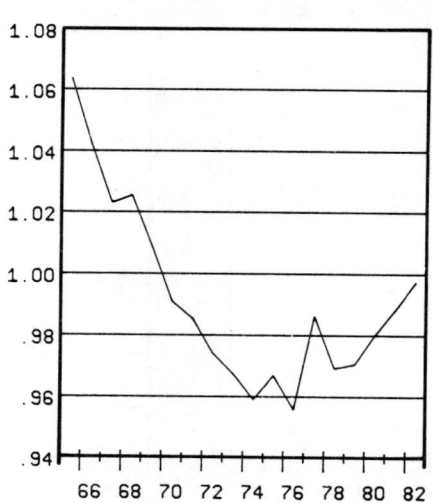

LEATHER PRODUCTS

The leather and products industry is shrinking in this country despite its strong resource base. The United States is one of the principal suppliers of hides to the world, yet this industry is a classic illustration that, with today's low transportation costs, the availability of the raw material at home is not a decisive advantage.

Industrial production of leather and products is down by 41.2% since 1968. Employment, which is now 220,000 workers, is down 37.7%, or 134,000 workers, since 1968. Relative wages, which have long been below the manufacturing average, have been falling, and in 1983 were 69% of the economy-wide average. The productivity trend is 1.0% and gives only slight signs of slowing.

The main use of leather is in the manufacture of shoes, a labor-intensive industry. The shoe industry has been declining in this country for many years; and, with the development of strong export industries in Italy, Brazil and Taiwan, much of the American shoe market has been taken over by foreign suppliers. While official data on import penetration are not available, industry sources estimate that foreign shoes are taking almost half of the market. Federal policy has rejected industry appeals for higher tariffs in a series of decisions since 1980. Of all U.S. industries, the leather and footwear industry is probably closest to extinction due to imports. The trade balance was a minus $11.2 billion in 1982.

LEATHER PRODUCTS

PRINCIPAL PRODUCTS
Tanned leather, shoes, luggage, and gloves

RECENT TRADE DATA
(Millions of dollars)

	1981	1982	1983 (Est.)
Exports	1,430	1,442	1,358
Imports	3,043	3,357	3,570
Trade Balance	−1,613	−1,915	−2,212

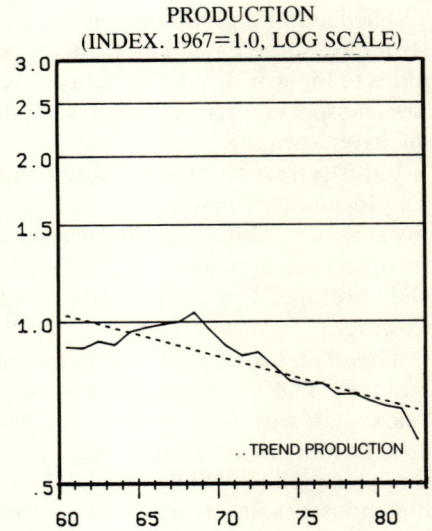

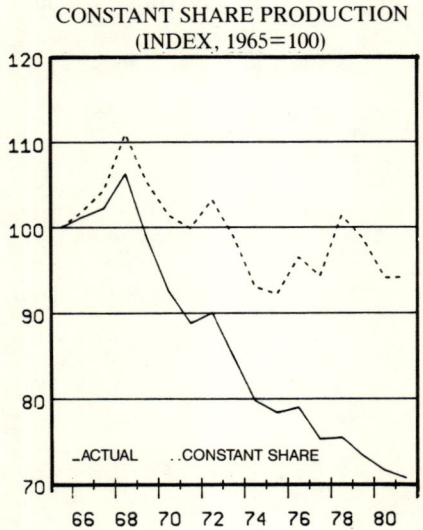

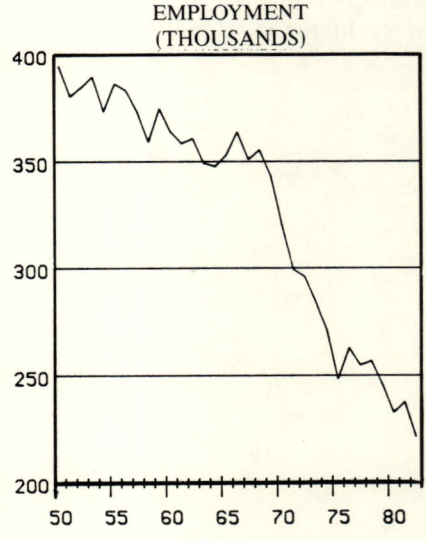

LEATHER PRODUCTS

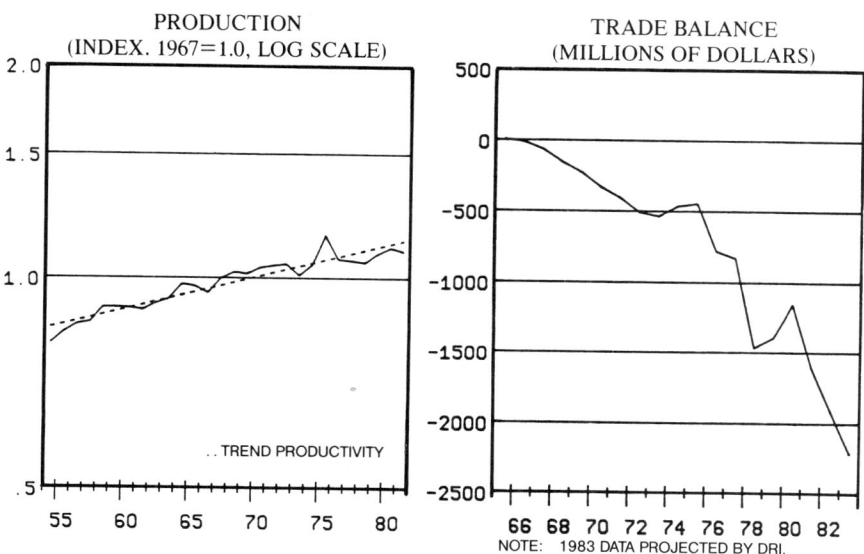

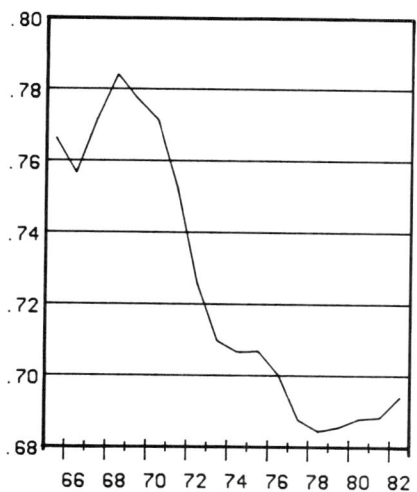

STONE, CLAY AND GLASS

The stone, clay and glass industry is affected particularly by high interest rates and the resultant instability of its markets, principally the construction industry. The growth rate of its production was 3.1%, with increasing variations around the trend.

The industry provides 580,000 jobs. There is relatively little employment growth. Productivity shows an above-average trend of 2.8%, and there is no sign of a slowdown. Relative wages have moved from slightly above the economy-wide average to substantially above average. The relative wage gain of the 1970s was a little over 10%, to a level nearly 16% above the average.

The industry experiences variations in the utilization rate of its capacity because of its dependence on the construction industry. As a result, profit margins have been falling, and in the recent business cycle remained barely positive. Industry investment has been relatively high, as the industry has made much progress in improving materials and products. Research and development outlays are low but stable.

The import penetration ratio rose sharply from the mid-1960s to 1980, and the U.S. share in world export markets declined. As a result, the industry trade deficit, which used to be negative but small, expanded and reached -$0.5 billion by 1982.

STONE, CLAY AND GLASS

PRINCIPAL PRODUCTS

Flat glass, glass containers, cement, ceramics, and abrasives

RECENT TRADE DATA
(Millions of dollars)

	1981	1982	1983 (Est.)
Exports	1,748	1,528	1,404
Imports	2,163	2,051	2,194
Trade Balance	−416	−523	−790

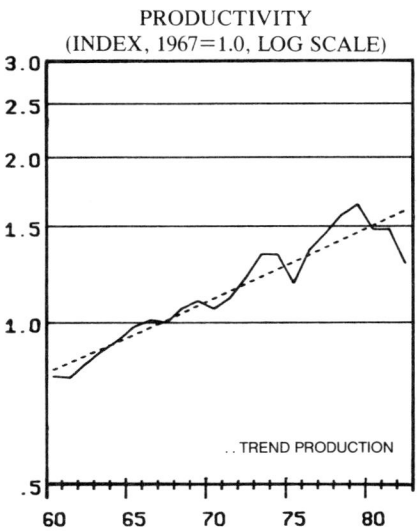

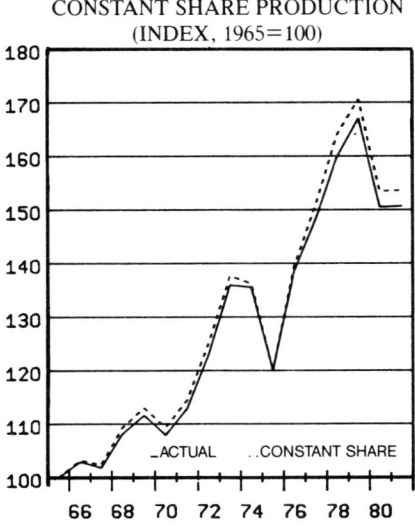

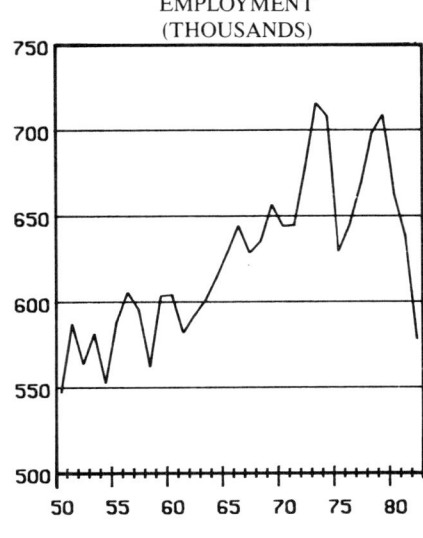

STONE, CLAY AND GLASS

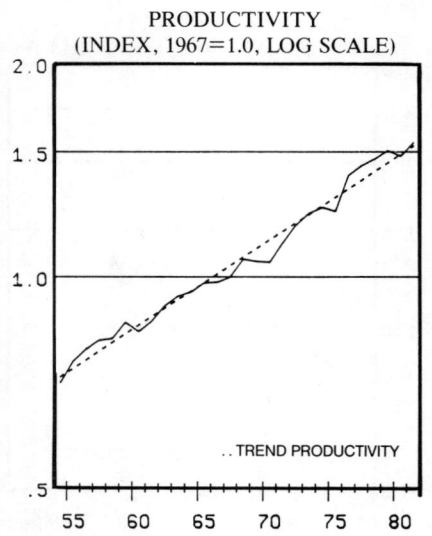

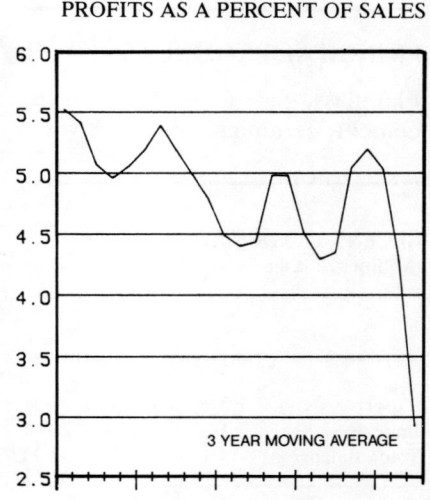

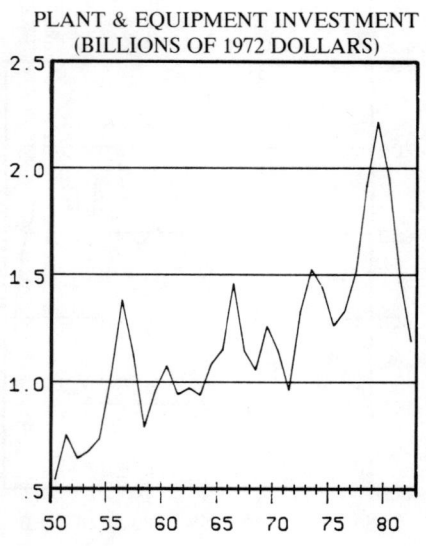

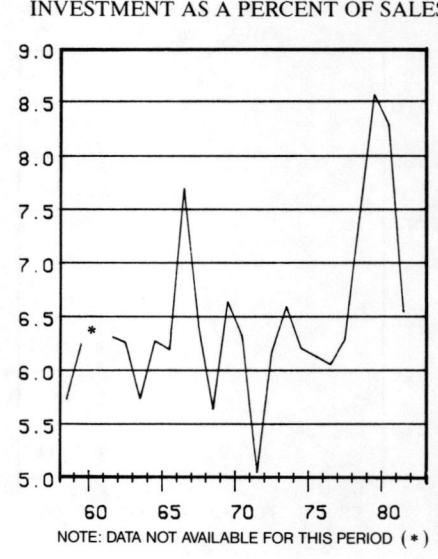

STONE, CLAY AND GLASS

R&D AS A PERCENT OF SALES

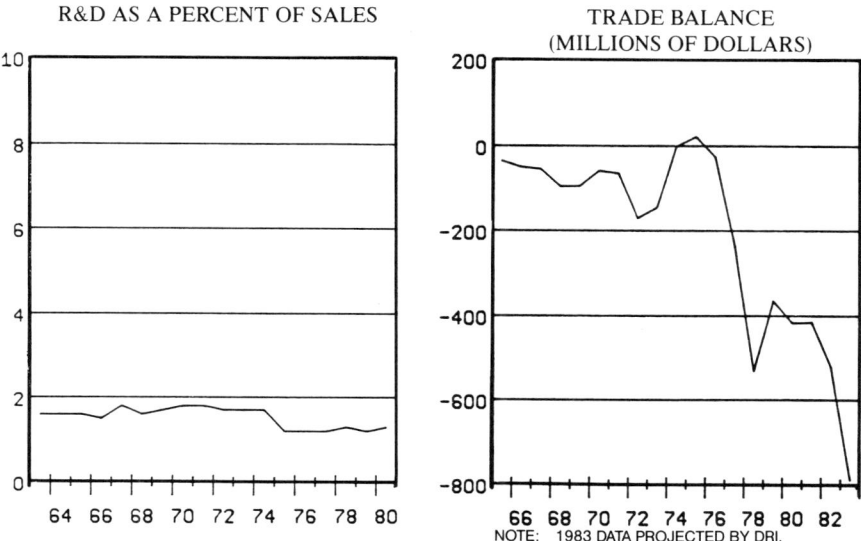

NOTE: 1983 DATA PROJECTED BY DRI.

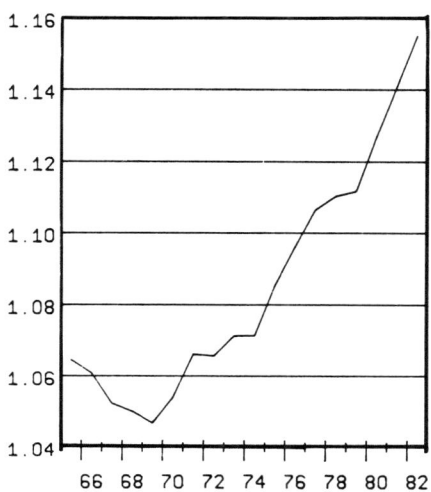

PRIMARY METALS INCLUDING STEEL

The primary metals industry has been shrinking under the impetus of its declining international position. Production expanded sharply during the 1960s, partly because of the Vietnam War and the space program, but has now returned to the levels that prevailed 20 years ago.

Industry employment was 922,000 last year, compared to 1.3 million in the better years of the 1950s and 1960s. Productivity rises at a modest 2.2%.

Despite the sharp decline in employment, wages in the industry have risen very sharply to a level nearly 50% above the economy-wide average. Primary metals have always been high-wage industries, and they were paying above average at the beginning of the 1970s. The wage explosion in the face of increasing industry difficulties was caused by the surprisingly high cost of escalator clauses in the wage contracts, a subnormal sensitivity of wages to variations in the labor market, and to the imbalance in collective bargaining caused by the fear of further foreign inroads in case of strike.

The profit margin of the industry has been trending downward since the 1950s, though there are occasional good years when the business cycle temporarily expands markets. In the recession of 1982, the industry incurred large losses that threatened the survival of some of the companies.

Investment in this capital-intensive industry has been falling recently. Further, an increasing share of the investment is no longer devoted to the modernization or creation of metals capacity, but is devoted to some of the newer fields into which the companies have diversified. The import penetration ratio has been rising rapidly, and in 1982 approached 20%. The industry trade deficit in primary metals was a very large minus $11.3 billion.

Steel

Separate data for steel show even more negative results. Production of basic steel was trendless from 1965 to 1981, though somewhat cyclical. But during the past year, production dropped by nearly 40%. Employment, which was near 600,000 workers until 1957, declined considerably in the succeeding years, and at the bottom of the recent recession fell below 300,000 workers. Investment of the industry has been highly unstable and also trendless. The import share of shipments has increased from 6% in 1965 to well over 20% in 1982. The 1982 trade deficit was $9.3 billion.

The rising import share is a surprising result, given the series of programs designed to limit total import volume. The Trigger Price Program adopted six years ago was relatively ineffective because of difficulties in properly enforcing the program. More recently, the United States and the European

Economic Community have signed a steel trade agreement which is having a major effect on limiting Europe's share of our steel markets to around 5%. Japan has been operating under an informal voluntary restraint program for some time, which provides her exporters with a roughly constant market share. However, a broad range of suppliers of steel are not covered by any program; they include Korea, Brazil, Canada, Spain, Mexico and South Africa. The share of U.S. imports provided by these countries has risen dramatically in recent years.

Governments have been deeply involved in the steel industry in recent decades. In some countries government ownership plays a major role. In others, government agencies are heavily involved in such basic decisions as investment, production and pricing, and may provide subsidies. These interventions affect relative costs and prices, and help determine the pattern of trade.

In the absence of import restraints, foreign steel would be taking an increasing share of the market, given the excess of world capacity and the openness of U.S. markets coupled with high U.S. labor costs, a modest productivity trend, a very high dollar exchange rate, and a still fractional share of capacity with the modern continuous casting and basic oxygen furnace technologies. According to DRI's steel analysis group, the quantity based import share would rise from 19% in 1983 to the 22-25% range. Smaller companies operating minimills, which now hold 10% to 15% of the domestic market, are providing a new competition for imports. While limited to certain products and processes largely based on the reprocessing of scrap, their productivity is sufficiently high to provide them with a competitive cost structure.

PRIMARY METALS

PRINCIPAL PRODUCTS

Steel mill products, steel castings, smelted or refined nonferrous metals, and rolled, drawn or extruded nonferrous metals

RECENT TRADE DATA
(Millions of dollars)

	1981	1982	1983 (Est.)
Exports	11,822	7,842	7,551
Imports	22,573	19,120	17,273
Trade Balance	−10,751	−11,279	−9,721

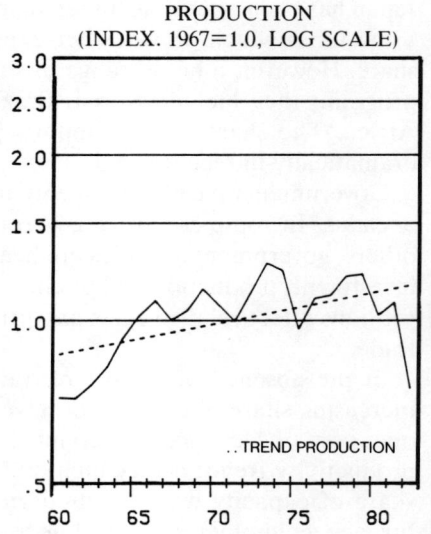

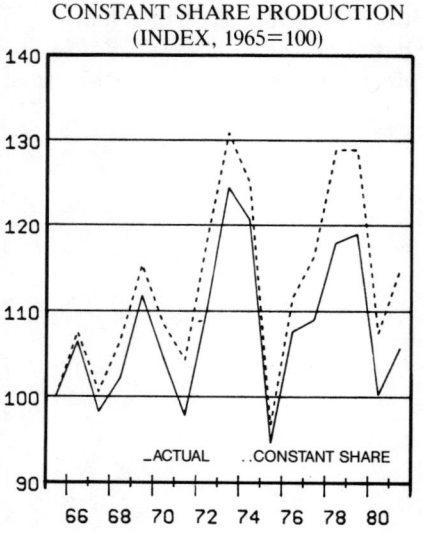

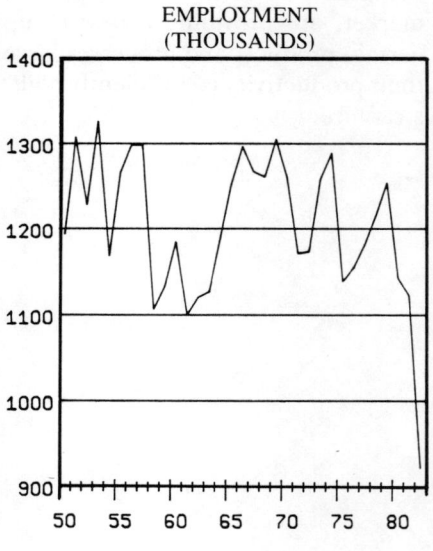

PRIMARY METALS

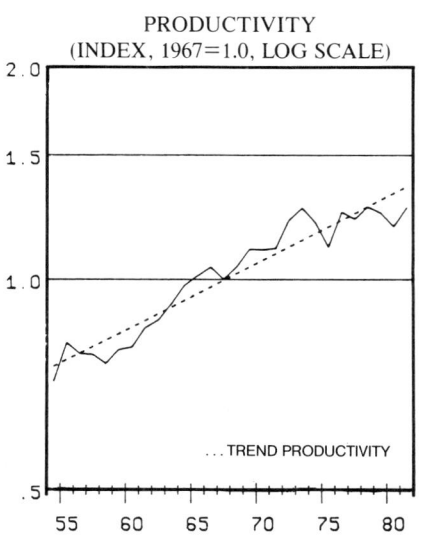

PRODUCTIVITY
(INDEX, 1967=1.0, LOG SCALE)

... TREND PRODUCTIVITY

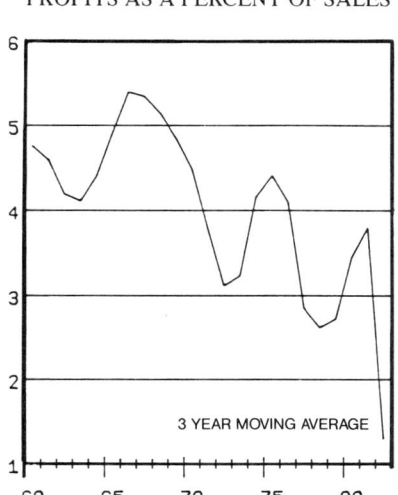

PROFITS AS A PERCENT OF SALES

3 YEAR MOVING AVERAGE

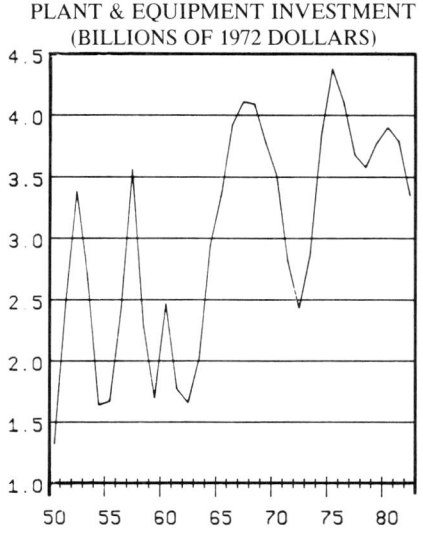

PLANT & EQUIPMENT INVESTMENT
(BILLIONS OF 1972 DOLLARS)

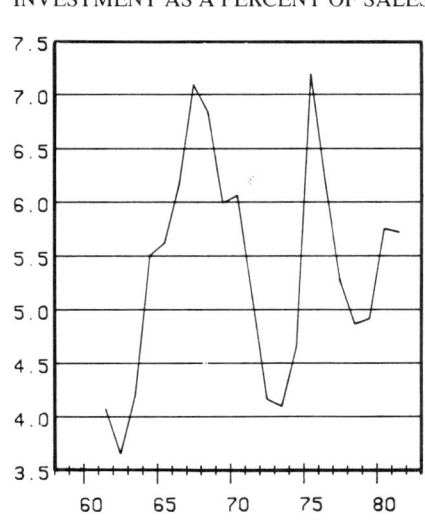

INVESTMENT AS A PERCENT OF SALES

PRIMARY METALS

R&D AS A PERCENT OF SALES

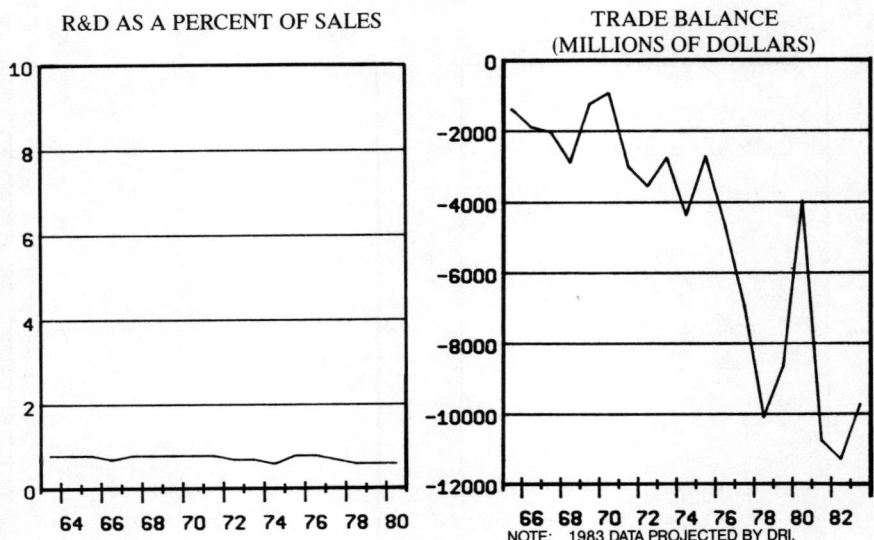

NOTE: 1983 DATA PROJECTED BY DRI.

WAGES RELATIVE TO TOTAL ECONOMY

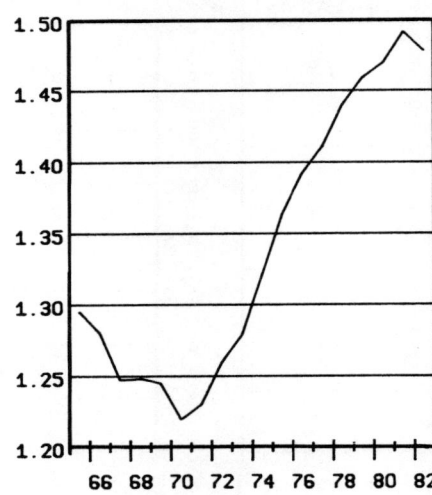

STEEL MILL PRODUCTS

PRINCIPAL PRODUCTS

Blast furnace products, drawn or rolled steel, and steel piping

RECENT TRADE DATA
(Millions of dollars)

	1981	1982	1983 (Est.)
Exports	900	779	738
Imports	11,262	10,071	5,901
Trade Balance	−10,362	−9,293	−5,163

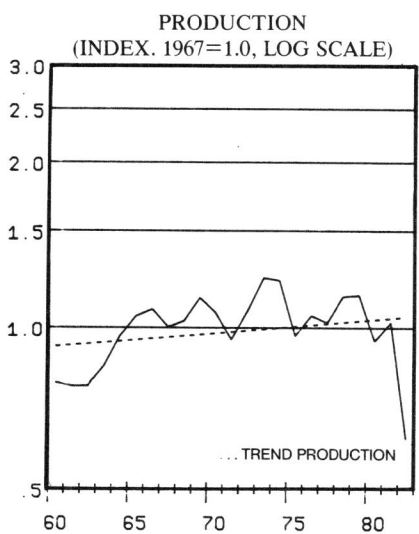

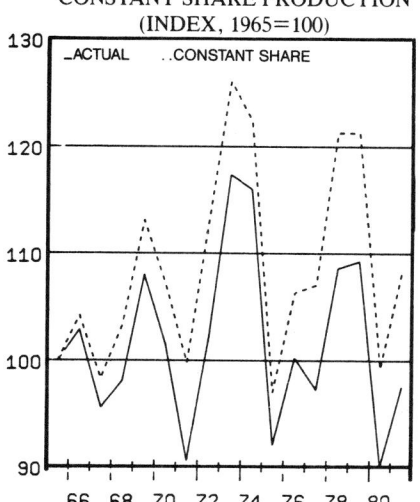

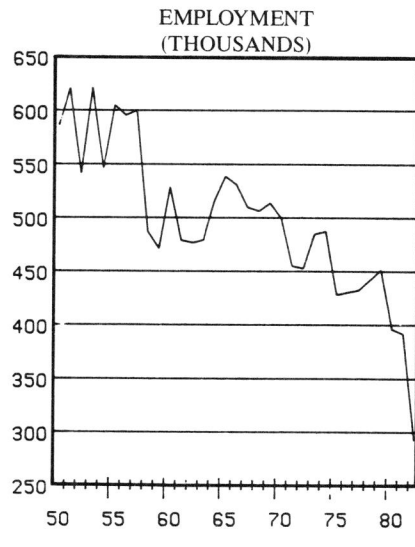

STEEL MILL PRODUCTS

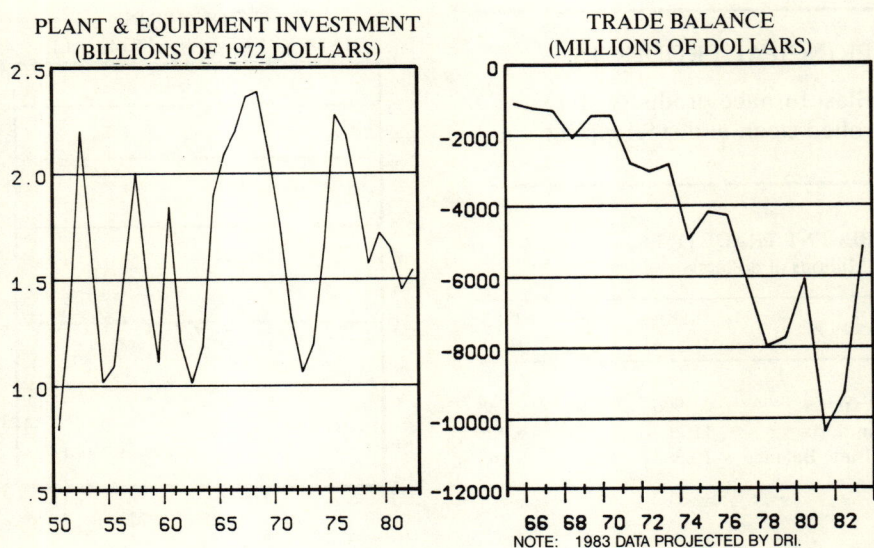

NOTE: 1983 DATA PROJECTED BY DRI.

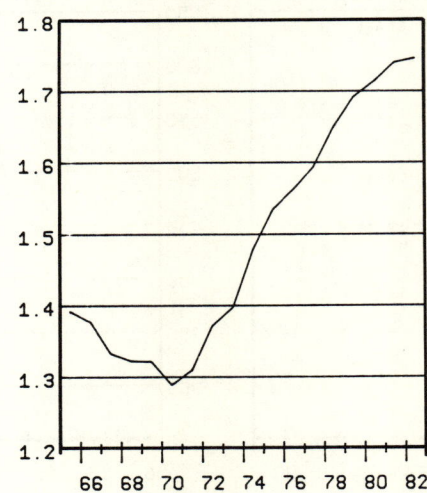

FABRICATED METALS

The fabricated metal products industry grew rapidly from the early 1960s to the late 1970s, but suffered a precipitous decline during the recent recession. The growth trend, 1960-1982, is 3.1%. A worsening international competitive position is becoming a major factor for the industry.

The industry employs 1.4 million people. The employment trend is positive, unlike many other manufacturing industries. The productivity trend is 2.2% and shows no signs of slowing. Wages are about 14% above the economy-wide average, and do not show dramatic changes. Profit margins remained positive in the recent recession, but industry investment has dropped sharply since 1974.

The import penetration ratio has been rising, and was 3.3% in 1980. The U.S. share in export markets has fallen, but we still provide approximately 10% of world exports. The industry trade balance turned negative in 1968 and was minus $900 million in 1982.

FABRICATED METALS

PRINCIPAL PRODUCTS

Cans, tools, plumbing fixtures, structural metal products, metal forgings and stampings, and guns and ammunition

RECENT TRADE DATA
(Millions of dollars)

	1981	1982	1983 (Est.)
Exports	2,388	1,969	1,818
Imports	2,747	2,874	2,758
Trade Balance	−359	−905	−940

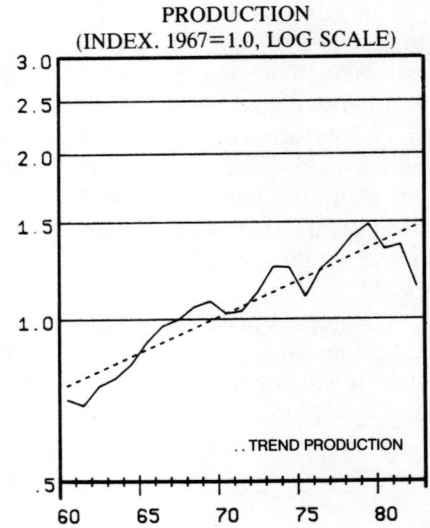

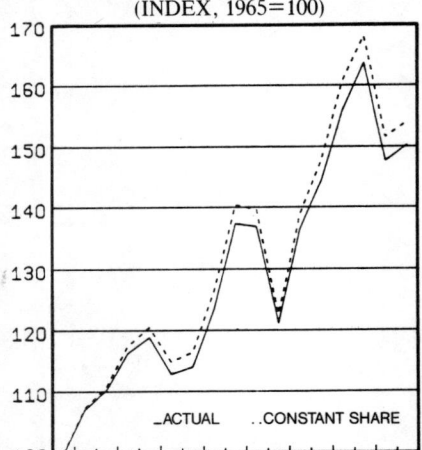

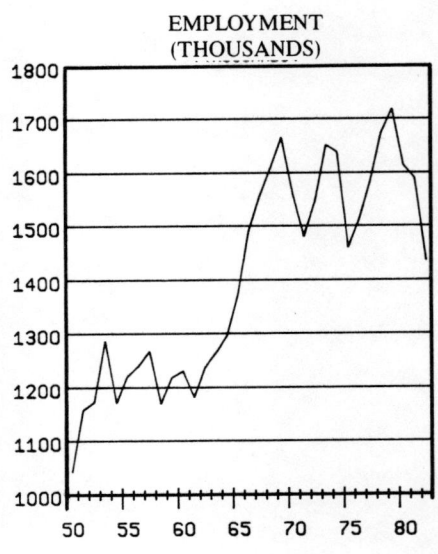

FABRICATED METALS

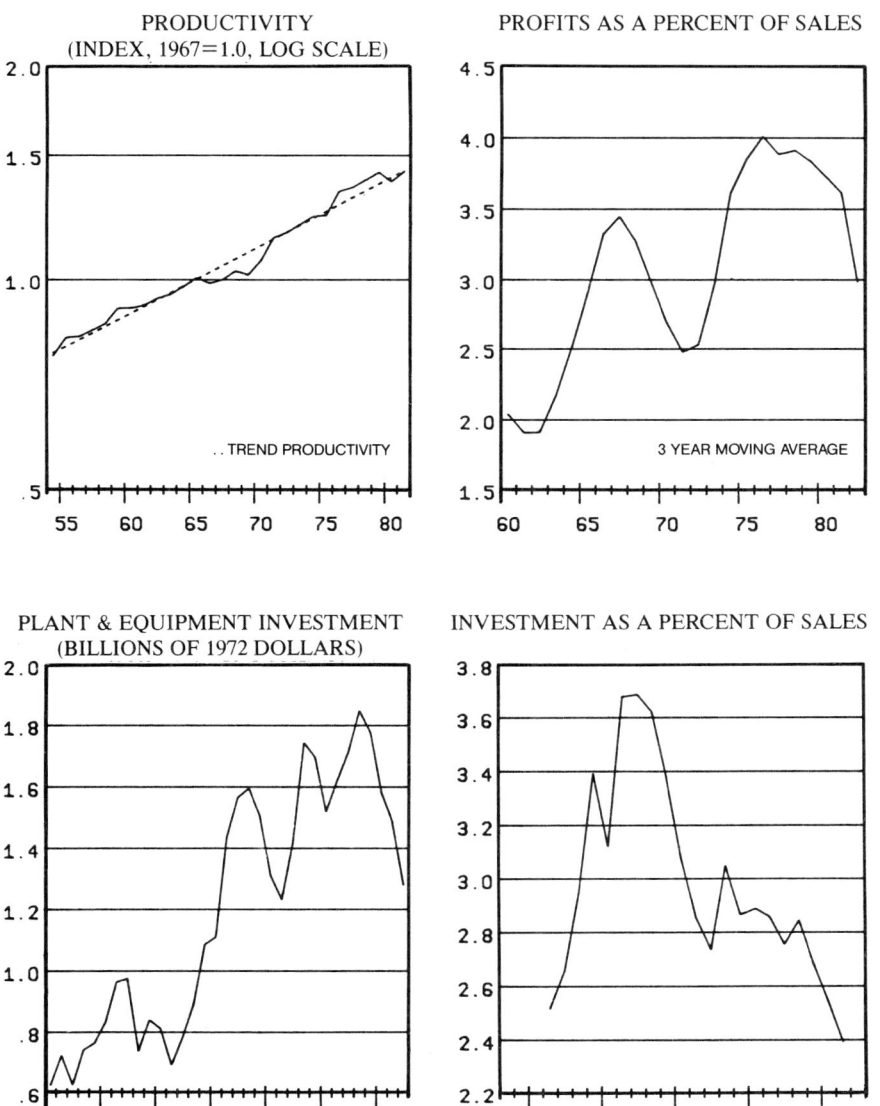

FABRICATED METALS

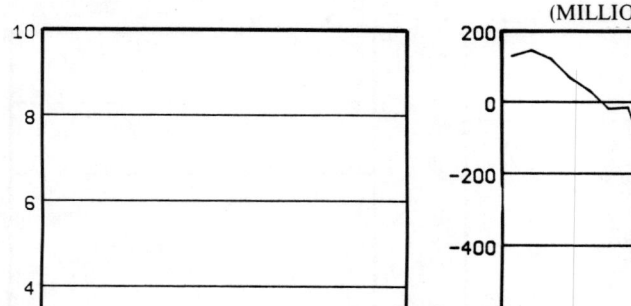

R&D AS A PERCENT OF SALES

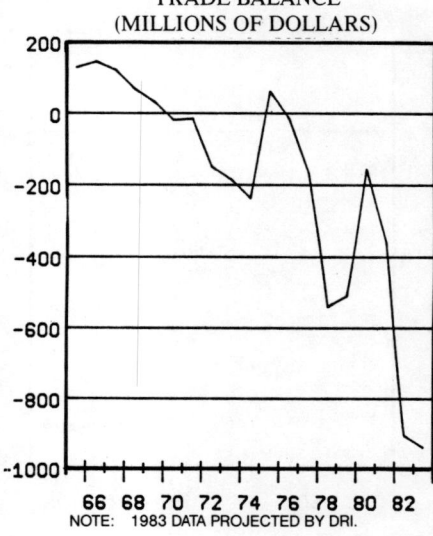

TRADE BALANCE (MILLIONS OF DOLLARS)

NOTE: 1983 DATA PROJECTED BY DRI.

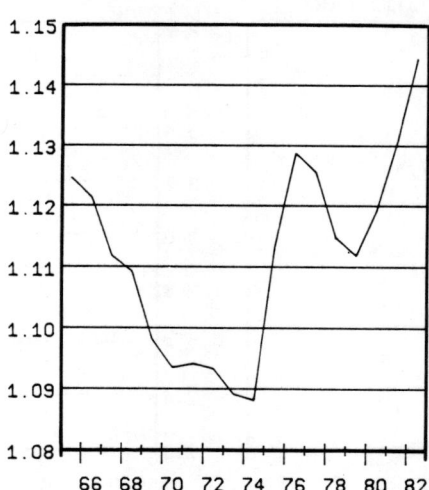

WAGES RELATIVE TO TOTAL ECONOMY

NONELECTRICAL MACHINERY

The United States has long been a major producer of capital goods and continues to play that role. The nonelectrical machinery industry has shown a growth trend of 5.0%, 1960-1982. While imports are taking a rising share of the American market, the net industry trade balance remains very favorable.

The industry employed 2,266,000 workers in 1982. The productivity trend is 3.0%, allowing a significant rate of increase of employment. Wages are 21% above the economy-wide average, and have not shown major changes.

Profit margins in the industry are highly cyclical, but the experience of the recent recession was not significantly worse than before. Margins show no secular erosion, and cash flow actually shows a gradual improvement.

The nonelectrical machinery industry shows a strong positive trend in its investment outlays. This is dramatically better than the results for most of the manufacturing industries. Of course, the industry manufactures a broad range of products; and there are big differences in relative performance. The computer industry is classified in this category, and it has been leading the way. More traditional machinery lines, such as general industrial machinery, do not show such strong positive results; and some product lines, such as agricultural equipment and construction equipment, are suffering severely from a worldwide weakness of their markets, as well as tough new competition from Japan. The machine tool industry has faced a particularly strong challenge.

Nonelectrical machinery enjoys the largest trade surplus of U.S. manufacturing industries, $31 billion in 1982.

NONELECTRICAL MACHINERY

PRINCIPAL PRODUCTS

Engines, turbines, farm and garden machinery, construction and mining machinery, and office machinery (includes computers)

RECENT TRADE DATA
(Millions of dollars)

	1981	1982	1983 (Est.)
Exports	55,649	51,468	44,271
Imports	19,637	20,098	21,713
Trade Balance	36,012	31,370	22,558

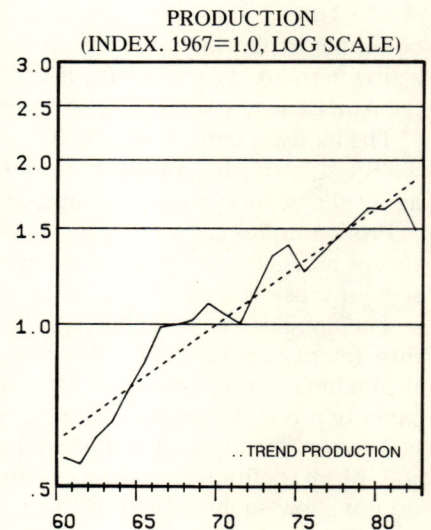

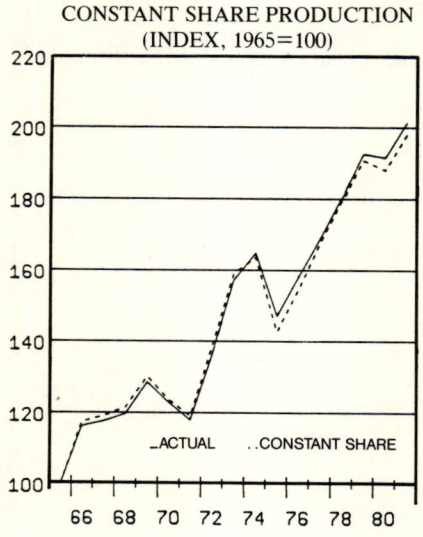

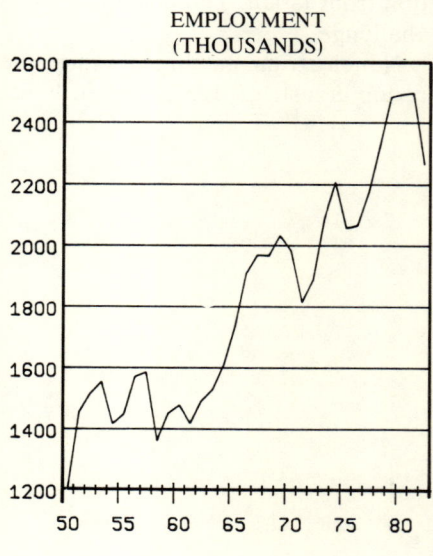

NONELECTRICAL MACHINERY

PRODUCTIVITY
(INDEX, 1967=1.0, LOG SCALE)

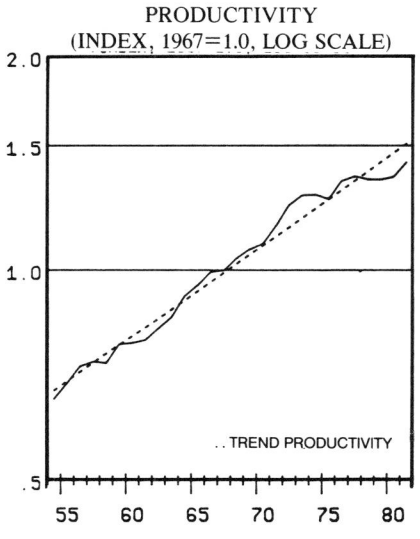

.. TREND PRODUCTIVITY

PROFITS AS A PERCENT OF SALES

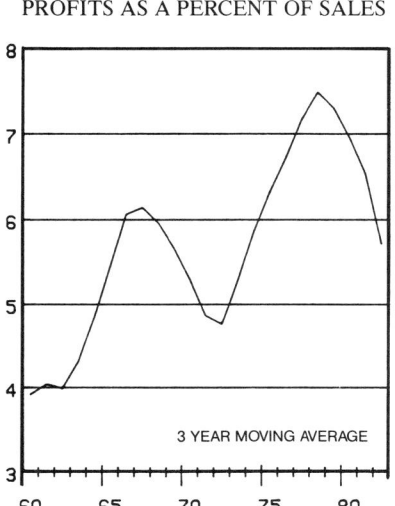

3 YEAR MOVING AVERAGE

PLANT & EQUIPMENT INVESTMENT
(BILLIONS OF 1972 DOLLARS)

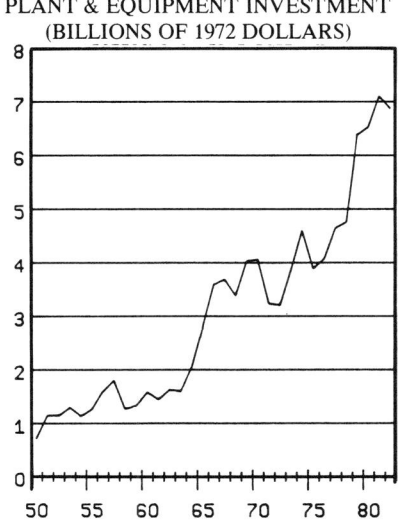

INVESTMENT AS A PERCENT OF SALES

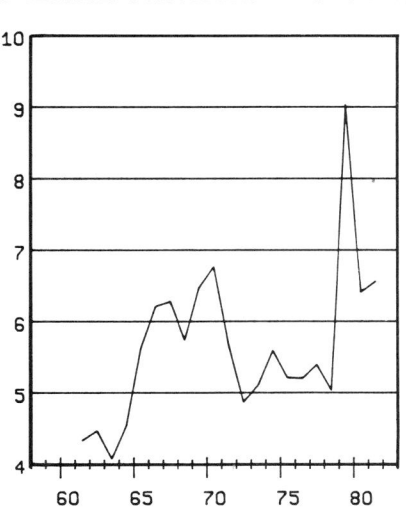

NONELECTRICAL MACHINERY

R&D AS A PERCENT OF SALES

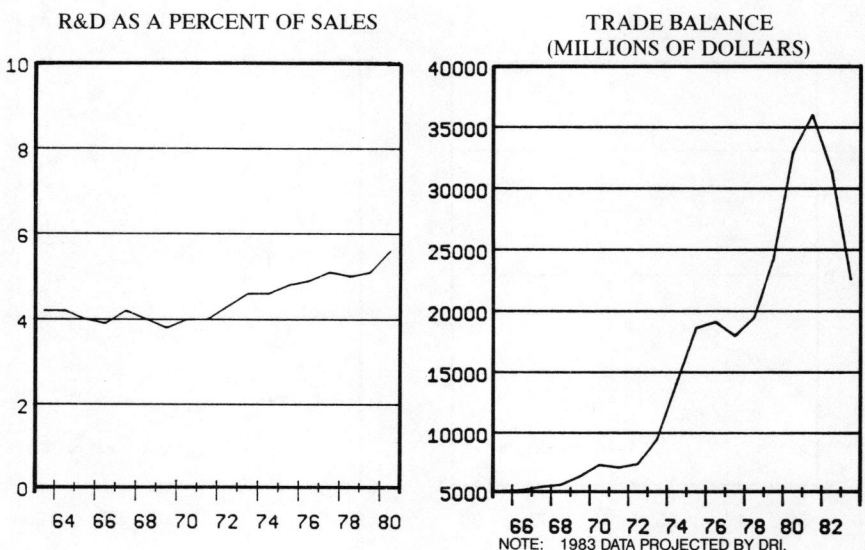

NOTE: 1983 DATA PROJECTED BY DRI.

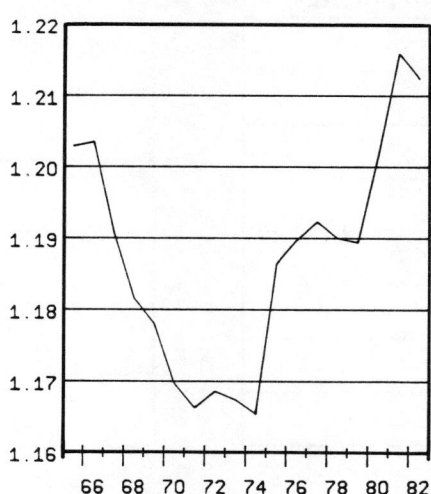

ELECTRICAL MACHINERY

The electrical machinery industry shows a growth trend of 5.6% a year and is a major leader of U.S. manufacturing. The industry employs 2.02 million workers. Productivity grows at a strong 4.5% rate. Wages are just 7% above the economy-wide average and are relatively constant.

Industry profitability is highly variable, but does not show a downtrend. Investment has been expanding rapidly. The industry also invests heavily in research and development.

The import penetration ratio has been rising, to 13.8% in 1980. The U.S. export share of world markets has been falling, but not as badly as in many other industries. The industry's trade balance was an $8.0 billion surplus in 1982.

The electrical machinery industry includes a highly diverse range of products, and international performance has differed strongly among them. Major segments of the TV and radio markets have been largely taken over by foreign producers, particularly after the expiration of voluntary marketing agreements with Japan and Korea in 1980. Household appliance markets are also seeing increasing foreign products, but their share is still modest. Communication equipment has a rapidly rising import share, but this large industry is still principally supplied domestically. With the dissolution of the Bell System, imports will leap. The electronic components industry has lost its lead in some products to Japan, including the famous case of the 64K chip. The major electrical equipment industry, including utility equipment, has suffered some loss of position in world markets, but still is the principal supplier for our own needs.

ELECTRICAL MACHINERY

PRINCIPAL PRODUCTS
Electrical power transmission equipment, household appliances, lighting equipment, radio and television equipment, communications equipment, and electronic components

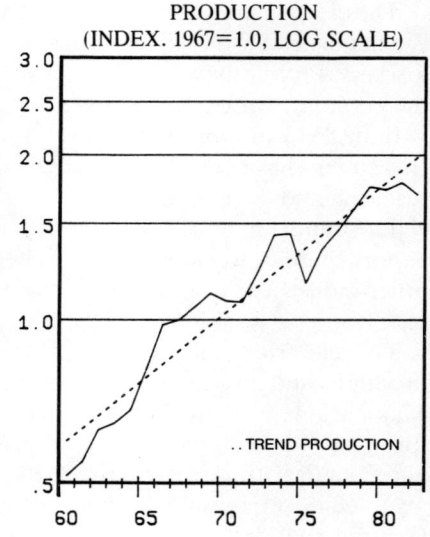

RECENT TRADE DATA
(Millions of dollars)

	1981	1982	1983 (Est.)
Exports	24,370	24,268	24,806
Imports	15,789	16,317	17,232
Trade Balance	8,581	7,951	7,574

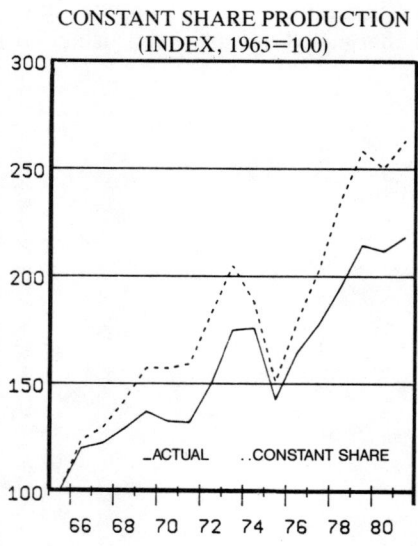

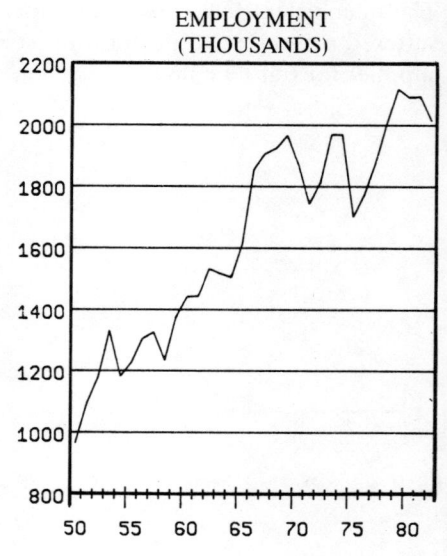

ELECTRICAL MACHINERY

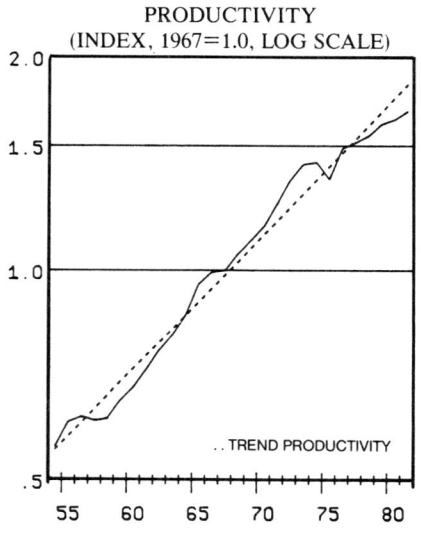

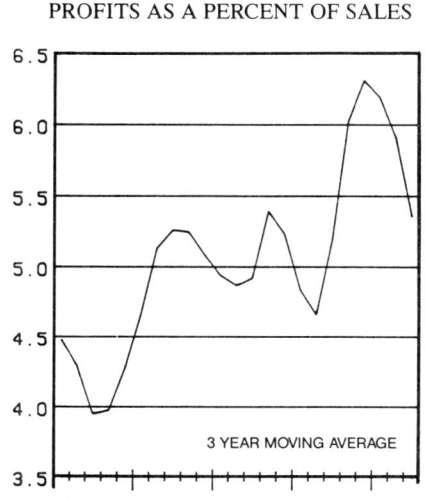

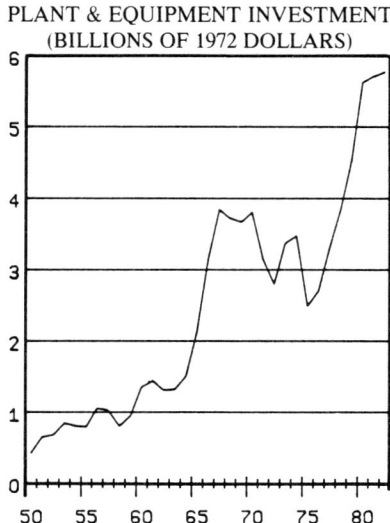

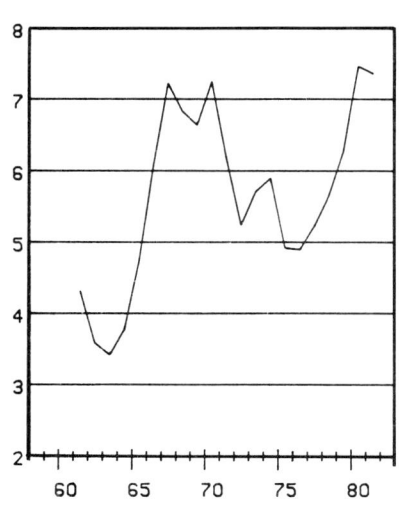

ELECTRICAL MACHINERY

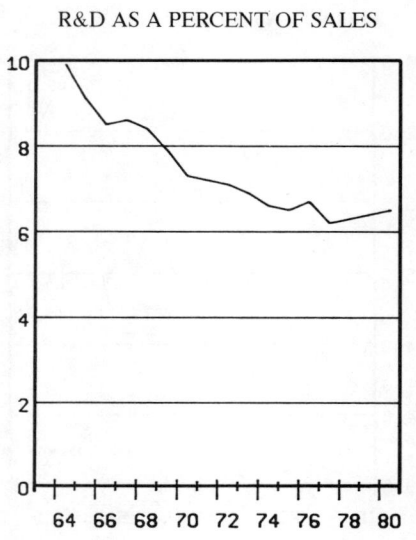

R&D AS A PERCENT OF SALES

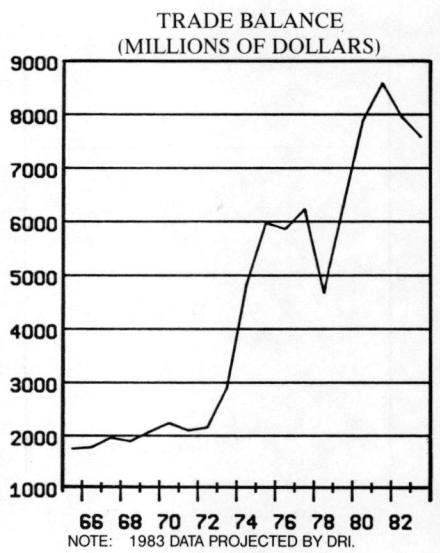

TRADE BALANCE (MILLIONS OF DOLLARS)

NOTE: 1983 DATA PROJECTED BY DRI.

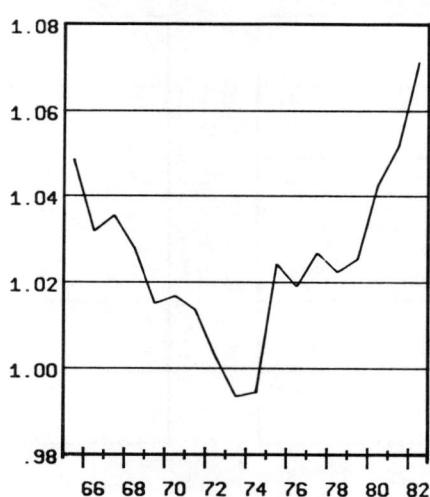

WAGES RELATIVE TO TOTAL ECONOMY

TRANSPORTATION EQUIPMENT INCLUDING AUTOMOBILES

The transportation equipment industry, which manufactures automobiles, trucks, airplanes, ships, railroad equipment and mobile homes, has experienced slowing growth of output both because of the energy revolution and the impaired international competitive position. The trend growth of industrial production, 1960-1982, is 2.6%, but growth has been nearly flat since 1968. If the industry had been able to maintain its share of domestic and foreign markets, its production would have been 5.3% higher.

The industry employed 1.74 million workers in 1982, 19% below its 1968 peak of 2.16 million. The productivity trend is 3.0% and shows little evidence of slowing. Production and productivity are quite unstable because of the cyclical vulnerability of its markets.

The industry's wages are 45% higher than the economy-wide average. This represents a 15% relative wage gain since 1970, despite the poor employment experience. Wages in this industry are less sensitive to fluctuations in employment than in most industries, and the surprisingly high cost of escalator clauses accounts for this relative wage gain.

The profit margin of the industry has fallen since the mid-1960s, and was close to zero during the recent recession. Investment has been high, albeit unstable, and does not show a downtrend. The need of the auto industry to modernize its product and improve its quality has sustained a high level of investment even in the face of shrunken profits.

Automobiles

The experience of the motor vehicle component of the transportation equipment industry has been considerably more negative. Production showed increases until 1978, though this increase was not in passenger cars but rather in trucks and in equipment. Employment, which has always been unstable, was barely more than 500,000 workers in 1982, compared to over 700,000 workers in the mid-1950s and in other good years for the industry. Profit margins fell sharply, and were slightly negative by 1980. The profits of the automobile manufacturers were substantially worse, of course, representing large losses in 1982, though equipment manufacturers did somewhat better. Investment has been rising as the industry has striven to modernize its product, and actually represented a larger percentage of sales in the last few years than was historically typical. The import share of shipments of the entire industry has risen from less than 6.1% in 1965 to nearly 30% in 1982. The trade balance for the motor vehicles and equipment industry was a large negative $17.6 billion in 1982.

The industry is devoting an exceptionally large share of its revenue to research and development expenditures at this time. In the case of the auto industry, this includes some of the outlays for modernizing the product. In the aircraft industry, R&D is always important because of the rapid advance of the technology, as well as the need to develop improved missiles for military purposes.

TRANSPORTATION EQUIPMENT

PRINCIPAL PRODUCTS

Motor vehicles, aircraft, ships, railroad equipment, and guided missiles

RECENT TRADE DATA
(Millions of dollars)

	1981	1982	1983 (Est.)
Exports	35,514	30,699	34,260
Imports	36,378	39,271	45,190
Trade Balance	−864	−8,572	−10,930

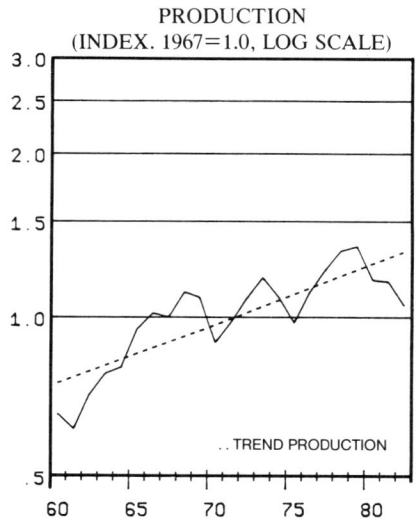

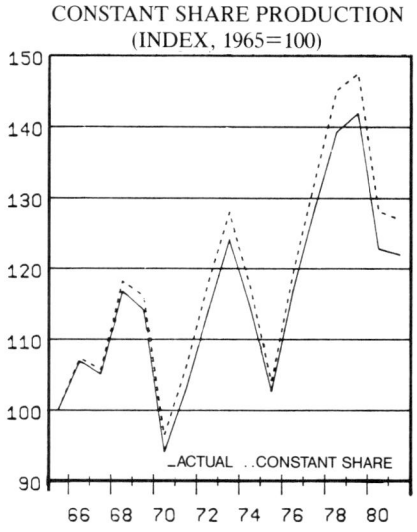

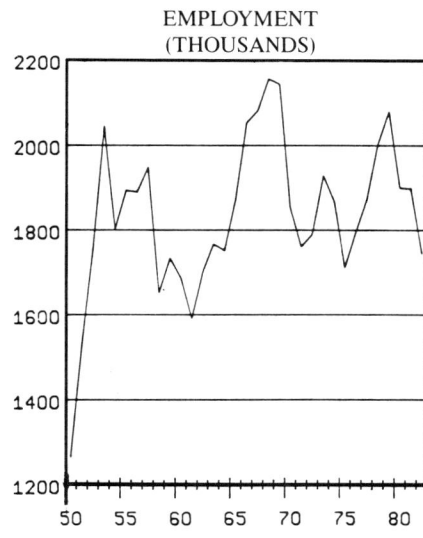

TRANSPORTATION EQUIPMENT

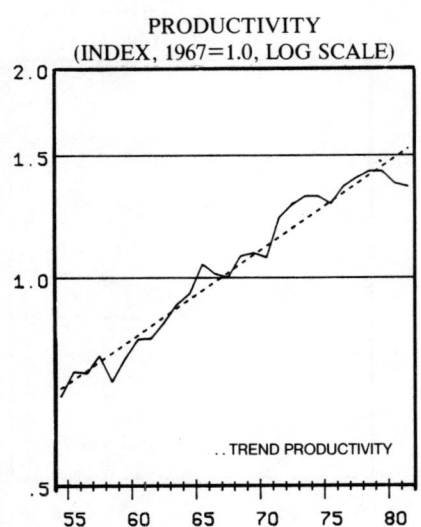

PRODUCTIVITY
(INDEX, 1967=1.0, LOG SCALE)
..TREND PRODUCTIVITY

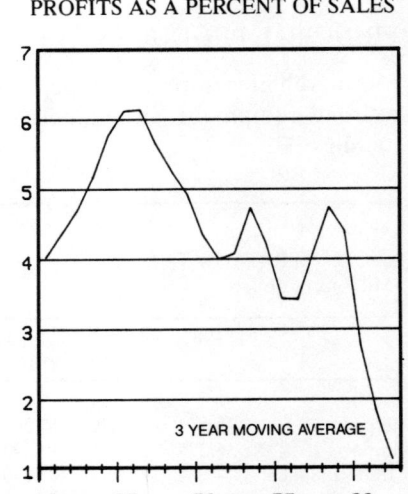

PROFITS AS A PERCENT OF SALES
3 YEAR MOVING AVERAGE

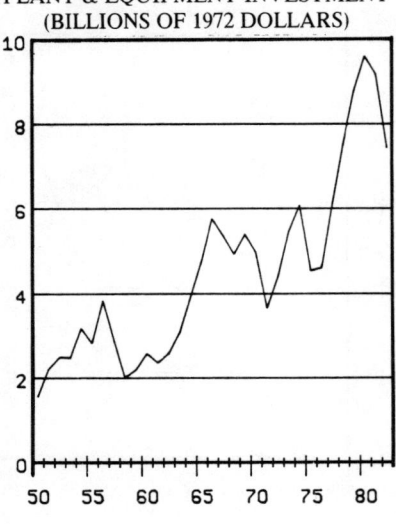

PLANT & EQUIPMENT INVESTMENT
(BILLIONS OF 1972 DOLLARS)

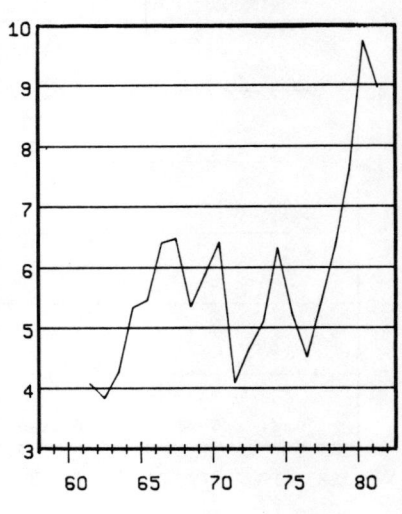

INVESTMENT AS A PERCENT OF SALES

TRANSPORTATION EQUIPMENT

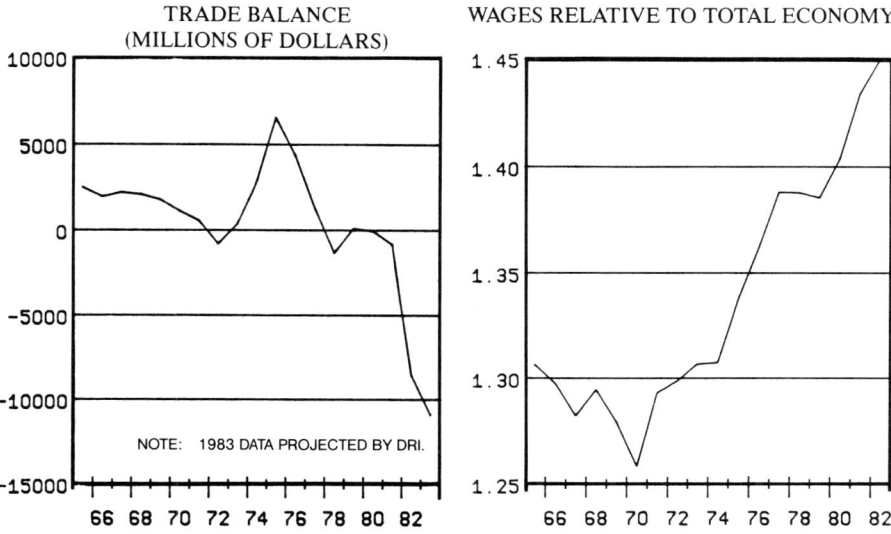

MOTOR VEHICLES AND PARTS

PRINCIPAL PRODUCTS

Motor vehicles, trucks, truck trailers, and motor vehicle parts

RECENT TRADE DATA
(Millions of dollars)

	1981	1982	1983 (Est.)
Exports	17,987	15,672	17,012
Imports	29,737	33,250	39,670
Trade Balance	−11,750	−17,579	−22,658

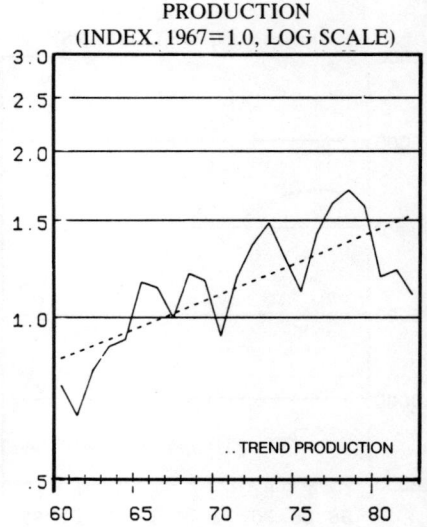

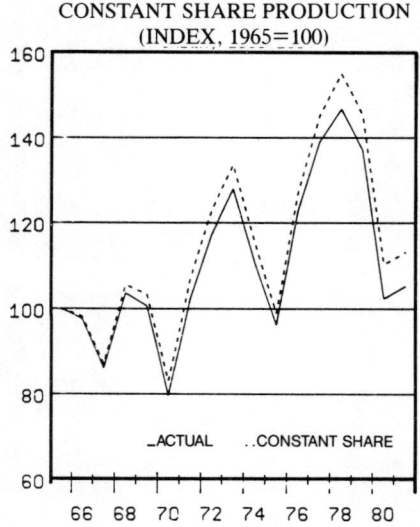

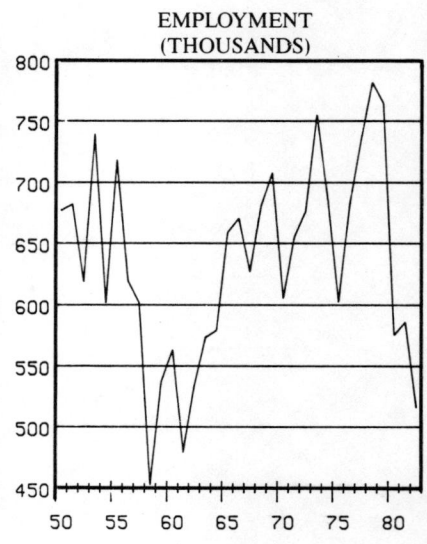

MOTOR VEHICLES AND PARTS

PROFITS AS A PERCENT OF SALES

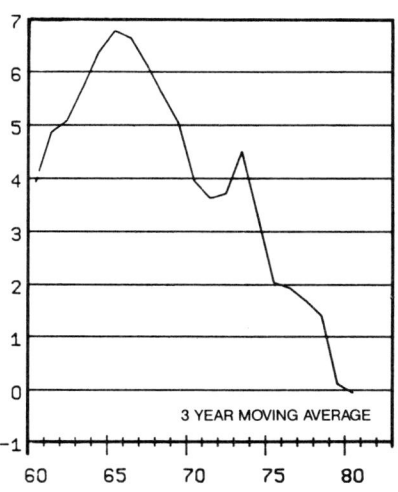

PLANT & EQUIPMENT INVESTMENT
(BILLIONS OF 1972 DOLLARS)

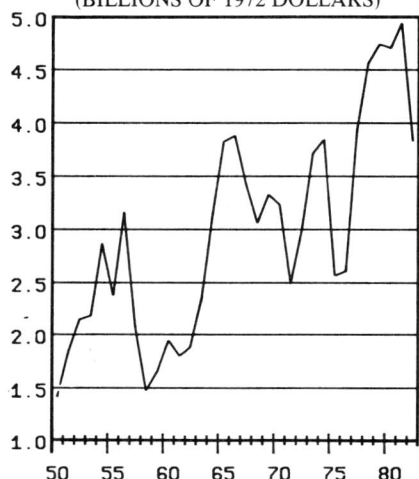

TRADE BALANCE
(MILLIONS OF DOLLARS)

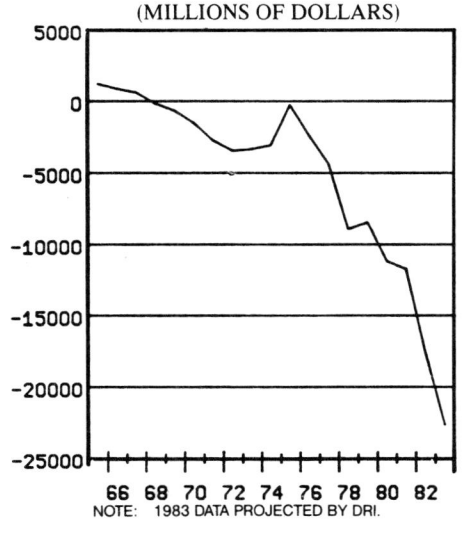

NOTE: 1983 DATA PROJECTED BY DRI.

WAGES RELATIVE TO TOTAL ECONOMY

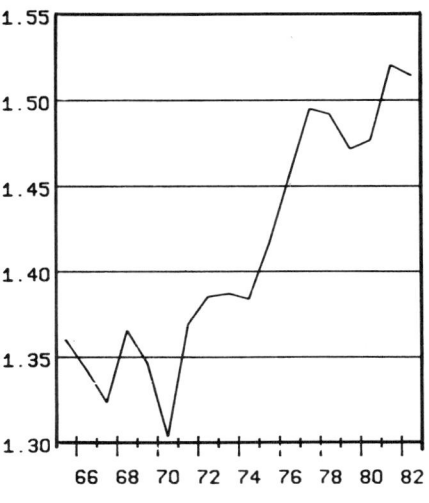

INSTRUMENTS

The instruments industry, consisting principally of scientific and industrial measurement equipment and consumer products such as cameras, continues to be one of the success stories of American manufacturing; but the international competitive position is changing. The trend rate of growth of production has been 5.5%. While always responsive to the business cycle, the production drop created by the most recent recession was substantially greater than before.

Employment was 716,000 persons in 1982, slightly higher than in 1979 before the recessions began. The trend rate of growth of employment has been 2.9%.

The productivity trend has been 3.5% and showed no sign of deceleration until the recent recession. Wages are just 6% above the economy-wide average and have not showed large variations.

The industry spends heavily on research and development, devoting about 6% of revenues to R&D for the last 20 years.

The import penetration ratio has gone from 4.3% to about 10%, and the U.S. share in world export markets is down quite substantially. Nonetheless, we continue to be a major exporter of instruments. The industry posted a trade surplus of $1.9 billion in 1982.

INSTRUMENTS

PRINCIPAL PRODUCTS

Scientific and research equipment, measuring and controlling instruments, optical instruments, medical instruments, and photographic equipment

RECENT TRADE DATA
(Millions of dollars)

	1981	1982	1983 (Est.)
Exports	5,767	5,364	4,983
Imports	3,607	3,434	3,835
Trade Balance	2,161	1,930	1,148

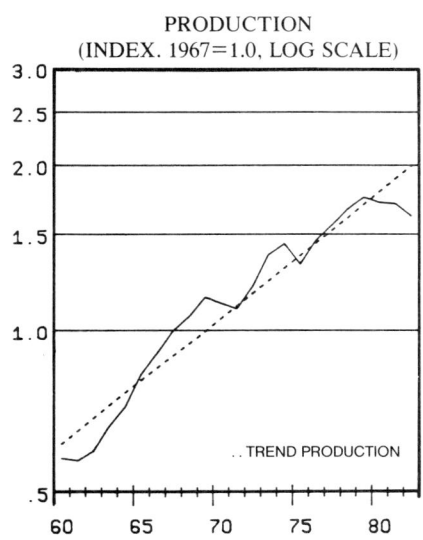

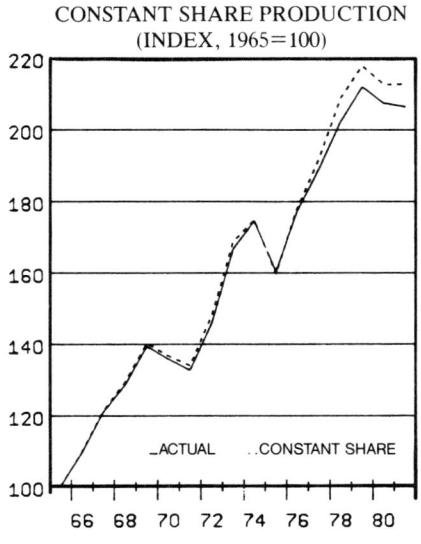

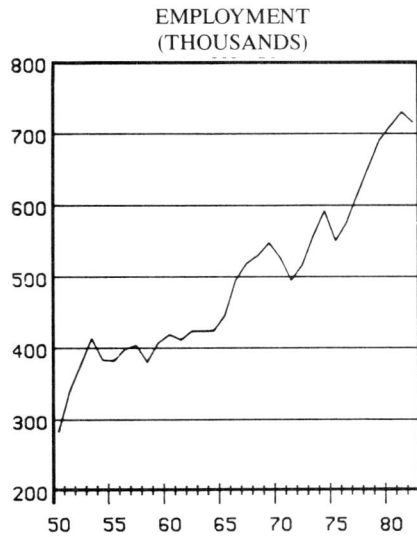

INSTRUMENTS

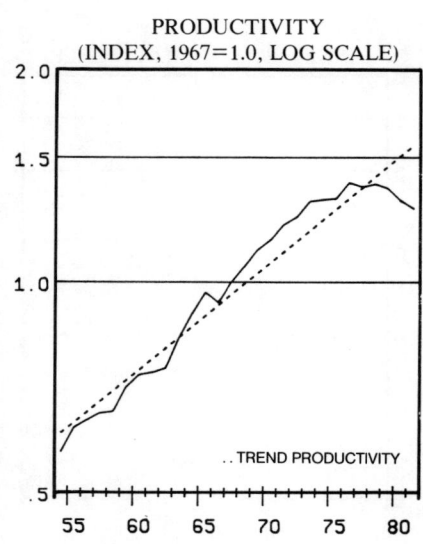

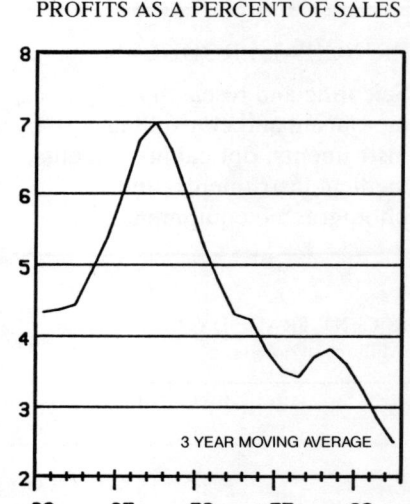

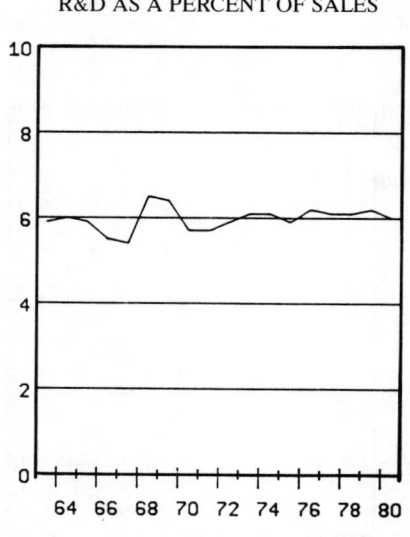

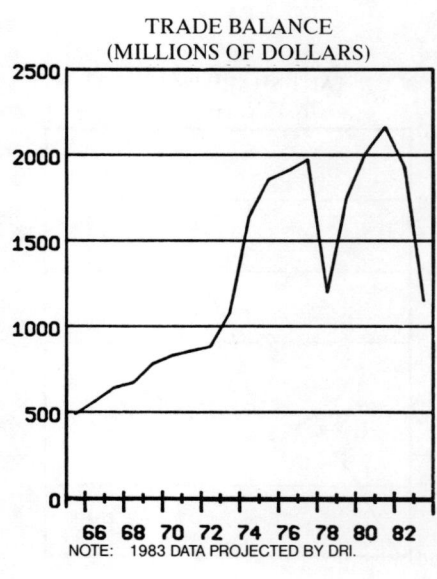

INSTRUMENTS

WAGES RELATIVE TO TOTAL ECONOMY

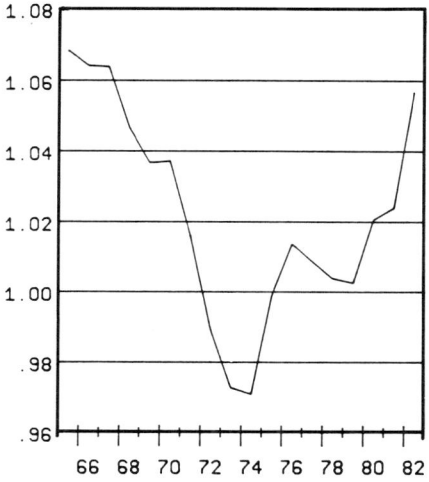

MISCELLANEOUS MANUFACTURING

PRINCIPAL PRODUCTS
Jewelry, silverware, musical instruments, toys, and sporting goods

RECENT TRADE DATA
(Millions of dollars)

	1981	1982	1983 (Est.)
Exports	4,208	3,795	3,538
Imports	5,728	6,680	6,311
Trade Balance	−1,520	−2,885	−2,772

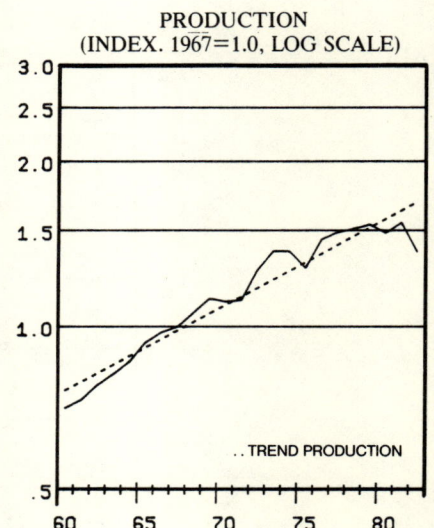

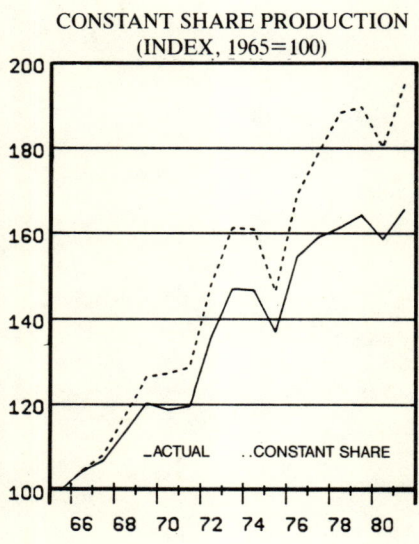

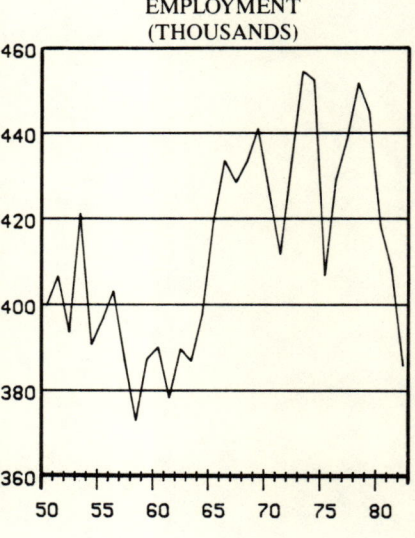

MISCELLANEOUS MANUFACTURING

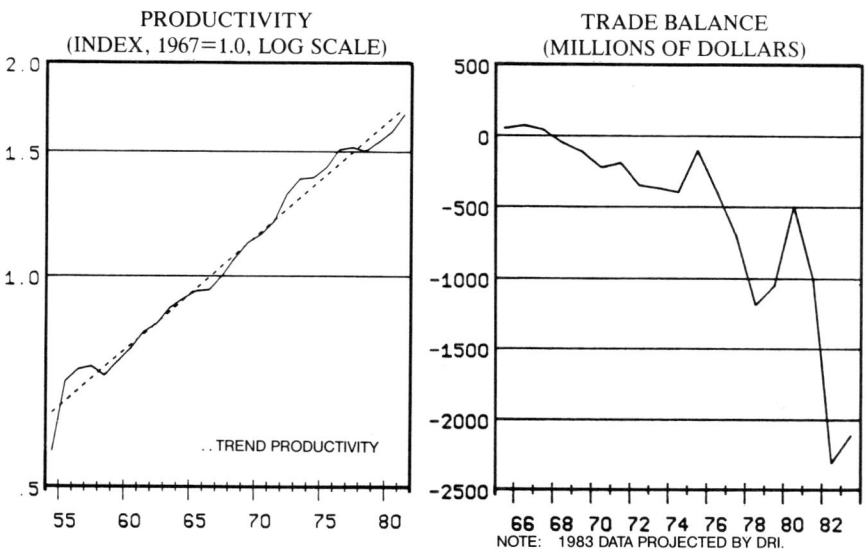

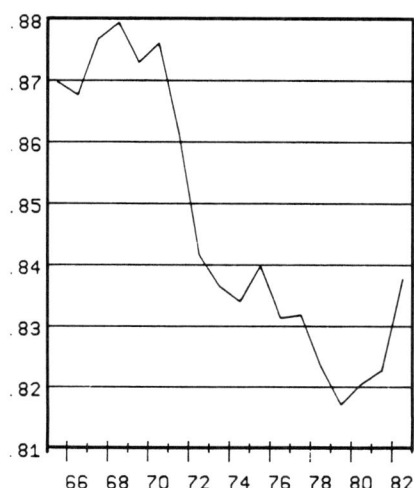

WAGES RELATIVE TO TOTAL ECONOMY

INDEX

Accelerated Cost Recovery System
  impact of, 32
Africa, 71
Aggregate supply, 13
Agricultural equipment
  investment shifts in, 27
Aircraft and parts
  production of, 7
  production projections, 95
Airplanes, ships, and railroad equipment
  investment shifts in, 27
Apparel, 25
  production, 8,61
  key concepts, 60
  constant share analysis, 62
  productivity, 63
  employment, 64
  trade balance, 68
  relative wages, 69
  exports, 72
  imports, 73
  production projections, 95
  employment projections, 96
  detailed summary, 121-123
Appliances, 7
Appliances, TV and radio
  production of, 8
Asia
  capital inflow from, 51
  east, 71
  mideast, 71
Austria, 39
Automobiles, 25
  growth of Japanese industry, 24
Automotive vehicles and parts
  current account balance, 70
Autos, trucks, and buses
  investment shifts in, 27

Balance of payments
  influence on policy, 48-50
Basic chemicals
  production of, 7
Bell, Daniel, 13n

Bell System, 171
Bergson, Abram, ed., 40
Black, Carl, 1n
Blades, Derek W., 35
Blast furnace, steel works
  investment projections, 97
Bluestone, Barry, 2n
Boeing, 79
Brazil, 55,110,149,157
Brinner, Roger, 44n
Britain,
  see United Kingdom
Bureau of Economic Analysis (BEA), 32,59
Bureau of Labor Statistics (BLS), 58
Business cycle
  role in slowing growth, 13-15

Canada, 70,71,130,157
  productivity, output per hour, 45-46
  compensation per hour, 45-46
Capital goods
  current account balance, 70
Capital income
  total taxation of, 32-34
Capital inflows, 51
Carter, Walter, 1n
Caves, Richard E., 86n
Central Europe
  capital inflow from, 51
Chemical products
  production of, 7
Chemicals, 25
  pollution abatement expenditures, 42
  key concepts, 60
  production, 61
  constant share analysis, 62
  productivity, 63
  employment, 64
  profit margins, 65
  investment, 66
  R&D, 67
  trade balance, 68
  relative wages, 69
  exports, 72

imports, 73
production projections, 95
employment projections, 96
investment projections, 97
detailed summary, 137-140
China, 56, 121
Clark, Colin
    stages of economic development, 12
Communications equipment, 26
    production of, 7
Communications machinery, photo and
    electronic equipment
    investment shifts in, 27
Communist countries, 71
Constant share analysis of foreign trade
    results of, 18-20
Construction activity
    pattern of, 27
    compared with Japan, 27
Construction equipment, 26
    investment shifts in, 27
Consumer goods except autos
    current account balance, 70
Cost of capital
    in U.S. manufacturing, 28-29
    in Japan, 29-31
    in Germany, 31
    in France, 31
Cotton fabrics
    production of, 8

Denison, Edward F., 79n

EEC, 44, 110, 151-152
Eckstein, Otto, 80n
Economic impact of the dollar's 1980-1982
    appreciation, 53
Economic Recovery Tax Act, 32
Electrical machinery, 25
    pollution abatement expenditure, 42
    key concepts, 60
    production, 61
    constant share analysis, 62
    productivity, 63
    employment, 64
    profit margins, 65
    investment, 66
    R&D, 67
    trade balance, 68
    relative wages, 69
    exports, 72
    imports, 73
    production projections, 95
    employment projections, 96

investment projections, 97
    detailed summary, 171-174
Electrical supplies, 7
Electronic components
    production of, 7
    Japanese takeover in, 24
    investment in, 26
Engines
    farm and construction equipment
        production of, 8
    investment shifts in, 27
Equity capital, 29
Exports, 18-19
    and imports, 59
    discussion of, 68

Fabricated metals, 25
    production, 8, 61
    pollution abatement expenditures, 42
    key concepts, 60
    constant share analysis, 62
    productivity, 63
    employment, 64
    profit margins, 65
    investment, 66
    R&D, 67
    trade balance, 68
    relative wages, 69
    exports, 72
    imports, 73
    production projections, 95
    employment projections, 96
    investment projections, 97
    detailed summary, 163-166
Federal Reserve Board (FRB), 58
Federal Trade Commission, 59
Feldman, Robert A., 50n
Food and products, 25
    production, 8, 61
    pollution abatement expenditures, 42
    key concepts, 60
    constant share analysis, 62
    productivity, 63
    employment, 64
    profit margins, 65
    investment, 66
    R&D, 67
    trade balances, 68
    relative wages, 69
    exports, 72
    imports, 73
    production projections, 95
    employment projections, 96
    investment projections, 97

detailed summary, 109-113
Foods, feeds, and beverages
   current account balance, 70
France, 55,71,81,85,86
   share of total employment, 11
   job decline, 11
   savings rates, 35
   productivity in output per hour, 45-46
   compensation per hour, 45-46
   devlauation of exchange rate, 47
   strong dollar simulation, 52
   annual percent growth rate, 83
Fuels and lubricants
   current account balance, 70
Fullerton, Don, ed., 33
Furniture and fixtures
   production, 8,61
   key concepts, 60
   constant share analysis, 62
   productivity, 63
   employment, 64
   trade balance, 68
   relative wages, 69
   exports, 72
   imports, 73
   production projections, 95
   employment projections, 96
   detailed summary, 127-129

Galenson, Walter, 80n
Gault, Nigel, 44n
General Agreement of Tariffs and Trade, 44
   impact of, 55
Generalized System of Preferences, 55
Germany, 39,71,81,85,86,
   share of total employment, 11
   job decline, 11
   manufacturing productivity, 12
   savings rate, 34,35
   R&D as percent of GNP, 40
   productivity, output per hour, 45-46
   compensation per hour, 45-46
   devaluation and appreciation in
      exchange rate, 47
   strong dollar simulation, 52
   annual percent growth rate, 83
Gold
   crises, 48
   standard, 50
Gross Domestic Product (GDP), 82
Gross National Product (GNP)
   potential GNP, historical trends, 15
   versus Japan, 24
   for Japan, 27

R&D as percent of, 40
real, 53
in strong dollar simulation, 53
in alternative scenarios, 88,89,90,92

Hammond, John, 1n
Harrison, Bennett, 2n
Hatsopoulos, George N., 30
Heston, Alan, 45n
High-tech equipment
   investment shifts in, 27
High technology industries, 25,26
Holland
   see The Netherlands
Hong Kong, 55,121

IBM, 79
Import penetration ratio, 16-17
Index of Industrial Production, 58
Industrial and metalworking machinery
   production of, 8
Industrial construction
   versus total nonresidential, 27-28
Industrial machinery, 26
   investment shifts in, 27
Industrial production, 58
   discussion of, 59-61
   constant share analysis, 62
Industry employment, 58
   discussion of, 64
Instruments
   production, 7,61
   key concepts, 60
   constant share analysis, 62
   productivity, 63
   employment, 64
   profit margins, 65
   R&D, 67
   trade balance, 68
   relative wages, 69
   exports, 72
   imports, 73
   production projections, 95
   employment projections, 96
   detailed summary, 182-185
Investment, 59
   discussion of, 66
Iron and steel foundries
   production, 8
Italy, 71,81,86,149
   savings rate, 35
   productivity in output per hour, 45-46
   compensation per hour, 45-46
   strong dollar simulation, 52
   annual percent growth rate, 83

J-curve effect, 54
Japan, 23,27,55,57,71,74,78,81,85,86,121,171
   share of total employment, 11
   manufacturing production, 12
   export share, 18
   employment decline, 19-20
   manufacturing investment, 23-25
   as share of GNP, 24
   real cost of fixed asset services, 31
   cost of capital, 34,38
   savings rates, 34,35
   technological challenge to U.S., 39
   supply of engineers, 39-40
   R&D as percent of GNP, 40
   pollution abatement costs, 42
   productivity in output per hour, 45-46
   compensation per hour, 45-46
   strong dollar simulation, 52-53
   annual percent growth rate,
     in manufacturing, 83
Johnson, Sara, 51n
Jorgenson, Dale W., 36

King, Mervyn, ed., 33
Korea, 55,57,121,157,171
Krause, Lawrence B., 86n
Kravis, Irving, 45n
Krugman, Paul, 2n

Latin America, 71
Lawrence, Robert Z., 18n-19n
Leather products
   production, 8,61
   key concepts, 60
   constant share analysis, 62
   productivity, 63
   employment, 64
   trade balance, 68
   relative wages, 69
   exports, 72
   imports, 73
   production projections, 95
   employment projections, 96
   detailed summary, 149-151
Leibenstein, Harvey, 80n
Leonard, James, 1n
Levine, Herbert S., ed., 40n
Lumber and wood, 7
   production, 8,61
   key concepts, 60
   constant share analysis, 62
   productivity, 63
   employment, 64
   trade balance, 68
   relative wages, 69
   exports, 72
   imports, 73
   production projections, 95
   employment projections, 96
   detailed summary, 124-126

MFA (Multi-Fiber Arrangement), 117,121
MITI (Ministry of Industry and Trade)
   for Japan, 56
MacKethan, Edwin R., 1n
Machinery and household equipment
   investment shifts in, 27
Magaziner, Ira C., 2n
Major electrical equipment and parts
   production of, 8
Malmquist, D.H., 25n
Manufacturing as output-per-worker
   leader, 76-78
   role of advance of productivity in, 78
   economies-to-scale, 79-80
   production of savings and investment, 80
   relationship with national defense, 83-84
   prosperity and regional
     development, 84-85
Manufacturing, capital stock
   growth of, 23
Manufacturing growth
   history of, 6-7
   slowdown of production, 7-8
   slowdown of employment, 8-9
   slowdown abroad, 10-11
Manufacturing investment
   rate of, 22
Manufacturing sector
   employment in, 9
Manufacturing scenarios
   pessimistic, 87-90
   optimistic, 90-101
Marginal tax rates on capital income following
   the Tax Equity and Fiscal Responsibility
   Act of 1982, 33
Marginal tax rates, relation to
   financing methods, 33-34
Merchandise trade
   current account balances, 70
Metal cans, 7
   production of, 8
Mexico, 55,71,157
Middle East
   capital inflow from, 51
Militzer, Kenneth, 1n
Miscellaneous electrical supplies
   production of, 7

Miscellaneous manufacturing
    key concepts, 60
    production, 61
    constant share analysis, 62
    productivity, 63
    employment, 64
    trade balance, 68
    relative wages, 69
    exports, 72
    imports, 73
    production projections, 95
    employment projections, 96
    detailed summary, 186-187
Mobile homes, 7
Morgan Guaranty Bank trade-weighted index, 88,90
Motor vehicles, 7
Motor vehicles and parts
    key concepts, 60
    production, 61
    constant share analysis, 62
    productivity, 63
    employment, 64
    investment, 66
    trade balance, 68
    relative wages, 69
    exports, 72
    imports, 73
    production projections including trucks, buses, and trailers, 95
    investment projections, 97

National Science Foundation, 39,59
Netherlands, The, 39,71
Non-cotton textiles
    production of, 8
Nonelectrical machinery
    pollution abatement expenditures, 42
    key concepts, 60
    constant share analysis, 62
    productivity, 63
    employment, 64
    profit margins, 65
    investment, 66
    R&D, 67
    trade balance, 68
    relative wages, 69
    exports, 72
    imports, 73
    production projections, 95
    employment projections, 96
    detailed summary, 167-170
Nonferrous metals, 7
    production of, 8

    production projections, 95
    investment projections, 97
Nonfuel industrial materials
    current account balance, 70
Norsworthy, J.R., 25n

OECD, 10,59
    measures of hourly compensation, 45
OPEC, 7,19,71,99,137,141
Office equipment, 7,26
Office machinery
    investment shifts in, 27
Office of the Trade Representative, 55
Office, service and miscellaneous equipment
    production of, 7
Ordnance, private and government
    production of, 8
    production projections, 95
Overvaluation of the dollar, 44
    effects on U.S. competitiveness, 45-46
    historical trend, 47
    manifestation of, 48-51

Paper and products, 25
    production, 8,61
    pollution abatement expenditures, 42
    key concepts, 61
    constant share analysis, 62
    productivity, 63
    employment, 64
    profit margins, 65
    investment, 66
    R&D, 67
    trade balance, 68
    relative wages, 69
    exports, 72
    imports, 73
    production projections, 95
    employment projections, 96
    investment projections, 97
    detailed summary, 130-133
Petroleum products, 7
    production, 8,61
    refining, 25
    pollution abatement expenditures, 42
    key concepts, 60
    constant share analysis, 62
    productivity, 63
    employment, 64
    profit margins, 65
    investment, 66
    R&D, 67
    trade balance, 68
    relative wages, 69

Index

exports, 72
imports, 73
production projections, 95
employment projections, 96
investment projections, 97
detailed summary, 141-144
Photographic equipment, 26
Plastics products, nec
    production of, 7
Policy
    balance of payments, influence on 48-50
    MITI (Ministry of Industry and Trade)
        role in policy-making, 56
    Office of the Trade Representative, 55
    regulatory
        general foci of, 41
        pollution abatement, 41-42
        wage-price controls, 43
        indirect costs of, 43
    trade, weakness of, 55-57
Pollard, Sidney, 86n
Pollution abatement, 23
    expenditures for, 42
Primary metals
    pollution abatement expenditures, 42
    key concepts, 60
    production, 61
    constant share analysis, 62
    productivity, 63
    employment, 64
    profit margins, 65
    investment, 66
    R&D, 67
    trade balance, 68
    relative wages, 69
    exports, 72
    imports, 73
    production projections, 95
    employment projections, 96
    investment projections, 97
    detailed summary, including steel, 156-162
Printing and publishing
    production, 8,61
    key concepts, 60
    constant share analysis, 62
    productivity, 63
    employment, 64
    trade balance, 68
    relative wages, 69
    exports, 72
    production projections, 95
    employment projections, 96
    detailed summary, 134-136
Proctor, Allen J., 50n

Productivity-output per manhour, 58
    discussion of, 63
Profits as a margin on sales, 59
    discussion of, 65

Railroad equipment, 7
Reexports, military, nec
    current account balance, 70
Regulatory policy
    general foci of, 41
    pollution abatement, 41-42
    wage-price controls, 43
    indirect costs of, 43
Rehmet, Paul, 1n
Reich, Robert B., 2n
Recession
    discussion of, 35-36
    simulation on effect on manufacturing
        investment, 36-38
Relative wages, 59
    discussion of, 69
Research and development expenditures, 59
    discussion of, 67
Rich, D. W., 1n
Rubber, 25
    tires, 7
Rubber and plastics
    pollution abatement expenditures, 42
    key concepts, 60
    production, 61
    constant share analysis, 62
    productivity, 63
    employment, 64
    profit margins, 65
    investment, 66
    R&D, 67
    trade balance, 68
    relative wages, 69
    exports, 72
    imports, 73
    production projections, 95
    employment projections, 96
    investment projections, 97
    detailed summary, 145-148
Rubber products except tires
    production of, 8

Saudi Arabia, 71,137
Savings rate
    discussion of, 35
Schultze, Charles L., 2n
Services
    growth of, 12-13

meaning with respect to international trade, 50
Shipbuilding, 7
Ships, RR equipment and mobile homes production of, 8
Singapore, 55
64 K chips, 171
Smith, Adam, 76,80
South Africa, 157
South America
　capital inflow from, 51
South Korea, 55,57,71
Soviet Union, 40,56,83
Spain, 157
Steel, 7
　Japanese industry, 24
　see primary metals for detailed summary
Steel mill products
　production, 8,61
　key concepts, 60
　constant share analysis, 62
　employment, 64
　investment, 66
　trade balance, 68
　relative wages, 69
　exports, 72
　production projections, 95
Stone, clay and glass
　production, 8,61
　pollution abatement expenditures, 42
　key concepts, 60
　constant share analysis, 62
　employment, 64
　profit margins, 65
　investment, 66
　R&D, 67
　trade balance, 68
　relative wages, 69
　exports, 72
　production projections, 95
　employment projections, 96
　investment projections, 97
　detailed summary, 152-155
Strong dollar simulation, 51-54
Sturm, Peter H., 34
Summers, Robert, 45n
Switzerland, 39
Synthetic materials
　production of, 7

Taiwan, 55,121,149
Technology
　U.S. goals and achievements, 38-39
　training for careers in 39-40
　lack of sufficient engineers, reasons for, 41
Textile mill products, 25
　pollution abatement expenditures, 42
　key concepts, 60
　production, 61
　constant share analysis, 62
　productivity, 63
　employment, 64
　profit margins, 65
　investment, 66
　trade balance, 68
　relative wages, 69
　exports, 72
　imports, 73
　production projections, 95
　employment projections, 96
　investment projections, 97
　detailed summary, 117-120
Thurow, Lester C., 2n
Tires
　production of, 8
Tobacco manufactures
　production, 8,61
　key concepts, 60
　constant share analysis, 62
　productivity, 63
　employment, 64
　trade balance, 68
　relative wages, 69
　exports, 72
　imports, 73
　production projections, 95
　employment projections, 96
　detailed summary, 114-116
Total nonfarm sector
　employment in, 9
Trade
　deficits in, 70-74
　discussion of, 70-74
Trade policy
　weaknesses of, 55-57
Transportation equipment
　investment shifts in, 27
　pollution abatement expenditures, 42
　key concepts, 60
　production, 61
　constant share analysis, 62
　productivity, 63
　employment, 64
　profit margins, 65
　investment, 66
　trade balance, 68
　relative wages, 69

exports, 72
imports, 73
production projections, including aircraft and parts, 95
employment projections, 96
investment projections, 97
detailed summary, 175-181
Trigger Price Program, 156
Trucks, buses and trailers
production projections, 95

U.S.S.R.
see Soviet Union
Underdepreciation
discussion of, 31-32
Unemployment rate, 15
United Kingdom, 81
savings rate, 34, 35
productivity in output per hour, 45-46
compensation per hour, 45-46
devaluation of exchange rate, 47
strong dollar simulation, 52
annual percent growth rate, 53
manufacturing decline, 85-86
Utilities
cost of capital, 29

Vietnam War, 16, 156

Walters, A.A., 79n
Wendt, Robert A., 1n
Western Europe, 71
Whitfield, Ronald, 1n
World War I, 83
World War II, 83